The Red Book

Labour Left

Edited by Dr Éoin Clarke and Owain Gardner

Copyright © Labour Left 2012

The contents of this publication, either in whole or in part, may not be reproduced, stored in a data retrieval system or transmitted in any form or by any means, electronic, mechanical, photocopying, recording or otherwise without the written permission of the copyright owner and publishers. Action will be taken against companies or individual persons who ignore this warning. The information set forth herein has been obtained form sources which we believe to be reliable, but is not guaranteed. The publication is provided with the understanding that the author and publisher shall have no liability for errors, inaccuracies or omissions of this publication and, by this publication, the author and publisher are not engaged in rendering consulting advice or other professional advice to the recipient with regard to any specific matter. In the event that consulting or other expert assistance is required with regard to any specific matter, the services of qualified professionals should be sought.

This book has been produced by Labour Left – a Labour Party campaign grouping within the UK Labour Party. For any queries please email the chief editor, DrEoinClarke@LabourLeft.co.uk. Each author retains sole responsibility for their work, and full intellectual property rights accordingly. You can find out more about Labour Left by visiting www.LabourLeft.co.uk.

First published 2012 by Searching Finance Ltd, 8 Whitehall Road, London W7 2JE, UK

ISBN: 978-1-907720-43-7

Typeset by Brooke Balza

The Red Book

Labour Left

Edited by Dr Éoin Clarke and Owain Gardner

Searching finance

About Labour Left

Labour Left formed in June 2011 as GEER, but changed its name in September to take account of the rapidly expanding membership. It was originally intended as a think tank to generate policy but it was clear that the influx of new members wanted much more than that. They wanted a place within the Labour Party where they could share in camaraderie and discussion with like-minded socialists. To an extent Labour had been lacking a coherent voice for those disillusioned with aspects of New Labour.

The ambition of Labour Left is to generate ethically socialist policies for inclusion in the next Labour General Election manifesto. We aim to intellectually reclaim what it means to be left and we wish to help Ed Miliband steer a course away from Neo-Liberalism. It is clear from the surge in new members, especially younger ones since the General Election in 2010, that there is an appetite for socialist policies that tame the excesses of capitalism and re-balance the UK economy in a way that is fairer to the have-nots.

The old battles of the 1980s are part of UK history, and the brand that was 'New Labour' is no longer new. Thus, Labour Left looks forward to a radical new age of communitarianism, solidarity and a new morality in politics. In Labour Left, we offer you our view of ethical socialism.

About Searching Finance

Searching Finance Ltd is a new voice in knowledge provision for the financial services, economics and related professional sectors. For more information, please visit www.searchingfinance.com

Acknowledgements

The book is the end product of three months (August-October 2011) of very hard work by a great number of people, many of whose names do not appear as chapter authors. One example is Margaret Waterhouse who is the life blood of Labour Left. Her unstinting positivity maintains the morale of our members and the professional/political advice which she offers to our organisation is indispensible. James Leppard generously provides our press coverage. He dedicates much time to networking and putting Labour Left ideas to important stakeholders. We are very grateful to him and deeply value his services.

David Hough, Alex Sobel, Darrell Goodliffe, and Daniel Wood were valued intellectual sounding boards for many of our ideas. Much of the policy contained herein was modified and fine-tuned based upon their nuanced feedback. Labour Left would be largely unknown were it not for the efforts of our online team in putting our ideas out there. We wish to thank and recognise the hard work of Andy Hicks, Brian Johnson and David Harney for their excellent professionalism in the way they have handled our public image in social media.

There are many more who will go unmentioned but who are growing in prominence within Labour Left. I am sad that I cannot mention all of their names herein but I am consoled by the fact that they have much to offer the future of Labour Left. Lastly, can I thank my co-editor Owain Gardner. He has a great Labour future ahead of him and I hope he'll always regard his work on the Red Book as a valued milestone.

Disclaimer

The ideas contained herein are the responsibility of each individual author. Although an effort has been made to find commonality of purpose this has not always been possible or indeed desirable. There are, in parts, some competing messages, and interests, but we in Labour Left opted to be flexible in how we dealt with that in an effort to promote tolerance and inclusivity of ideas. On matters of energy policy, Europe and religion there are clear differences of emphasis within Labour Left. We cherish that and hope that you view it as a positive.

The veracity of each piece has been scrutinised by the editorial team, but in the event we missed something that a reader may take exception to can we both apologise in advance and remind the reader that each author alone is accountable for their words. In circumstances where a writers ideas conflict with that of the stated policy position of an elected representative, may I remind the reader that this is not in any way inconsistent, as only the author is accountable for their words.

Lastly, whilst many clear policy differences exist with various elements of the wider Labour Party, we can only win the 2015 General Election as a fully united party. Thus, we both recognise and accept many competing arguments will be vying for their ideas to be included in the 2015 manifesto. We wish our extended fraternity best wishes as we all strive to put Labour first. Labour works best when it is counter-hegemonic.

Contents

Part 1: Introducing Labour Left and Ethical Socialism	**1**
A Place for Labour Left in the Great Labour Debate	3
The Human Face of Socialism	11
Part 2: What Now for the NHS?	**21**
The Betrayal of our NHS	23
An NHS Which Belongs to Us	33
The Commercialisation of Public Services	43
Part 3: Education: Unequal Resources,	
Social Mobility and Poverty of Aspiration	**51**
Archimedes or Stephenson?	53
Education: 'a debt due, from the present to future generations'	63
Part 4: Labour Left and the Importance of Ethical Economics	**77**
Consumer Debt	79
A Living Wage	91
Tax at the Heart of Labour Left	97
Private Renters – the Forgotten Millions who Abandoned Labour	109
Houses not to Blame	135
Labour's Co-operative Future	141
Recession: the Socialist Solution	149
Part 5: Can Academic Philosophy Help us to Learn	
the Lessons of our General Election Defeat?	**157**
Understanding the Psychology of the Working Class Right Wing	159
The Real Lesson of New Labour	171
Labour Winning in the South	183
Part 6: Making Affordable Energy Compatible with Sustainable	
Energy	**197**
Energy Efficiency Provides One of the Keys to Affordable Energy	199
Financial Benefits of Green Energy Can Help Pay its Price	207
Making the Case for Opening New Coal Mines	215
Part 7: Labour Left and Issues Beyond Class	**227**
LGB&T and the Next Generation of Reforms	229
What now for Gender Equality?	243

Harsh Lessons for Labour if they Wish to Recapture the Christian Vote	253
A New Ethical Foreign Policy for Labour	261
Labour Must Champion the Cause of the 'Working Poor' if We Want to Win the 2015 General Election	269

Part I

Introducing Labour Left and Ethical Socialism

A Place for Labour Left in the Great Labour Debate

By Andy Shaw

Andy Shaw is a Labour Member based in Sheffield. He has worked on various Scottish Holyrood and General Election campaigns during his time as a university student in Scotland. Andy was a founding member of Labour Left and designs and maintains the Labour Left website.

Introducing Labour Left and Ethical Socialism

On 11 May 2010, Gordon Brown left 10 Downing Street for the final time, in the wake of Labour's worst general election performance since 1983. Since that moment, it would seem efforts to reshape the Labour movement have been ongoing, with strands within the party pulling in often wildly different directions.

These conflicting efforts – sometimes termed 'the battle for the soul of the Labour Party' – have taken place under intense scrutiny amongst the politically-attuned sectors of the media. Our opponents will, of course, seek to make the most of this internal dialogue, painting the robust debate as some kind of terminal fracture within the movement.

But it is an inevitable and necessary part of recovery from the resounding defeat in May 2010 to discuss the future direction of the party. It is certainly not enough to say, as Tony Blair did in a 2010 interview with the BBC's Andrew Marr, that the best way to return a Labour government to office is to 'not move a millimetre' from the positions of his own 'New Labour' project.[1]

More recently, in a speech to the think tank Progress, Tony Blair lamented that Gordon Brown had abandoned 'New' Labour when he became Prime Minister in 2007, claiming that under Brown, Labour 'lost the driving rhythm that made us different and successful.'[2] The subtext of this is clear: that Brown's handling of the party, and his supposed move away from New Labour, is what cost us the last election.

'New Labour won us three elections and remains the best approach for winning again in the future', is a common refrain that we hear from Blairites. But, Blair's attempt to distance himself from Labour's defeat does not stand up to scrutiny. Of the 13.5 million people who voted for Labour in 1997, nearly four million of those had already ceased to vote for the party in 2005. Between 2005 and 2010, Labour lost less than a million voters, meaning that by the time Blair left office in 2007, much of the damage had already been done. The New Labour project may have won over many British voters in 1997, but these figures indicate that, nearly a decade and a half down the line, such an approach has become outdated and irrelevant.

However, most of those involved in the 'Great Labour Debate' acknowledge that the party does have to change in order to achieve future electoral success. It is the directions in which that change needs to take place which is the matter under dispute. A number of potential solutions have been proposed, such as Maurice Glasman's 'Blue Labour,' which aimed to combine a rejection of neo-liberal economics with social

5

conservatism in order to win back white working-class voters; the group he correctly identifies as having abandoned the Labour Party.

While many, particularly on the left of the party, were concerned about the nature and extent of Blue Labour's social conservatism, fresh perspectives in the debate must *always* be welcomed. In some respects it is a shame that Glasman's over-concentration on issues such as immigration have detracted from an important debate.

Then there is the 'Purple Book,' backed by Progress and others, who claimed that it contains modernising ideas for the Labour Party in the hope of attracting centre-ground voters to the party. There are some concerns that this would simply be a case of New Labour reheated, or worse still an advocacy of a further shift to the right. Certainly, Blairites have not been shy about their insistence that Labour should not tack left in the wake of our defeat. In this respect I cannot be alone in believing the view that the party of 42-day detention, ID cards, two long-running foreign wars, a widening wealth gap, lost the election was because they weren't right-wing enough to be ill judged.

Indeed, analysis by Dr Éoin Clarke suggests that it was not a loss of middle-income (A/B) voters – traditionally thought of as the centre ground – that cost us the 2010 election. Instead, it was the haemorrhaging of poorer voters (C2) that brought about our defeat.[3] This suggests that exploring the concerns of our former core voters, the working classes, is the best electoral strategy for attracting those voters that left us between 1997 and 2010.

This is where Labour Left, and the Red Book, has its place. Only by reaffirming Labour's core values, but updating them for the modern setting, can we hope to reconnect with our traditional base, and this is the surest way of delivering a new Labour government. The resulting Labour government, brought about according to these values, would not be hamstrung by the kind of right leaning compromises and contradictions that defined New Labour. Bad capitalism exposed the right of the Labour Party to accusations of not understanding the concerns of those on modest incomes, but only ethical socialism can make the cost of living affordable to the bottom two thirds of society.

A further case for moving Labour away from the 'Third Way' and Blairite consensus is to look at how badly it has failed both the political establishment and the wider public. As a result of this, an extension of the neo-liberal economics of the 1980s, we have a political culture perceived by many as interested solely in its own enrichment, to the detriment of almost everything else. Scandals like MPs' expenses, bankers' bonuses and the like only serve to compound this perception. The Labour Party's result in the 2011 Scottish Parliament elections demonstrates this; the Scottish National Party effectively painted themselves as an 'anti-establishment' alternative to the major British parties, and consequently won by a landslide. The need for a clear alternative to this political cesspit cannot be clearer, and it is in Labour's interest to lead the way in finding that alternative, not determinedly cling to what remains of Blairite dogma.

Labour Left's view, is that 'moving to the centre ground' – that is, shifting the party to the right – is unnecessary in order to win elections. As Ed Balls memorably put it in his Bloomberg speech in the winter of 2010, politics is about shaping public opinion, not bowing slavishly to it.[4] I would add that if we have to sacrifice our principles in order to be elected, there is no point standing for election in the first place. 16 million voters did not cast their ballot at the last election, am I alone in thinking that energising turnout could yield electoral benefits for Labour? Labour Left values would not only make the Labour movement a principled force of democratic socialism, but also an electable one, as the analysis has shown.

With that in mind, it is surprising that Labour Left has met with such hostility from certain elements within the party. There are two major criticisms of Labour Left's approach and outlook that have been raised on multiple occasions by several commentators. I want to deal with these objections now, to dispel some of the mythology that has been circulated about Labour Left by its critics.

Firstly, Labour Left's former name – GEER – did indeed stand for 'Gender, Environment, Equality and Race.' So many of the attacks on Labour Left had homed in on this name, implying or stating outright that these are not core Labour values, and that the efforts of a group intending to regain Labour's lost base would be best directed elsewhere.

A cursory glance at Labour Left's website, or ideas contained within the Red Book, would indicate to even the laziest of critics that these four issues, while important, are far from being exclusively Labour Left's output. In particular, left-leaning Labour members and supporters have often asked where the issue of class, once so important to Labour, fits into the Labour Left worldview. Again, the importance of this issue and others to Labour Left is readily confirmed by reading its material, rather than interpreting its name alone.

The second objection most often raised against Labour Left is the very idea – abject fear, it would seem – that a pressure group or think tank made up of socialists within the Labour Party should dare to have any input into the future direction of the party. When its publication was announced, this Red Book was derided on Twitter – by a key Labour NEC member as a 'Peoples' Front of Judea' no less – as 'an even longer suicide note,' a reference to the party's ill-fated 1983 manifesto or 'the longest suicide note in history'. Never mind that this critic had not read a page of the Red Book.

Comparisons to the early 1980s and Labour's move to the left under Michael Foot are frustrating, since this misses the point entirely. Of course, it suits those on the right of the Labour Party well to draw comparisons between Labour Left and our worst electoral performance of the modern era, as if to imply that considering left-wing values as part of our next manifesto would bring about a similar result. Of course, what held true in the 1980s will not do so now; furthermore, when the political consensus is in such dire need of a shake-up, why should socialism not be the answer?

Some of Labour Left's supporters have sought to draw parallels between Labour Left and the Labour movement not in the 1980s, but in 1945, when Britain emerged from the Second World War and. A Labour government in power, on the back of a difficult financial situation constructed the NHS and the welfare state, instead of using economic difficulty as an excuse for ushering in Victorian-style austerity. There is merit to this argument, but I prefer to think of Labour Left as a forward-looking organisation rather than one which looks back; Labour Left offers unique solutions to the problems faced in the 21st century. It is 'New Labour', not Labour Left, which is stuck in the past, attempting to solve these same problems with outdated and bankrupt 1990s-style solutions.

A final point, in this regard, is that the ethical values upon which Labour Left is founded are not alien to the majority of Labour supporters in any case. Though its detractors have characterised Labour Left in a number of ways, including 'far left loyalism' (the loyalty being to Ed Miliband), the truth is that if Labour Left's values of equality, redistribution and fairness are perceived as 'far left,' then something has gone very wrong in the Labour movement as a whole, not with Labour Left.[5]

The Red Book, therefore, aims to cut through this prejudice by presenting a clear vision for a Labour Party and government of the future. There is plenty herein that can find support across broad swathes of our party; we should not be deterred by the sound and fury of our detractors. Labour Left has found its voice – and that, in and of itself, is just the beginning.

---

1 'The Tony Blair Interview with Andrew Marr.' BBC News Online, 01/09/2010. http://www.bbc.co.uk/news/uk-politics-11157485. Retrieved 24/07/11.
2 Curtis, P. (2011). 'Tony Blair: New Labour died when I handed over to Gordon Brown.' *The Guardian*, 08/07/11. http://www.guardian.co.uk/politics/2011/jul/08/tony-blair-new-labour-gordon-brown. Retrieved 24/07/11.
3 Clarke, E. (2011). 'Exposing the myth that appealing to Middle England is the key to electoral victory.' Labour Left. http://www.labourleft.co.uk/?p=23. Retrieved 24/07/11.
4 Balls, E. (2010). 'There is an alternative – Ed Balls' speech at Bloomberg.' Ed Balls. http://www.edballs4labour.org/blog/?p=907. Retrieved 20/08/11.
5 Burnell, E. (2011). 'The disorganised left.' LabourList. http://www.labourlist.org/the-disorganised-left. Retrieved 20/08/11.

The Human Face of Socialism

By Professor Beverley Clack

Professor Beverley Clack is a Labour member and a candidate in the upcoming election for St Clements in Oxford. Beverley teaches philosophy and religion at Oxford Brookes University. Her interests lie in the role ethics plays in politics. Beverley also blogs at www.theaccidentallabouractivist.com

Introducing Labour Left and Ethical Socialism

"If you want a picture of the future, imagine a boot stamping on a human face – forever."[6]

Of all the memorable images in George Orwell's Nineteen Eighty-Four, this is the most powerful. In the action of a boot stamping remorselessly on a human face, all individuality is obliterated; any trace of the personal is destroyed. There is one reality and that is the reality of Big Brother: the overwhelming might of the state and those who control it.

While Orwell's intention was to depict the fate of the individual in the fascist and communist regimes of his day, that image of the individual crushed by an ideology that has no place for them or their desires suggests something of the fears that have come to dominate ideas about what socialism involves. At its most basic, socialism aims at an economic system that enables a more equal society where the needs of all are taken seriously, and none are left powerless in the face of the powerful. But that ideal of equality has all-too-often been associated with a levelling down of individual circumstances, resulting in drab conformity. Linked to a certain kind of faceless, bureaucratic joylessness, best illustrated by the rules and regulations attending to council house tenancies, it seems inevitably to promote the collective at the expense of the individual.

Seen in this way, socialism has little to offer western liberal societies that take as given the importance of fostering individual creativity. In shaping left-of-centre politics, one solution to this apparent mismatch has been to avoid using the 'S' word. We are now 'social democrats' or followers of 'the Third Way'. At best, this means smuggling a socialist agenda in by the back door: a good example of this being found in Gordon Brown's tax policies which surreptitiously allowed for some redistribution of wealth.[7] At its worst, it means denying the relevance of socialism reflects a fatalistic attitude about the current economic and social system. 'There is no alternative' therefore all that left-of-centre parties can do is design policies that mitigate the excesses of the market. The problem with this strategy is that it leads to the disappointing reality of a Labour government leaving office, as it did in 2010, with the inequalities between top and bottom of society largely intact and in some instances worse than before.[8]

As we reflect on the kind of Labour manifesto to be offered in the future, an honest assessment of the failings of the New Labour project is needed. More importantly, though, we need to confront the changing context which forms the backdrop for such deliberations. The financial crisis of 2008 and the bailing out of financial institutions by governments worldwide revealed the failures of free market economics. The UK's expenses scandal exposed the lack of connection between political institutions (elected representatives, Parliament, Councils and the like) and the communities they were supposed to serve. More recently, the phone-hacking scandal revealed widespread lawlessness in the way parts of the media operate. That scandal has also suggested the possibility of police corruption, while at the same time raising questions about the kind of people we are when the meaning we ascribe to our lives is grounded in salacious gossip about the lives of others. This question has been given even greater urgency in the face of the widespread rioting and looting that took place in August 2011 in several major English cities.

We are at a point when it is not a case of whether we can create a different kind of society; we must. The old ways of doing things have failed – if they ever worked properly in the first place. And for those of us on the Left, this presents a real opportunity to consider the place there might be for a revived socialism in the policies we formulate.

My suggestion for the kind of socialism that might underpin this endeavour involves revisiting a particular strand of thought and practice in the history of the British Labour movement. We might call this 'ethical socialism'; a type of socialism that, rather than destroying the individual in the way described in Orwell's dystopia, seeks ways of aiding its flourishing.[9]

As Peter Kellner notes, the word 'socialist' first appeared in 1827 in the Co-operative magazine of Robert Owen. For the visionary Owen, a socialist was 'someone who co-operated with others for the common good'.[10] By defining socialism in this way, Owen directs our gaze to the individual who seeks to act ethically in society. This notion of the practical socialist challenges bureaucratic accounts of what socialism entails; but it also highlights the need to think again about the neo-liberal model of the 'self' that has dominated the political scene for the last thirty years.

This account of the self has gone and still goes by various names, but it is best defined as 'neo-liberal'. Emerging out of the Thatcherite economics of the 1980s, it has remained largely unchallenged in British politics as the best way of understanding human beings and their desires. The late Labour leader John Smith summed up this concept rather neatly in an essay written in 1993. For the 'New Right', he wrote, 'individuals [are defined as] decision making units, concerned exclusively with their self-interest, making transactions in the marketplace'.[11] This model of the self reflects the values of consumer capitalism, and, regrettably, was little challenged by New Labour. Rather than developing more holistic accounts of the relationship between an individual and their community, Labour policies tended to reflect the idea that what was important was to find ways of freeing up individual potential. In this way, striving for a more equal society became equated with ensuring 'equality of opportunity' rather than economic equality. This shift in language drew attention to the experience of individuals rather than communities. The talented individual from a lower socio-economic group should be just as able to succeed as someone from a more privileged background. The downside of shaping policies in line with this aspiration was that if an individual failed to take advantage of these new opportunities, responsibility was located solely with their failings, rather than in any surrounding social conditions.[12]

In order to develop an ethical socialism, the vision of the individual at the heart of the neo-liberal account must be challenged, and this means considering once again the relationship between self and society. According to Aristotle, humans are 'social animals' not isolated units. Recent research by the New Economics Foundation lends empirical weight to this philosophical idea. Well-being, according to NEF, is to be found not just in the achievement of personal goals, but in a sense of oneself as socially grounded, part of a wider community. To focus on 'the individual' is to ignore the fact that we are human precisely because we find our fulfilment in our relationships with each other. We need each other. The challenge for today's socialists is to develop policies that reflect that social self and that enable individuals and the communities that they form – and that form them – to flourish.

In order to do this, we need to think about what it means to be a socialist. Owen's description of a socialist – someone who works with others for the common good – suggests a practical grounding for socialism. It is not merely a system of ideas; it describes a particular way of life.

This might come as something of a surprise. Ideas are not to be divorced from practice. Under this approach, the model for the socialist is less the academic Marx and more that forgotten leader of the 1930s Labour Party, George Lansbury (1859-1940). Lansbury did not use his position to improve his own finances, he refused the pension to which he was entitled as a former cabinet minister, and lived out his life modestly in the deprived community of Bow that he represented.[13]

Living out one's socialism in this way reflects forms of religious practice. Just as religious faith is never simply a matter of holding a particular set of beliefs but is also about how you live them out, so socialism is nothing if its practitioners fail to live in ways that further the socialist vision of how we might best live together. In the Christian socialism of Stewart Headlam (1847-1924) and William Temple (1881-1944), this more human and humane socialism was derived from the Christian belief that all individuals are created by God. Recognising that each individual is unique, valued by God, has an effect on how we behave: the needs of others are as important as our own.

The claim that all are brothers and sisters forms the so-called 'Golden Thread' that runs through the biblical tradition. The story of Cain and Abel provides a fine example of the interdependence that lies at the heart of the demand for social justice. Having murdered his brother, Cain is asked by God as to Abel's whereabouts. Cain's response – 'I am not my brother's keeper' – is a sign of his depravity, rather than an accurate reflection of the nature of human relationship (Genesis 4:1-8). Similarly, St Paul's claim that 'love of money is the root of all evil' (Timothy 6:10) identifies materialism as something which distorts the personality, thus leading to warped relationships. Forget Gordon Gecko: greed is never good because the sins of selfishness, avarice and cruelty that follow in its wake twist the mutual respect and concern that should form the basis for relationship. What this means in practice is summed up in Jesus' neat prescription for living: 'love God and treat your neighbour as yourself' (Mark 12: 30-31). No wonder, then, that Keir Hardie should have located his socialism not in Marx, but in the Bible.

Given the Right's easy acquisition of religion for its own purposes, we may well feel uneasy about grounding socialism in the biblical tradition. And there are plenty of other less than life-affirming biblical texts supporting genocide, tribalism and hatred. This should not surprise us. Christianity is, like socialism, a human creed that reflects the best and worst of its creators. What these ancient Christian texts do support, however, is the importance of responsibility – for others, but also for how we act towards others.

In the ethical socialist tradition derived from Christian socialism, this emphasis shifts attention from socialism as an abstract commitment to a consideration of what it means to live in harmony with each other. Yes, socialism identifies the state as an identity which ensures the means by which all its citizens can flourish. Yes, socialism involves working with others to achieve a more equal society. But it is more than that. It is also about how we, through the quality of our relationships, create socialism in our day-to-day lives.

This might sound irrelevant when thinking about the kind of policies that enable the flourishing of all. But an ethical socialism places our day-to-day practice at the centre of things. This acknowledgement has the power to transform our politics, and, as Labour refounds itself, to determine the direction that its policies take.

So how to live the socialist life? At the outset, it means committing ourselves to living in community with all who share our social space. This means, for better off socialists, refusing the option of buying out of that society alongside developing policies that challenge the choices of those who do. Private education and health provision mean those who can afford them do not have to share the experience of those who are not able to affect such an opt-out. The vision of a harmonious society lies at the heart of a socialist community: and a socialist community cannot exist where we relate only to those whose experiences mirror our own.

It follows from this that we must treat our fellow citizens with decency and respect. I am often shocked by the way people who profess to be socialist treat people who work in the service industry, retail and public services. Recognising that relationships form our communities, we must work at making them good relationships. Fraternity is not an abstract concept that can be detached from our ordinary dealings with others. It is nothing if it is not based in respectful, caring friendships.

Working at the relationships that bind society together has implications for Labour's organisation. That the political class is largely drawn from the same socio-economic groups, the same universities and the same professions means that it invariably operates with a view of the fulfilling life based upon the experiences of the professional middle class. As a result, there has been a failure to think more broadly about what makes for a fulfilling life and the contribution that all can make to the good society.

Consider New Labour's promotion of 'aspiration'. On the surface, encouraging people to aspire to 'better' ways of living seems perfectly proper for a left-of-centre party. And after the disaster of Thatcherism, which resulted in part from Labour's failure to sufficiently engage with the hopes and aspirations of its working class base, it made perfect sense to cultivate social mobility.

Yet the problem with such an ideal is that it targets the aspiration of 'gifted' individuals without thinking about the kind of society that enables all to flourish. Considering the way in which aspiration has been connected to education exposes the paucity of this vision. Enabling all to have a university education, so the logic goes, means that all will have the possibility of using that education to move into the middle class professions. In a society where monetary weight and considerable autonomy accompanies such professions, this aspiration makes a lot of sense. But as Owen Jones has shown, the model of society that accompanies this vision is sadly lacking.[14] What if all were to become lawyers, doctors, teachers, professors, accountants, bankers? What of the vital role of cleaners, shop assistants, secretarial staff, builders, plumbers? What is desperately needed is an holistic vision of society where the contribution of all its parts is recognised and treated with dignity and respect. Until Labour politicians reflect the diversity of British experience, not just the professional middle class, it is difficult to see how that more holistic vision of the good society can take hold.

But that is not to say that it is impossible. The expansion in the numbers of women and BAME in parliament and other institutions did not come about by accident. It is possible to address this issue and think imaginatively about how to connect the party to the communities that it serves.

Recognising that diverse experiences and talents would enable a richer account of what makes for a vibrant society to emerge necessitates developing a particular set of practical policies. A society recognising the value of all its parts would look rather different from ours. Pay differentials between the top and the bottom are shockingly out of proportion. These economic inequalities suggest a society that has failed to think about what makes for society in the first place; such failings must be addressed. This is far from impossible. Such societies already exist. In Japan and some the Scandinavian countries, the richest 20% are less than four times as rich as the poorest 20%. Compare that with the UK, where the richest 20% are more than seven times richer than the poorest 20%.[15] In London, this disparity in incomes is even starker, with the richest tenth of Londoners possessing 273 times as much wealth as the poorest tenth.[16] It is not impossible for the UK to change, and there are, indeed, already moves to narrow the difference between top and bottom pay in some of the UK's public institutions.[17]

Labour can go further. Given that more equal societies can be shown to be better places for all to live in, including the wealthy,[18] there is no reason why we should not campaign more explicitly about the value that comes from the redistribution of wealth: higher levels of trust, lower levels of mental illness, higher life expectancy, higher levels of educational achievement, less crime. Making this shift involves thinking again the role that work plays in the meaningful life. We have an unbalanced attitude to work. Long hours, stressful conditions, the struggle to balance family and other commitments with the demands of the workplace. We should promote better paid, part time work and job sharing, eliminating unemployment and enabling people to spend more time with their families, friends or doing the kind of voluntary work that makes communities good places to live. We should also look at tax breaks for businesses run along co-operative lines, giving workers a real stake in the place of their employment.

At this point the more sceptical reader will have decided that this is all too utopian and could never be achieved. But no society is a given; all arise out of the visions human beings pursue. Ethical socialism starts with the demand on the socialist to pursue just relationships in their own life. It ends with the reality of a society that values all and that understands the importance of strong communities as supportive places for individual flourishing. Grounding socialism in practice, in day-to-day life, avoids the brutality that Orwell feared in societies that had lost sight of the individual in their midst. In an age which is overly dependent on the mysterious working of the abstract forces of the financial markets, what better starting place for a socialism fit to confront the fears and anxieties of a rapidly changing world?

---

6 George Orwell, *Nineteen Eighty-Four*, Harmondsworth: Penguin [1949] 1954, p. 215.
7 See Danny Dorling, *So You Think You Know About Britain*, London: Constable, 2011, pp. 271-272, note 31.
8 Dorling, So You Think You Know About Britain, especially p. 149: 'The last time we were as unequal as we are in 2010 was around 1910.'
9 For an idea of the historical forebears of this approach, see Norman Dennis and A H Halsey, *English Ethical Socialism*, Oxford: Clarendon Press, 1988.
10 Quoted in Greg Rosen, *Serving the People: Co-operative Party History from Fred Perry to Gordon Brown*, London: Co-operative Party, p. 71
11 John Smith, 'Reclaiming the Ground: Freedom and the Value of Society' in *Reclaiming the Ground: Christianity and Socialism*, edited by Christopher Bryant, London: Hodder& Stoughton, 1993, p. 131
12 Contrast this with Bob Holman on the social context for poverty: 'a person's economic position, and hence risk of poverty, is decided largely by his family background, education, gender, race and occupation' ('Reconstructing the Common Good' in Reclaiming the Ground, p. 36).
13 For Lansbury's life and politics, see Bob Holman, *Good Old George: The Life of George Lansbury*, Oxford: Lion Publishing, 1990.

14 See Owen Jones, *Chavs: The Demonisation of the Working Class*, London: Verso, 2011, pp. 258-269.
15 See Richard Wilkinson and Kate Pickett, *The Spirit Level: Why Equality is Better for Everyone*, Harmondsworth: Penguin, 2010, introduction.
16 See http://www.guardian.co.uk/uk/2010/apr/21/wealth-social-divide-health-inequality
17 See for example Chris Patten's comments on becoming Chair of the BBC Trust, *The Guardian*, Wednesday 6 July.
18 Wilkinson and Pickett, *The Spirit Level*, chapter 13.

Part 2

What Now for the NHS?

The Betrayal of our NHS

By Richard Grimes

Richard tweets under the now infamous @RichardBlogger. He is a Labour Party member, an IT writer and consultant. He writes the left of centre NHSVault blog and the NHS blog for False Economy and is an occasional writer for Liberal Conspiracy http://nhsvault.blogspot.com

The NHS in England is in crisis. Two decades of marketisation have resulted in a system vulnerable to private sector cherry picking and asset stripping. The Coalition government's health policy is merely the final part of a long process of moving from a carefully planned, equitable, high quality service to a system where the market decides the care patients get. At the same time the NHS is under the tightest financial constrains it has ever faced.

The combination of a move to a market-based system with public funding of care being cut will inevitably mean that health inequalities will rise, quality will fall and our cherished NHS principle of free-at-the-point-of-use will come under threat. This crisis can only be averted by moving away from the market so that healthcare is delivered according to need, rather than market forces.

Laying the foundations of the NHS

In 1946 the government issued a white paper describing the new NHS (Cmd 6761). The document starts with these paragraphs:

> "The Bill provides for the establishment of a comprehensive health service in England and Wales. A further Bill to provide for Scotland will be introduced later.
>
> "All the service, or any part of it, is to be available to everyone in England and Wales. The Bill imposes no limitation on availability – for example, limitations on financial means, age, sex, employment or vocation, area of residence or insurance qualification."

From the very beginning of our NHS this was the pledge – to provide a comprehensive and universal service; that was available to all regardless of income or location. These principles are precious yet vulnerable. Reforms over the last two decades have chipped away at these principles and the final push to abolish them takes the form of the Coalition government's Health and Social Care Bill.

Funding the NHS adequately

Throughout its six decades finance has always been a problem for the NHS. Even the rise in funding during the Blair years depended partly by offsetting capital payments over 30 to 60 years through off-balance sheet Private Finance Initiatives. The issue is not that the NHS is wasteful in its healthcare spending; in fact, the situation is quite the opposite. The UK spends less than France, Germany, Canada and the US (OECD figures) both in terms of spending per head of population and percentage of GDP. Indeed, a recent study by the Journal of the Royal Society of Medicine showed that the NHS is one of the most cost-effective healthcare systems in the Western world, not only in terms of how much money is spent, but how effectively the money is spent. The JRSM paper shows that the NHS was second only to Ireland in getting the most improvements in terms of the lives saved for the least extra expenditure.

The government 'justifies' its bill by attacking the most vulnerable: the elderly and those with long-term conditions (LTCs). Earlier this year, David Cameron tried to justify his new health bill by saying:

> "The number of people with three or more long-term health conditions is set to rise by 30% in just 8 years. The cost of drugs has been growing by £600 million a year and medical technologies are continuously advancing. Now ask yourself: do you think the NHS will be able to cope with all this if we just put in a little money and carry on business as usual? The answer's no. Fail to modernise, and the NHS is heading for crisis."

The facts are true, there will be greater demands on NHS funding in the future; however, it starts from a position of being efficient whilst being very low cost. So, we actually have scope to increase funding whereas the Coalition government intends to cut funding. Cameron rightly points out that the elderly and patients with LTCs depend upon the NHS, and it is these people – the most vulnerable in our society – who will be most affected by NHS cuts.

NHS England is now suffering the biggest squeeze in funding it has ever experienced. This year, and every year until the next election, it will only get inflationary rises. This means that in real terms the NHS will have the same money, yet, as the above figures show, the demand on the NHS will be greater every year. How can one of the most cost-effective healthcare systems in the world be able to survive with such funding constraints? The answer is: rationing.

Rationing through 'care footprints'

Mike Farrar, the chief executive of the NHS Confederation recently published his idea of 'care footprints' modelled on the idea of 'carbon footprints'. This idea is simplistic and is wrong, but it chimes with the government's own rationing plans. Farrar says: "As with carbon, if individuals or communities could see their care footprint, they might be motivated and empowered to work out ways of reducing it."

A person's carbon footprint comes through their consumption and this can be seen as consumption that is either necessary or optional. As consumers we choose to take the guilt of the optional part of our carbon footprint or we make an effort to reduce it. Government has a role in reducing carbon footprints – through regulation and tax incentives to use low carbon alternatives – but it is the individual who plays the largest part.

Similar to a carbon footprint, a care footprint assumes that some NHS care is optional and that the individual is responsible for reduction. These assumptions are dangerous. Patients should have choice about how they are treated. This is called co-production where the clinician and the patient work together to deliver the treatment. However, it is abhorrent to make the patient responsible for reducing the care they receive, yet this is central to the government's policy. The government's white paper, 'Equity and excellence: Liberating the NHS', makes this clear: "In return for greater choice and control, patients should accept responsibility for the choices they make, concordance with treatment programmes and the implications for their lifestyle."

The 'greater choice and control' is predominately exercised by the affluent few, yet the responsibilities and change of lifestyle will be imposed upon the majority: the elderly and those with LTCs.

Restricting unnecessary treatments

Aneurin Bevan said that NHS treatment was to be 'made available to rich and to poor alike in accordance with medical needs and no other criteria'. If care is delivered according to medical needs, what is there to reduce? In 2006, Croydon Primary Care Trust and the London Health Observatory conducted a study of treatments commissioned by the PCT with a view to providing guidelines about whether the NHS should fund the treatments. This became known as the Croydon List. The study provided a list of treatments that were regarded as 'relatively ineffective' or cosmetic, procedures that can be argued as not fitting in with Bevan's description of 'medical needs'.

However, the Croydon List also gives procedures that can provide significant 'savings' because the NHS performs them in high volumes: cataract removal, knee and hip replacements. The Croydon List says that such savings can be made by reducing the number of these procedures in the case where the medical need is 'mild'. For hip and knee surgery this is estimated to be between 15% and 30% savings; for cataracts they are between 5% and 25%.

The problem is the definition of 'mild' cases. A cataract takes years to develop and no responsible clinician would recommend the removal of a functioning lens if the cataract does not significantly impair vision. A cataract never gets 'better', so the replacement will have to be carried out at some point in time meaning that the 'saving' is merely a delayed payment. Cataract surgery is the most common surgical procedure undertaken in England, with around 300,000 operations performed annually in the NHS. A 25% saving on the numbers of cataract operations clear will save a large amount of money, but like PFI this 'saving' merely postpones the payment.

Rationing is happening now. From April 2011 GP referrals have gone down by 4.7% compared to 2010. The GP trade magazine *Pulse* surveyed 300 GPs and found that 41 trusts throughout England have added new procedures to their 'low clinical priority' lists, the procedures they will not fund. More concerning is that of the GPs surveyed 22% said their patients were facing restrictions in access to operations for uncomplicated hernias, 17% to hip and knee operations and 11% to vasectomy or female sterilisation. These are all procedures that have a clinical value and make a difference to a patient's life. Equally concerning are the cuts to diagnostic tests: 13% reported rationing of direct access to MRI and CT scans, alongside 16% said there were cuts to routine blood glucose testing. If patients are not getting diagnostic tests their conditions can get worse which will cost the NHS extra in the long run.

Not coincidentally, perhaps, since April the NHS has started the so-called QIPP 'efficiency savings' whereby NHS England has to increase 'productivity' by 4% for each year until the next election. The result is clear: in response to the demand for 4% 'efficiency savings' there has been a 4.7% drop in referrals: rationing.

Care footprint effects on long-term conditions

One of the biggest problems with the concept of a 'care footprint' is that it fundamentally misunderstands the motivation of people with LTCs. A patient with a long term condition will live with that condition all their life; they will die with it, and most likely from it. But more significantly, they live with the condition 24 hours a day. Someone wanting to reduce their carbon footprint can do so unevenly: insulate their home to reduce their heating fuel consumption so that they can justify their holiday air travel. Their holiday becomes a vacation from their carbon reduction, and so long as there is a net reduction in their carbon usage over the entire year, who can argue against a week off? A patient with an LTC cannot do this. They have the condition from which they never get time off; their treatment is ongoing and continuous with no possibility for respite.

Patients with long term conditions present a particular challenge to the NHS – the Department of Health says that there are 15 million people with at least one LTC in England and with LTCs accounting for two-thirds of the NHS budget. Patients with LTCs have just one primary goal: to manage their condition well enough that they feel as well as possible for as long as possible throughout the day. If this was a simple task then LTCs would not cost the NHS so much, however the pressure of reducing their 'care footprint' will be an intolerable burden on LTC patients. Further, to make any significant difference to the budget, Farrar's idea can only be successful if it is aimed at those patients who use the most healthcare. Since patients with LTCs use the majority of the NHS budget, Farrar's comments can only be taken as targeting the most vulnerable of patients who are least able to reduce their healthcare.

Creating consumers through personal budgets

The government intends to introduce 'personal budgets' for people with long term conditions. They tell us that these budgets enable greater patient choice over their care and because of this they say that personal budgets are 'popular'. In fact this is not the case. A recent pilot of personal budgets across the country was met with opposition by patients who feared that budgets meant rationing and refused to take part. NHS managers reported that when they did recruit patients to the personal budget scheme they required more resources and this had a detrimental effect on those not the pilot.

The government says that no patient on a personal budget will be denied care even if their budget is exceeded. This suggests that the budget will have to be more than is actually needed, further taking resources that would otherwise be spent on other patient care. Personal budgets clearly are costly and require increased administration, so why is the government so keen? Consumerism.

Patients are not, and should never be consumers. This contradicts Bevan's promise of care 'in accordance with medical needs and no other criteria'. The government has promised that (initially at least) personal budgets will be used to purchase care through a fixed price system; the rhetoric is 'patient choice' and 'competition on quality'. The argument goes that when the patient has a personal choice they will choose an option they prefer and so the treatment is more likely to be successful. However, healthcare is about need, not consumerist desires.

We also have to question how personal budgets fit in with the evidence based principle that underpins the NHS. We know that the only way to maintain it as one of the most cost-effective healthcare systems in the developed world is to ensure that only clinically effective treatments are offered. The 'personal' aspect is used as the main selling point of the programme, and the cost effectiveness of the NHS will diminish if patients use their choice to choose less effective treatments.

The National Institute for Health and Clinical Excellence (NICE) is highly regarded around the world for their evidence based approach. By using measures such as the Quality Adjusted Life Year (QALY) they attempt to provide clinicians a comparative measure of the benefits of different treatments. Personal budgets are based on 'patient choice', yet nowhere in the literature about personal budgets is there a mention of providing an equivalent of QALY so that patients can make an informed choice about the outcomes of their care. Quality of life is a significant concern for patients with LTCs and a patient with a personal budget will need to know the effectiveness of the treatment they are purchasing so that they can make an informed choice. If there is no independent measure of the effectiveness of a treatment, where will patients get their information from?

The National Mental Health Development Unit found that private sector providers were enthusiastic about personal budgets because of their 'customer-focused attitude, experience of marketing themselves to individuals, and greater workforce flexibility'. In other words, private sector providers see personal budgets as a way of turning patients into consumers. Marketing does not exist simply to persuade patients to switch providers, a significant part of marketing is to increase demand. Private sector providers will persuade patients that they need the service they provide, even when they don't. With consumers determining healthcare demand rather than clinicians, costs will skyrocket, and more seriously it could result in a conflict between the marketing departments of providers who want to increase demand and clinicians who want care to be provided only for those who need it.

These are all problems with personal budgets when they are well funded, however, the NHS will come under severe funding issues in the next few years and so there is little chance that they will ever be adequately funded. As austerity bites into the NHS budget personal budgets will be squeezed. Initial government reassurances that no patient will be denied care when their budgets are exhausted will become untenable. For a Conservative government, the natural solution to this is top-ups and co-pay.

The NHS already has co-payments: dental, optician and prescription charges are all co-pay. An NHS true to its founding principles would not have co-pay because it is effectively a tax on the sick. It is only a matter of time before there are charges for GP visits and routine outpatient appointments. Furthermore, as the private sector makes inroads into the NHS – through the government's Any Qualified Provider policy – patients will find that they will be offered additional treatments not available on the NHS and may be offered supplementary care paid through top-up payments. Again, we already see this in dentistry where patients can opt to have their treatment from a dentist's private price list and this has lead to a well established market in dental insurance plans. Once top-ups are introduced into the wider NHS, insurance plans will follow and gradually the government will reduce the care provided free-at-the-point-of-use.

Personal budgets, though sold as 'patient choice' are the quickest way to move from our cherished free-at-the-point-of-use system to a health insurance system where the sick pay more than the healthy.

What should Labour do?

An incoming Labour administration must put equity at the centre of its NHS policy. The actual policy name may be different, the term may be to eradicate the postcode lottery, or to give fair access, but the result will be the same: a return to the founding principles of the NHS where there is 'no limitation on availability, [no] limitations on financial means, age, sex, employment or vocation, area of residence or insurance qualification'. This means ditching the consumerist 'patient choice' agenda that has been at the forefront of government policy over the last two decades.

A Labour government must ensure that care is given according to need, and this means that it must rule out once and for all any move towards co-pay or top-ups for healthcare. Indeed, to be consistent and fair, a Labour administration should move towards abolishing prescription charges in England.

We must handle the new demands for healthcare from an elderly population through more, and adequate funding, rather than rationing care.

The German healthcare system costs half as much again as the NHS producing no better outcomes, so we can easily afford to spend at German levels: we just have to have the political will to spend more of our GDP on health and less on other areas. We should stop talking about those who need healthcare as being a burden on the Treasury, whether this attack is through talk of 'care footprints' or by using them as a justification to embark on a top down, evidence-free reorganisation.

An NHS Which Belongs to Us
By David Taylor-Gooby

David Taylor-Gooby lives in Peterlee, County Durham, where he is secretary of the Branch Labour Party. He was a member of the District of Easington Council for twenty years. He previously worked as a Senior Lecturer at East Durham College. More recently he worked for the Commission for Patient and Public Involvement in Health and has done research on Patient Involvement at Sunderland University. He is currently an Executive Member of LINks and a Lay member of the Durham Dales, Easington and Sedgefield Clinical Commissioning Group. For more, email david.taylorgooby@btinternet.com.

What Now for the NHS?

I think we are agreed on the basic socialist ideas of the NHS, why we should defend it, and try and stop the flawed Lansley proposals. I do not need to argue about that. The opportunities for privatisation, not overnight, but in many small little advances, are the most dangerous. A hard-pressed GP group here will accept the seductive offer of a cheaper service (for now) from a private provider because they want to balance their books, and a hospital there will decide it cannot provide a range of services, so will franchise some out. At first we will not notice, but then one morning we will wake up and find the comprehensive service based on need not ability to pay is no longer there. No 'big bang', just 'salami slicing'. It will then be very difficult to take it back. Look at all the pressure the private sector put on Obama and Clinton before him in America to sabotage what we would regard as quite moderate reforms.

But we should not be pushed into the position of always defending the NHS the way that it is. Some aspects of it do need reform without undermining the basic principles.

What I want to debate here is how to make the NHS more genuinely democratic and embedded in the community so there will be strong popular resistance to attempts to take it away from us. At the moment I feel much of its management is remote and perceived as bureaucratic and out of touch by the public.

There are some good things in the Lansley proposals which I think those on the Left should welcome. One is handing public health to local authorities, so long as it is properly funded. Then it can be more integrated with leisure provision, housing, social services and other local government initiatives. The other, more controversially is the abolition of PCTs and their replacement by Practice Based Commissioning. In any case this had its origins in proposals by the previous government in 2006.

Alan Milburn is not a popular figure in the Labour Party nowadays, but his ideas for PCTs which were established on his watch in 2002 were good ones. They were genuinely community based, with close links to community activists and local authorities. Not only did they commission health care for an area, but they also provided the community services. Because of their strong links with local authorities and other community groups they could work closely with them, and people felt involved with them.

Professor Hudson from Durham University described how this worked in Sedgefield County Durham in 2006. He completed a study of an Integrated Team Working in the Sedgefield area of Durham. This looked at a project involving Sedgefield Primary Care Trust, Sedgefield Borough Council and Durham County Council. These three partners established five locality-based teams, co-located from line teams across the Borough, each consisting of social workers, district nurses and housing officers. This project was a practical example of devolution down to non-hierarchical teams. The project meant professional boundaries and hierarchies were broken down. Hudson (2006) notes that it had the effect of producing faster responses since people talked to each other rather than go through lengthy procedures. Greater trust also developed between different professionals.

For the first time in many cases people were beginning to know who ran their health and how they could talk to them. Health care was focused on clearly identified communities. In 2006 the PCTs were merged into bigger organisations with the emphasis on efficient management rather than local involvement.

The Boards were dominated with managers rather than community representatives. Local representation and public involvement programmes were reduced. As a result the big PCTs are often seen as bureaucratic, remote, and excessively staffed. The last government did in fact recognise this by starting to reduce their staffing.

Practice Based Commissioning was introduced in 2006, and was intended to involve the community in the planning of health care. This was an attempt to promote greater public involvement. The original proposals were set out in 'Our health, our care, our say: a new direction for community services' (DoH 2006): Detailed guidance to GPs published in 2006 stated proposals would only be considered if a business case was established. The criteria for assessing business cases included:

Whether the specific needs of population groups such as disabled people (including those with learning difficulties or mental health needs), people from Black Minority Ethnic communities (BME), the differing needs of men and women and of the diverse age groups, different faiths and sexual orientation of individuals and groups accessing services have been taken into account; patient and stakeholder support. (DoH 2006)

Thus there was an incentive, if Practice Based Commissioning (PBC) was to work, for the GPs to have evidence that they have consulted the public, particularly 'hard to reach groups' (DoH 2006). A document published by the Department of Health in June 2009 identifies good practice, including an example of how COPD services were redesigned locally in Easington. These were all examples of where GPs had organised projects in the community and drawn down, or 'unbundled' funds from the PCT to do so. (Practice Based Commissioning in Action, a Guide for GPs, DoH 2009) The objective was for more care to be organised in the community rather than people having to be sent to hospital. The public were to be involved in this process.

Some PCTs, such as Cumbria and Northamptonshire devolved budgets to PBC groups and things have worked well. In Northampton back pain is treated locally rather than in hospital. But in many other areas, including Durham, relations between the PCTs and the PBC groups have been unsatisfactory with the Commissioning Groups feeling their efforts are being blocked by the PCT. I think it is this frustration by some doctors which convinced Lansley to abolish PCTs, that and the possibilities of privatisation, which he seems to believe, is always better.

Simply having Practice Based Commissioning (PBC) will not necessarily be good for patients. There is always the possibility that doctors will make more money and services will not improve. It needs to be regulated. But it is much easier to establish public involvement in smaller groups that have affinity with local communities. I studied the various NHS documents about what 'public involvement' means, and find that it is always assumed to be desirable, but actual definitions are often non-existent or vague.

There seemed to be four strands of thinking about involvement of public and patients as follows:

- Scrutiny: The work of the OSCs. These bodies consider and if necessary criticise the activities of the NHS. By law the NHS must respond.
- Partnership: Carers, patients and other interested parties work with the NHS to improve services. There are often groups to consider particular illnesses or conditions. Within this category can be placed individuals who are now taking a greater role to manage their own treatment or care, particularly those with long term conditions.
- Forward planning: The Commissioning role. PBC Boards, PCTs and to a lesser extent OSCs consider the future options. This is a role primarily for the PCTs, with local involvement such as practice based commissioning, since the Acute Trusts have to respond to what is commissioned. This role is developing.
- Customer feedback: With the increasing complexity and variety of NHS provision, those who commission care want to know whether that care is working and what improvements can be made. Public and

Patient Involvement has a role here. (Taylor-Gooby and MacDonald, Sunderland University 2010).

Real involvement of patients and the public, in a way where they would feel real ownership and identity with the NHS would incorporate all four.

Unfortunately, many in the NHS feel it is simply something they must do, or to 'tick a box' to use a phrase. A trusted group of volunteers are summoned, and the public is then deemed to have been involved. This is the easy way out, to which busy staffs often resort. The NHS itself admits that PPI is often inadequate:

While nationally there are many examples of innovative practice, there is still little evidence that involvement is a mainstream activity alongside other policy and performance requirements. There is scant evidence to show that involvement activity is stitched into all the strands of NHS organisations' work, including their decision-making processes; of how organisations have listened and responded to what users have told them; or of how health services have been shaped according to the needs and preferences of users. We also know that the NHS is not always sure about when it needs to involve users and clear about whether involving users is the same or different to consulting them. World class commissioning reflects the shift of involvement to the forefront of the policy agenda and establish it as one of the key developmental challenges for NHS organisations (DoH 2008: 'Real Involvement').

Public involvement does not simply mean going to meetings with nice lunches, as some NHS managers seem to think and approving decisions which have already been made. It means genuine involvement in the decision making progress, being made aware of facts and able to participate in decisions. Thus if difficult choices have to be made, such as closing a hospital, which may well happen when there is more community-based treatment, then people are involved in the debate at the beginning. It is when the public are confronted with a decision to close a facility without much warning that people become incensed and politicians jump on the bandwagon.

The ideas for commissioning, as set out during the last government, long before Lansley was on the scene, do reflect this idea that users of the service should be involved in the planning and execution of a service, not simply 'consulted' about it. It is important that these principles of commissioning are actually put into practice.

But I think involvement is about more than this. Many of the problems of health today deal with bad lifestyles and unhealthy habits. Our consumption-based market-driven society does not help, and expecting the culprits, such as the food, tobacco or alcohol industries to solve it is either naive or self-serving. These problems can only be solved by encouraging people to adopt healthier habits and lifestyles. Mobilising the public to do this, provided they are properly resourced, is more likely to do it rather than lectures by professionals. For example, someone is more likely to give up smoking if his mates encourage him than if he receives a lecture or leaflet from the NHS. In the professional jargon this use of volunteers to 'target' those at risk is known as 'social marketing'. Here is an example of what can be done, again from the Easington area.

Social marketing can employ a range of techniques, including videos and posters, but to be effective it needs one-to- one interaction between volunteers who are sympathetic to the person who wants to change their behaviour. The volunteer who was Chair of the Health Forum which had (until next year) access to funding, was proud to list the projects his group had promoted. They included promoting flu vaccination, fitting smoke alarms, providing lighting for the elderly to reduce the risk of falls, and promoting various activities organised by community groups to reduce loneliness and promote fitness. Projects needed financial help (although most also raised resources themselves), but none could have functioned without volunteers – to carry out the survey of elderly people's properties, for example. They all had a positive effect of health, either preventing accidents and illness or promoting good health, physical and mental, through exercise and social activity. A side effect was that the activity improved the health of the volunteers themselves (Taylor-Gooby and McDonald, Sunderland 2010).

This direct involvement of volunteers in the actual process of promoting good health and delivering health care can be called 'positive involvement'. Another description of it is 'co-production'.

Co-production of public services means the public sector and citizens making better use of each other's assets and resources to achieve better outcomes and improved efficiency (Governance International 2011-09-07).

Co-production means treating people as resources, not patients or customers. See 'A glass half-full: how an asset approach can improve community health and well-being' (IDeA 2010).

There remains the issue of the actual practicalities of commissioning, which is really booking and monitoring treatment. It would be wasteful for each Commissioning Group to set up its own mini-bureaucracy, and some commissioning, and the pooling of risk, needs to be done on a large scale.

This is where the private operators will try and move in. Accountants and consultants (of a non-medical kind) will see this as an area where they can readily offer expertise. The answer is probably social enterprises, jointly owned by the local authority and the GPs themselves, to make it harder for them to be privatised.

These could employ ex-PCT staff, but they would not need to be on such a large scale. If they were under the control of the local authority and the GPs then they would be obliged to carry out the commissioning instructions, which would now be decided with real popular involvement.

As socialists we want the NHS to continue as an example to the rest of the world that socialism does work. But the 'spectre of privatisation' will continue to prowl. We need to ensure genuine involvement of people in the NHS so they believe it is 'their 'NHS. Then they will want to make sure it stays that way.

I must conclude by observing that I do have my feet rooted in practicality. I have worked in patient and public involvement in health both in a professional and voluntary capacity, not simply thought and written about it. I know what the practical problems are. Many of the people attracted to it enjoy meetings for their own sake, and do not assess the effectiveness of their efforts rigorously enough.

Nor do I share the view of Trotskyists on the Left or 'Big Society' enthusiasts on the Right that all you have to do is remove real or imaginary barriers and suddenly many people will become involved. Involving people effectively is hard work. In many cases, however, they now perceive involvement as a waste of time. It is our challenge to convince them otherwise.

We do have to offer a new vision of the NHS. It is a service for the people which is responsive to the people. Thus they must be involved in the planning, and where practical, actual management of it.

Treatment is not something professionals 'do' to you, but the achievement of good health is a partnership between professionals and people. A socialist vision of the NHS makes it clear that it belongs to people, and they can shape and help run it. Then they will ferociously resist attempts at privatisation.

Bibliography
- Department of Health. (2006) Practice Based Commissioning, practical implementation. London: HMSO
- Department of Health (2008a) 'Real Involvement 'Working with People to Improve
- Health Services (Revised). London: HMSO.
- Department of Health. (2009) Practice Based Commissioning in Action: A guide for GPs, London: HMSO
- Easington Primary Care Trust. (2006) Half Year Report and Summary Financial Statements April – September 2006. Durham: NHS
- Health and Social Care Act (2001) Directions to local authorities (overview and scrutiny Committees, health scrutiny functions), London: Department of Health.
- Hudson, B. (2006): Whole Systems Working A Guide and Discussion Paper, NHS Care Services Improvement Partnership, Integrated Care Network. London: Department of Health.
- Dr Stephen MacDonald and David Taylor-Gooby; The Role of Public and Patient Involvement in Practice Based Commissioning within Easington NHS Services July 2010, University of Sunderland.
- NHS (2010) Equity and Excellence: Liberating the NHS. Cm 7881, London: Department of Health.
- 'Our Health, Our Care, Our Say' A new direction for community services. (2006) London: HMSO.
- Townsend, P., Phillimore, P., & Beattie, A. (1994). Inequalities in Health in the Northeast Region: Northern Regional Health Authority and the University of Bristol

The Commercialisation of Public Services

By Grahame Morris MP

Grahame Morris MP is the Chairperson of Labour Left as well as the Labour MP for Easington, an area blighted by the Tory misgovernment of the 1980s. Having spent his early career in the NHS, Grahame began working with John Cummings, MP in 1987 and has served as a Labour Member of Easington District Council for fifteen years. Grahame is a member of the Health Select Committee, and he writes for the Morning Star on matters related to the NHS. Grahame's passion lies in narrowing the health inequality gaps brought about by the unequal society in which we live.

What Now for the NHS?

The Left should champion dynamic responsive public services. We need a dynamic, responsive, publicly funded and publicly provided model for the UK's public services. We must be bold and reclaim our public services for the sake of our people, our economy and our country.

The recent trend in delivering public services in the UK has seen a move away from the large centrally driven publicly provided service model which characterised the welfare state in the immediate post-war period. Across the public sector we have seen the introduction of competition as well as large sections of services passed over to the private sector. The drive behind this commercialisation has been from right-wing critics of the old-style monolithic services who believed that it would be impossible to achieve improved outcomes, greater efficiencies and a consumer focus without such significant reform.

The desire of governments to reform key public services and extend the commercialisation agenda as they seek further efficiencies has entered a new phase under this Coalition. While New Labour brought competition into the NHS, the Coalition is seeking to break it up and remove any distinction between public and private providers of health services. The Health and Social Care Bill will turn the NHS into little more than an insurance fund.

There were those in the Labour Party who warned that the split between commissioners and providers, the introduction of competition, commercial practices and the incorporation of the private sector into public service delivery would risk opening the floodgates to further ideological change in the future. While Margaret Thatcher would have struggled to pass current Tory-led reforms to the NHS back in the 1980s, once the private sector had a foot in the door and the public service ideology was broken down under a Labour government, these policies became a Trojan horse for privatisation.

At the last election, all three main political parties seem to have lost faith in the ability of public service workers to improve public services from within. 'Reform' itself had become almost entirely associated with further marketisation, the extension of competition or a greater role for the private sector at the heart of our public services.

The ideological drive behind reform of this nature has also deepened. The extension of commercial practices into public services is now pursued regardless of the impact or assessment of how its implementation will affect the costs, accessibility or quality of service delivery. The government's own impact assessment of the Health and Social Care Bill suggested that 'the majority of quantifiable [financial] distortions work in favour of NHS organisations' – for example, NHS providers have a lower cost base than the private sector even before taking into account the latter's need to make a profit.

The evidence suggests that the contracting out of public services to the private sector has a poor record. There is often a negative impact for employees with the prevalence of short-term contacts and the increasing use of employment agencies. UNISON commissioned a report on the rise of the multi billion pound Private Public Services Industry raising significant concerns about the increased dependency on private firms. Public services have become a huge industry from which the private sector receives more than £80 billion of taxpayers' money every year. Yet private sector delivery of services has become characterised by increased cost, deteriorating quality, the loss of accountability and greater risk of service failure. The Southern Cross Care Homes debacle has brought just these sorts of issues to the fore once again.

More and more services are being transferred to the private sector, leading to a situation where there is a danger that we lose control over our public services altogether. In 2007 the Local Government Association warned that because of the amount of local authority spending on external private sector contracts, the ability to make efficiency savings without damaging services was not realistic. It should be even more evident at a time of financial restraint how important it is that we retain control over our public services.

The central argument in favour of the increased commercialisation and privatisation of public services rests on the importance of consumer choice as a driver of increased efficiency, accountability and value for money. Yet there are serious limitations to the idea of the 'well-informed consumer' as examples show.

While there were many faults with the nationalised rail services provided by British Rail, privatisation has not resulted in increased efficiency or competitive ticket pricing. On the contrary, disruptions to rail services remain, commuters suffer from chronic overcrowding on rush hour trains and prices have increased dramatically year-on-year. In fact, privatisation has not resulted in increased choice for consumers at all: in the case of the railways it is not possible to make a choice about which rail company to use. High fares and poor conditions have to be accepted. This is not a 'free market'. It is the result of the State granting a licence to specific companies to make money through market domination. We must be very wary indeed of allowing this situation to develop in the provision of healthcare and other welfare services.

One area which it is argued does feature genuine consumer choice is the provision of utilities. In most parts of the United Kingdom, it is possible to choose a provider of gas and electricity from a handful of companies. Yet here too prices have increased above inflation and the profits of the energy companies have soared, to the extent that during the autumn of 2011, Labour Leader Ed Miliband looked to hold the 'big six' energy companies to account for their excessive price increases.

Of course, energy companies claim that they are only reflecting the vagaries of the international markets in coal, oil and gas. However, their increased profits and continued price increases suggest that not only have they made no attempt to insulate people from any increased costs but that they are making money rather than working in the best interests of their customers. The reason is that the energy companies are well aware that the idea of the well informed consumer is largely a myth. People are often confused by the proliferation of similar sounding deals or are reluctant to get involved in changing supplier.

Similarly, people are traditionally very reluctant to change the bank which provides their current account, even when there are tangible financial benefits from doing so. That is why banks create incentives to those who do switch their current accounts. It is also why there are so many attractive add-ons to opening a student account. Banks know full well that once a person has opened an account with a bank as a student, they will most likely use the same bank for the rest of their life.

There are very few people indeed, irrespective of income or education, who sit down every month, work out which energy company or bank account offers best value, and, crucially, act by changing their utility provider or switching their current account. And even if they want to do so, there are usually financial tie-ins and penalties for leaving their existing deal. It seems that the 'big six' energy companies know these things, hence the steep increase in fuel bills and their reluctance (as evidenced by their increase in profits) to insulate their customers from the increase in the market prices of fuels.

It is worth remembering that Left politicians at the end of the nineteenth century argued for municipalisation on the grounds of efficiency, in that it enabled councils to run utilities at a lower cost to ratepayers and to avoid the wastefulness and high costs incurred through the use of private companies. There are certain services which it seems natural for the state to provide - no one would seriously suggest replacing police forces with private security firms – and the increasing consumerisation of public services not only undermines our welfare state, but also the health of our economy and society.

Milton Friedman and Friedrich Hayek did not advocate a 'small state', as many commentators on both the right and the Left have mistakenly argued. On the contrary, they saw the state as vital for securing private property, protecting the market and incentivising trade. They recognised that for a nation to succeed economically it was not simply a matter of low taxation and regulation. They did not believe the simplistic argument that capital and human resources simply move from an area of high taxation to one of low taxation, as though through osmosis – but rather that security and infrastructure needed to be provided and the only institution able to provide this was the state.

As a nation, we cannot expect to attract leading industries without leading excellent state education. We cannot expect to have a motivated, healthy and happy workforce without comprehensive welfare provision; and we cannot expect our innovators and entrepreneurs to take risks with borrowed capital if their main concern is whether they can afford treatment should they be ill. Given that the vast majority of start-up companies fail within the first twelve months, and given that many small businessmen and women build up large amounts of debts while starting up businesses, they are less likely to take these risks if they are liable for ruinous healthcare or welfare payments should they be ill, pregnant, or unable to work. Essentially, if we are to have a vibrant and vital economy which can attract the most innovative industries and keep the brightest people in the United Kingdom, we need robust public services. There are certain areas which benefit from consumerisation – the welfare state is not one of them. For the health of our people, our economy and our society we need to keep it in the public sphere.

The welfare state has a proud history and has embedded itself into the British psyche. The NHS has perhaps been one of the most robust drivers behind the welfare state with its guiding principles and values which are supported wholeheartedly by the public at large. We do not need to protect the welfare state merely for ideological reasons, nor do we need to resist the consumerisation of the NHS and other public services simply out of a suspicion of change and a desire to protect the status quo. Indeed, the last Labour government sought to use the private sector in the NHS to increase capacity, for instance in reducing waiting times for cataract and hip operations. However, once the distinction between our public services and the private sector was blurred by the centre-left it was clear that this would be abused once those on the political right took power. While this government denies its motives are to privatise NHS services, there is growing evidence that NHS providers and social enterprises are continuing to lose out to commercial companies for major NHS contracts. Private healthcare firms have on numerous occasions beaten social enterprise projects even where these projects reinvest profits into the local community. The direction of travel that of this government, forcing new commissioning groups and hospitals to operate in the private sector, is certain to lead to much more of this privatisation of our NHS services.

Aneurin Bevan argued that abuse in the health service occurred when the incompatible principles of private acquisitiveness and public service were married together. This is true throughout the welfare state. The scale of the privatisation in public services receives little or no attention in the media and often goes unnoticed apart from by those that it directly affects – such as the cleaner or cook that loses their job. Yet around 20-30% of government spending on public services goes to the private sector – almost a third. It is not that we should simply oppose any money going to the private sector from the public purse. What should be opposed is the direction of travel and rapid growth of the private sector within public services. The benefits of good public services are clear for all to see. They should be characterised by:

- Reliable employment practices;
- Greater democratic control over service delivery; and
- Greater accountability.

However, the most basic benefit of public services should always be the ability to deliver an effective service for better value for money than private competitors.

We must set out an agenda which puts confidence back into public services and the public sector workforce and which can fashion change and improvements from within. There have been clear failures in the state-owned public services model which must be addressed if those of us who support this model are to win the arguments over future reform. Slow moving monolithic bureaucracies at local and national level need to become more responsive and we must recognise that the move towards the private sector was in part inspired by the refusal of some services to adapt and change. Trade unions and staff associations must become part of the solution to improving services – indeed, there are examples where unions have worked with local authorities to redesign services for the benefit of staff and services users, such as in my own area, in commercial vehicle maintenance and refuse collection. As we look to the future, we must consider today how we will respond to creeping privatisation and outline a clear plan to reclaim our public services.

There are many powerful, pragmatic arguments for robust public services. Any attempt to undermine the social provision of these services is a grave mistake – for our economy, for our society and for our country. We on the Left should be bold and we should not allow ourselves to be hoodwinked by the falseness of the 'choice' argument. Nor should we be taken in by the neo-liberal consensus of recent years that reform of public services must inevitably lead to commercialisation. A dynamic, responsive, publicly funded and provided model can deliver services more efficiently and with greater accountability than the private sector.

Part 3

Education: Unequal Resources, Social Mobility and Poverty of Aspiration

Archimedes or Stephenson?

By Chi Onwurah MP

Chi Onwurah is the MP for Newcastle Upon Tyne. Chi's educational and employment expertise is in science and innovation and she was, before becoming an MP, head of Telecoms Technology at Ofcom as well as holding various roles in the private sector. In 2010, Chi was appointed shadow minister for Business, Innovation and Skills. Chi is not a member of Labour Left but was keen to participate in a debate about the future direction of the Labour Party.

Education: Unequal Resources, Social Mobility and Poverty of Aspiration

I cannot remember a time when I was not interested in science. On the council estate where I grew up there were no scientists but there were libraries full of science books. And teachers at my primary school did not so much bring text books to life as enchant you into science so you were captured by the magic of it.

I clearly remember learning how Archimedes was inspired to discover the principle of displacement after immersing himself in a hot bath. His cousin the King was worried his crown was made of silver and bronze instead of the more expensive gold he had paid for. As the water slopped over the side of his bath, Archimedes realised that the amount of water he displaced was equal to his volume, and that once he knew the volume of the crown, and its weight, he could tell the King if it was pure gold or not.

Archimedes leapt from the bath and ran naked through the streets of Syracuse shouting 'Eureka'. I ran home, filled the kitchen sink with water and proceeded to submerge all manner of pots and pans until I had proven Archimedes discovery to my own satisfaction. My mother was not best pleased but I explained that she was lucky I was fully dressed and she would have to grow accustomed to this sort of behaviour now she had a scientist in the family.

Fortunately for my mother's sanity, my teachers had less flamboyant role models to offer me closer to home.

George Stephenson grew up in poverty in Wylam, a mining village ten miles from where I lived. Illiterate until the age of 18, he was fascinated by the machinery of the mines in which he worked. At night he paid a local farmer to teach him to read, so he could follow engineering manuals. During the day he was inspired to put science to the service of his fellow colliery workers tackling the dangers they faced. His own father was blinded in a mining accident. In 1812, 92 men and boys died in the Felling Pit explosion, eight miles from where Stephenson lived.

Through a process of trial and error Stephenson set about designing a 'safety lamp', which could be used in mines without causing explosions. In 1815 he succeeded. There followed a long drawn out battle with Sir Humphry Davy, inventor of the Davy lamp, an eminent scientist who could not believe that an illiterate colliery worker could have matched his own invention. The battle reputedly gave Stephenson a life-long distrust of London-based, theoretical, scientific experts.[19] Something many of his compatriots share to this day.

After the safety lamp Stephenson turned his attention to the most visible part of the coal mining industry, the movement of coal. With his son Robert, he improved upon the existing rudimentary steam engines. In 1829 their engine 'the Rocket' won the competition for the Liverpool to Manchester Railway. George Stephenson was now world famous.

Archimedes went on to invent the screw that bears his name and the principle of the lever. Stephenson's trains went all around the world and his screw arch bridge was the first to cross a railway at an angle.

I have huge admiration for Archimedes, but my respect is tempered by the knowledge that he was a rich and privileged man in a slave society that gave him the leisure to solve some of the great scientific problems of the age. Stephenson, on the other hand, was born with nothing, was self-taught and addressed his genius to tackling the problems that the people around him faced.

The question I find myself asking is, why is it that, 2,223 years after the death of Archimedes but only 153 years after the death of Stephenson, scientists resemble the former so much more than the latter?

I write as someone with an enduring love of science and technology. But I am much less enamoured of the fact that when I attend Royal Society events or other gatherings of eminent scientists I am all too literally in a class of my own. Engineering is less affluent but drawn even more exclusively from a narrow male demographic. That cannot be right.

Class, science and getting your hands dirty

The predominance of those from more privileged backgrounds is not limited to science or to the UK. In his book 'Chavs, the demonisation of the working class'[20], Owen Jones describes at some length the limited socio-economic make-up of much of the media and its detrimental consequences. Though the book was reviewed in papers of all political colours, not one journalist took issue with Owen's characterisation of the media or contested his conclusion that media from which working class people were absent were more likely to actively or passively allow for the demonisation of working class people.

I am not implying that science demonises the working class, it is not science's role to construct narratives and therefore science has much less power to determine the representation of a particular group in our society. But the consequences of drawing science and technology's skill base from a narrow socio-economic group may be equally far-reaching at a time when many of the major challenges we face as a country appear to have technological solutions. Across politics and media there is a general

Education: Unequal Resources, Social Mobility and Poverty of Aspiration

consensus that we need more scientists and engineers and that is unlikely to happen if we continue to fish in the same narrow, shallow pool.

Why it is that scientists and engineers are so unrepresentative of the British people? I am not a social scientist so in the tradition of the best engineers including Stephenson, the analysis I offer is based on empirical evidence rather than theoretical study. As an engineer I have lived and worked in Denmark, France, the US, Nigeria and of course the UK. I have also travelled extensively for work. Before the financial crash changed views in the UK I would have said there was no other country which has such a negative attitude to practical science – that is applied science and engineering.

When working in France I was surprised by the high status in which engineers were held – the highest compliment was to be called an engineer, in fact, Napoleon was praised for being an engineer rather than a general or, indeed, an Emperor.

In Germany and Portugal Engineer is a title of a similar or even higher standard than Doctor. In the UK, until recently, an engineer was someone who cleaned your boiler. The reasons for this are no doubt complex but I suspect related to England's (as opposed to Britain's) well documented history of anti-intellectualism, particularly amongst the upper and parts of the working classes albeit for different reasons.

Additionally, idleness was traditionally seen as not only the mark but the duty of a gentleman. English literature from the 16th to the 20th century makes it clear that any occupation apart from the army and perhaps the law was an absolute bar on being considered a gentleman, or a lady

It is ironic, and at the same time tragic, that this rigid upper-class veneration of worklessness went hand in hand with attacks on the workshy lower orders given over to sedition, godlessness and drink.

Today everyone, from the Duke of Cambridge to the school-leaver on the most deprived council estate, is expected to get a job. But the legacy of that reverence for genteel inactivity lives on in a distaste for occupations which require you to 'get your hands dirty' – and almost anything involving applied science or engineering is thought to involve a little wear and tear on the hands.

In fact, and as good careers advice can make clear, science, engineering and technology are excellent groundings for a wide range of careers. I find it very useful in politics, and science graduates are also valued in the civil service, project management, operations, financial services, accountancy and all forms of management and logistics.

But good careers advice is rare and getting rarer. So the UK's unique history of class, anti-intellectualism and idleness is able to have a profound impact on the place of science and engineering in our culture today

If we consider that impact together with the decline of engineering apprenticeships and the fact that only a small proportion of the less well off make it to university to study anything then the absence of those with a working class background from the top of science and engineering becomes easier to understand if not accept.

The 2009 Sutton Trust report *The Educational Backgrounds of Leading Scientists and Scholars*[21] found that the backgrounds of Royal Society and British Academy Fellows closely mirror the student intakes to Oxbridge and other elite universities in the 1960s, when many entered higher education. 42% of top UK scientists went to private schools as opposed to 7% of the general population.

While this may be lamentable the real cause for concern is that there is little sign of change. Private school students still account for one-third or more of top grades in key subjects like physics and chemistry.

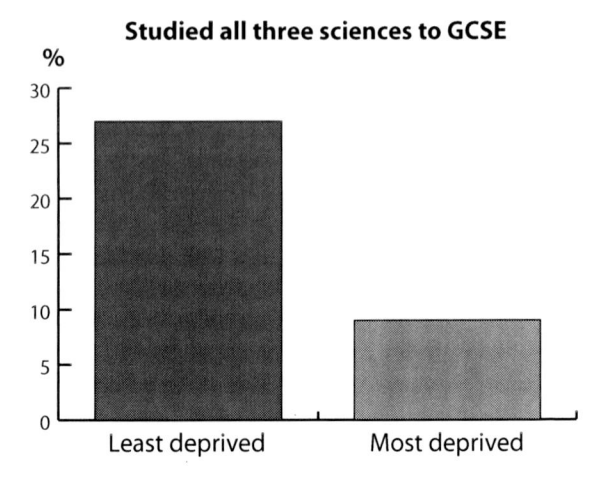

Studied all three sciences to GCSE

The graph above shows that in state schools, only 8% of children from the most deprived backgrounds studied all three sciences at GCSE, compared to 27% of those from the least deprived backgrounds. The Sutton

Education: Unequal Resources, Social Mobility and Poverty of Aspiration

report concluded that current trends in student intakes to leading research universities suggest that independent school pupils will continue to be significantly over-represented among the next generation of leading scientists.

The impact of the tripling of university fees on both the provision of, and attendance at, science and engineering degrees is yet to be understood and has certainly not been factored in.

As well as being from more privileged backgrounds scientists and engineers tend to be overwhelmingly male. In both the Royal Society and the Royal Academy of Engineering the proportion of female Fellows is under 10%.

The comparison with Archimedes is therefore more appropriate than might first appear. As a male, literate citizen of an aristocratic family I estimate he represented the top 2% of Greek society at best.

With a household income of 12 shillings a week the Stephenson family was on close to the average income for the early 1800s. Around 40% of the population of the time was illiterate and about 50% lived in cities. George Stephenson was therefore far more representative of the country and time in which he lived than Archimedes. And his work still touches most of our lives today.

I am very grateful to my teachers for ensuring I learned that science was not only a matter of lying in baths, or for that matter sitting under apple trees, but also about working hard to develop practical solutions to working peoples' problems.

Science of the people, by the people, for the people

So does it matter? Anti-intellectualism is a national rather than a demographic characteristic, applied science is too dirty or too difficult or both, and if these attitudes are exaggerated in less privileged children by the challenges of getting an apprenticeship or getting to university and knowing what to study, then so what?

My concern is not simply that science is unrepresentative. That is both a cause and a consequence of the real problem. Which is that science is incapable of speaking to or for the people.

And that matters. Not only because rebalancing the economy towards manufacturing requires more engineers and scientists. Not simply because China, India, Russia and many other emerging economies value engineering and science more highly, as we ourselves did when we were going through our industrial revolution. Not even because it is estimated that 85% of economic growth is due to innovation[22].

A more representative science establishment matters for social as well as economic reasons because science plays a significant part in some of the key decisions that society needs to take. For example:

- Do industrialised countries respond to climate change by changing our behaviour, do we adapt to changing climate or do we try to change the climate change through geo-engineering?
- Do we need genetically modified crops to feed a world population of seven billion and rising?
- Can non-industrialised countries deliver middle class lifestyles without going into carbon overload?

I am not going to include here the host of social networking questions around the nature of privacy and trust which have technology at their heart, as these can be answered without understanding the underlying technology. But taking an informed view of genetically modified foods without understanding GM technology is much harder.

And these decisions are going to be taken whether the majority of people understand them or not. Science, like all professions, does not lack for arrogant practitioners. All too often scientists or engineers tell me the British public is far too stupid to understand GM/climate change/cloud computing and so should just learn to do what their betters tell them. This is not an acceptable approach for a progressive party.

So we need more scientists and engineers able to speak to and for the mass of people so these decisions can be taken by, and in the interests of, an informed people.

In October I was in Kyoto in Japan for a conference on Science in Society. Fukushima was present even when it was not on the agenda, a constant reminder of science's duty to society. Not surprisingly perhaps, protests have been part of the metaphorical fall-out of the nuclear accident in Japan. Some do question whether nuclear power is an acceptable price to pay for the clear blue skies that have replaced the coal-fired Tokyo smog of yesteryear. But for many of the protesters the key question is whether the Japanese people were well enough informed to take that decision. Were the risks of nuclear energy openly debated and the population fully informed of earlier safety lapses? Was enough done to ensure informed decisions representing the informed views of an informed people?

Education: Unequal Resources, Social Mobility and Poverty of Aspiration

What, then, do we need to do to enable informed decision making? This is a subject for social scientists. But I have a few suggestions:

- A general expectation that an understanding of science is, like numeracy and literacy, an essential skill.
- Recognition by the Left and centre-left that a wider understanding and democratisation of science is part of a progressive agenda.
- Informed debate on key questions which does not patronise or ignore the people – who are ultimately most concerned by the consequences of the decision
- Real effort by the science and engineering establishment to open up these professions to a wider range of backgrounds. They would claim that much is being done, and to a certain extent this is true, right now the Institute of Physics is running a scheme in my school I went to aimed at getting more girls into science. But rather than working hard at failing we need effective change. Policymakers must make sure the right incentives are in place. Timescales need a sense of urgency.
- Support within the media for science and technology debate. The media is very good at simplifying complex arguments – not necessarily in ways which policy makers like! So far, this has rarely been applied to science and technology, perhaps because media professionals with science and technology backgrounds are few.

If these suggestions were implemented I might then live to see what science and technology that is representative of the people looks like. Where might technology lead us if it were being led by the many not the few?

Far too often the technology we meet today seems openly hostile, expecting us to adapt to it rather than that it should serve us. I am writing this on a PC running a well known operating system with applications from different companies. Between crashing, hanging, sending me unpleasant messages and threatening me with dire consequences if I don't do what it says – buy a printer cartridge or a software upgrade - it hardly engenders a relationship of mutual respect.

If I dial customer service to complain my call will be 'handled' by a machine which will treat me as if I, too, am a machine.

And if I decide to relieve my frustration by buying a snack at the supermarket I risk having an automatic teller shout at me because I have had the audacity to put my own bag in the bagging area.

These examples may appear trivial, but they are defining a relationship between people and technology which reduces the likelihood of productive engagement. The Rocket never talked back. Over the last 20 years technology has found a voice and it is not a particularly pleasant one. If the train had been invented today I fear it would refuse to move until all luggage had been securely stowed and then berate passengers who dared to bring their own refreshments.

I harbour the hope that science of the people by the people and for the people might result in technology that was not only useful but compassionate, humble and, even, considerate.

---

[19] Davies, Hunter (1975). *George Stephenson*. Weidenfeld and Nicolson. ISBN 0-297-76934-0.
[20] Owen Jones, *Chavs: The Demonisation of the Working Class* Verso. ISBN-10: 184467696X
[21] http://www.suttontrust.com/research/scientists-and-scholars/
[22] Josh Lerner, *Boulevard of Broken Dreams* Page 44 Princeton University Press ISBN-10: 069114219X

Education: 'a debt due, from the present to future generations'

By Dan Young
(with input from Andy Shaw)

Dan Young lives in Romford and is a member of Romford Labour CLP. He is the Co-op party, London youth rep. As well as this, Dan works as an assistant for Jon Cruddas MP.

Education: Unequal Resources, Social Mobility and Poverty of Aspiration

Education: 'a debt due, from the present to future generations'. These famous words by George Peabody, well-known banker and philanthropist, show he knew way back in the 19th century that education was the central pillar to social mobility. It is education that can ensure the most gifted child from the most disadvantaged background can still realise his potential in life. This core belief of George Peabody's is as true today as it was in the 19th century. Education is still the best platform for growth but it is now under attack. The Coalition is currently pursuing policies that put social mobility through education at risk and the Labour Party can do far more to attack the Coalition on a number of issues; from free schools to academies Labour must set out its stall.

Imbalances in higher education provision

At present, higher education provision is skewed towards those who attended schools in the independent sector. Figure 1 shows the rates of successful admission to Oxbridge, in the top 30 performing schools in

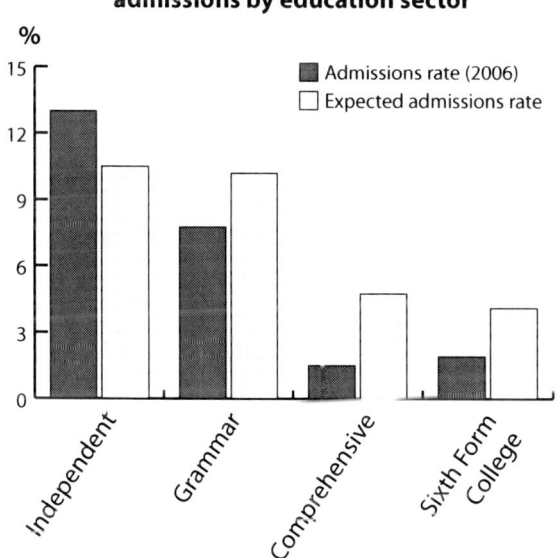

Figure 1: Oxbridge University admissions by education sector

Source: Oxbridge admissions rates by education sector, compared with admission rates expected according to average A-Level results in that sector. Data taken from Sutton Trust report (2008): University Admissions by Individual Schools

different school sectors. Figure 2 shows the rates of successful admission to the 13 'Sutton Trust' universities, those 13 universities considered by the Sutton Trust as the highest-ranked universities across an average of published university league tables. In both cases, successful admission rates are contrasted with "expected" admissions rates – that is, the admissions rate that each sector should expect to achieve, given the average A-Level results of pupils attending the schools in that sector. For both figures, it is clear that the independent school sector is the only one to significantly outperform its "expected" admissions rate, with the problem particularly exacerbated when all 13 Sutton Trust universities are considered.

Figure 2: Sutton Trust univesity admissions by education sector

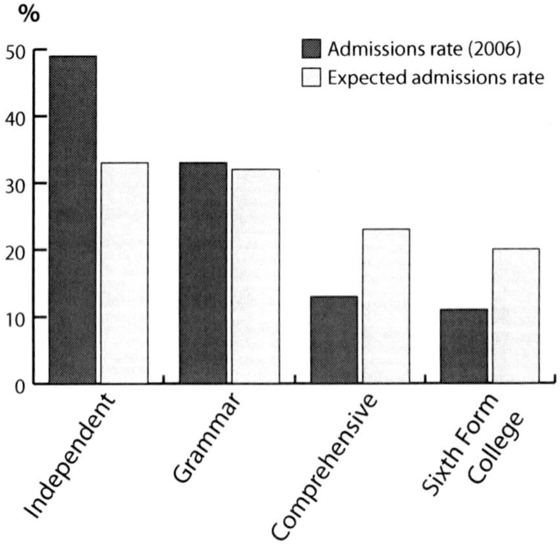

Figure 2. Admissions rates to the 13 Sutton Trust universities by education sector, compared with admission rates expected according to average A-Level results in that sector. Data from Sutton Trust report (2008): University Admissions by Individual Schools

The independent school sector represents just 7% of schools, and 15% of A-Level candidates. Yet according to figures obtained under the Freedom of Information Act in 2006, 38% of students at Cambridge University came from the independent sector; at Oxford, this figure was 43.4%.

Education: Unequal Resources, Social Mobility and Poverty of Aspiration

The 2008 Sutton Trust report 'University Admissions by Individual Schools' identified the poverty of aspiration as one of the key reasons why university admissions were so skewed towards the independent (and, to a lesser extent, grammar) school sector.

Further research published by the Trust in 2006 revealed that every year approximately 3,000 state school students do not gain admission to the Sutton Trust universities – even though they are academically qualified to do so. This 'missing 3,000' would make up about 10% of the 30,000 undergraduates entering this group of universities each year.

This research suggested that some state school pupils are simply not applying to elite academic institutions even when they have the required A-levels grades, something confirmed by a study by the National Foundation for Education Research for the Universities of Oxford and Cambridge. This showed that comprehensive school pupils – all other things being the same – are less likely to apply to Oxbridge than grammar school pupils. Unfortunately, this research did not look at the application rates for independent school pupils.

As Lord Browne led a review into the previous tuition fee scheme and what changes should be made in the future, the Sutton Trust[23] led an investigation into what the possible consequences could be of a rise in fees. They found that 80% of current A-Level students would pursue a degree if the system was not changed. That figure dropped to 45% when the figure is raised to £7,000. More alarmingly, when the students with unemployed parents were asked if they would go to university if the fee was £7,000, only 33% said they would consider it, let alone take it up. This information clearly shows students from low-income backgrounds would be deprived of the opportunities afforded to those from wealthier backgrounds if a rise in fees was agreed upon.

With this information from the Sutton Trust taken into account you would assume that Lord Browne would try to find an alternative to rising fees or at least the Coalition would look to an alternative to accepting Lord Browne's proposals. This, as we all now know, did not occur and no matter how many thousands of people marched and called for the Coalition to see sense, the calls fell on deaf ears. So what did the Coalition changes amount to?

The Independent Review of Higher Education Funding and Student Finance (Browne Review), published in October 2010, recommended that university tuition fees be uncapped, in exchange for a cut to the teaching grant passed from central government to universities.

The effective outcome of these recommendations would have been to shift the burden of funding university teaching from the government to students. In December 2010, the House of Commons approved a modified version of the Browne recommendations, with the tuition fee cap being raised from £3,290 to £9,000. To accompany these measures is an estimated 80% cut in the teaching grant.

Browne's proposals would have effectively generated a free market in higher education, though this has been mitigated against somewhat by the government's decision to impose a cap on fees, albeit one almost three times as high as the cap that preceded it. Nonetheless concerns have been raised that the new fee levels will be unaffordable for many poorer students, and that saddling graduates with up to £27,000 of debt for a three-year degree course will prove to be a disincentive for those from poorer backgrounds. Despite the Coalition government's assertion of their commitment to social mobility, it appears that the new tuition fee regime will have precisely the opposite effect.

Nonetheless, the Browne proposals, and the modified form accepted by the Coalition government, represent a genuine attempt to address a growing problem in higher education: how to ensure widespread provision of high-quality higher education to those deemed capable of it, particularly at a time when government spending is being restricted. Here I outline some of the basic inequalities in higher education provision at present, and propose a new policy for funding higher education, based on principles of equality, redistribution and fairness.

The new scheme takes effect this academic school year and allows each university to set their own fee level up to a maximum of £9,000 with different levels of scrutiny imposed on the university based on the fee they set.

Ministers claimed fees should only exceed £6,000 in exceptional circumstances. Institutions imposing higher fees will be required to take more poor students and spend more of their additional fee income on outreach programmes and bursaries. However, we now know the average fee to be £8,393.[24]

As part of the Coalition proposals, repayments will not kick in until graduates are earning £21,000 (and this will rise with inflation). The interest rate on student loans will remain at zero until graduates earn £21,000 – when they will be charged 3%, plus inflation. If debts are not repaid after 30 years, they will be wiped out.

Students taking a three year course – with basic fees of £6,000 – can expect to owe around £30,000 when living costs are added.[25]

Another interesting point of this new scheme is that the IFS believe that, assuming fees of £7,500, for about half of graduates, the plan is essentially a 9% graduate tax for 30 years, because they will not finish paying off the debt by the 30-year cut-off point.[26]

This new policy has already had an effect on university applications which are running at 9% below last year's level, says the UCAS admissions service. When overseas applications are removed, the figures show a 12% drop in applications from UK only students. These are the first official application figures for the students who will have to pay higher tuition fees. The final deadline for most courses is January – but Oxford and Cambridge and medical school applications have now closed and these showed a 0.8% fall.

This 12% amounts to roughly 7,000 fewer students applying compared to this point last year – with the largest declines amongst mature and female students. Applications from people over 25 have fallen by over a fifth, and for those in their 40s, the drop is 28%.

We should be extremely worried about students who are no longer looking to study a degree later in life, "Studying for the degree people need to get the job they want in the future will be particularly important for those seeking to re-enter the labour market after losing their jobs," Professor Ebdon, chair of the Million+ group of new universities, said of declines in mature student applications.[27]

The new tuition fee scheme is likely to further compound these aspirational problems for pupils in the state sector, with many prospective students resolving that they simply cannot afford to go to university. The Sutton Trust report outlines a number of recommendations for addressing these issues, such as better provision of careers and higher education advice for pupils in state schools. However, these intentions, while well-placed, will not resolve the basic difficulty that, for some, university education is simply unaffordable. As such, tuition fee scheme that recognises the differing requirements of state- and privately-educated pupils, and incorporates that in a redistributive and fair manner, is required. I will outline such a scheme in the next section.

Problems with a graduate tax

The other idea gaining support at the moment in Labour Party is the graduate tax. Before the election Vince Cable had been pushing the idea of a 5% tax when a student starts earning £15,000 for a maximum of

25 years. On the face of it, this idea does seem valid and at the start of his leadership Ed Miliband was also mildly in support of the idea. Ed Miliband has outlined his policy on capping tuition fees, but has yet to outline if the Labour Party would support a graduate tax as an alternative as well as capping fees, and if so at what level he would set it. However, when asked in 2009 he said he would limit it to only 20 years and, instead of a 5% rate of taxation, would limit it to between 0.25% and 2%, since then we have heard no more on this.

Even the NUS supported Vince Cable's proposals. This is surprising because, if implemented, teachers, nurses and the low paid will be the greatest to suffer. For example;

- Teachers would pay £17,271 more than they currently do, which is half of their average annual salary of £36,837.
- Nurses and social workers would pay an extra £7,824 and £8,528 of an average annual salary of £29,494 and £30,040 respectively.
- Doctors would pay an extra £77,118, nearly a full year's average annual salary of £84,451.

This evidence shows that those in the most valuable and essential careers for our society will suffer under this graduation tax. This is clear proof that a graduate tax is clearly not the answer to the important question of how we put forward a viable alternative to the government's policy on rising tuition fees. So is there an alternative to rising tuition fees and a graduate tax? Below I outline one of the solutions we should consider in how we tackle this problem.

Option 1 (proposed by Dan Young)
Those in the most valuable and essential careers for our society will suffer under this new system or a graduate tax. So, is there another option? An option fairer to all that will aid realisation of potential, regardless of background, and still ensure the education system is well funded? What if we rewarded people who took those essential jobs by removing the fee? If you are studying medicine at university, you could still have a tuition fee loan but at the end of your course there could be multiple options available to you, such as:

1. You apply for a job and pay for your fees as usual.
2. The NHS could offer you a job which will, in turn, pay off your tuition fee loan over time, but the agreement will include you being

contracted to work for the NHS for a set period of time before you can work privately or move and work abroad. For example a 10 year contract would see 10% of your debt removed every year. If you wear sacked after six years you would then pay back the last four years as normal. There could also be break parts in the contract so after every three years you would have the option of leaving the agreement and paying the rest back as normal.

This would work for all public sector jobs from teaching to the army and would not only be limited to course specific degrees. You might study a subject such as art but then train as an art teacher so you would also be entitled to your fees being waived. This ensures that the brightest minds remain in the public sector and help to provide for the whole of society rather than simply being lumped with huge debts that force them into either the private market or abroad.

The benefits for the individual are that they will no longer have to worry about money being a factor in their pursuit of further education and that they will also have more than one option available to them when they graduate.

To society the benefits are even greater, as you will see the top minds that may have been put off teaching or the civil service willing to work in the public sector. This will prevent a brain drain and ensure jobs/industries such as maths teachers, which have previously been struggling to employ the highest achieving graduates, become able to compete with private companies, not through wages but through incentives.

This system would need to be funded by central government and with most students leaving with roughly £30,000 of debt under the new system the government would only have to set aside £30 million a year, which is only 0.09%[28] of central government's education budget, which would allow you to keep 10,000 people in the public sector for anything between five to ten years. Note that this system is one possible consideration for principally public sector workers. My colleague Andy Shaw has another suggestion which I would also ask that you give consideration.

Option 2 (proposed by Andy Shaw)
We can envisage the likely nature of a "free market" in tuition fees by looking at the rates charged by universities for overseas students, who are not subject to the cap on fees applied to students from the European Union. Though precise figures are unavailable, it has long been suspected that disproportionate numbers of overseas students are accepted into the

UK's top universities, due to the significantly greater fees they are required to pay. Figure 3 shows the undergraduate fees requested in the 2010/11 academic session for an EU student, a non-EU student studying a science course, and a non-EU student studying an arts course at four UK universities: Oxford, Leeds (a 'red-brick, Russell Group university'), York (a 1960s university) and Worcester (a post-1992 university).

Figure 3: Tuition fees at UK universities by student category

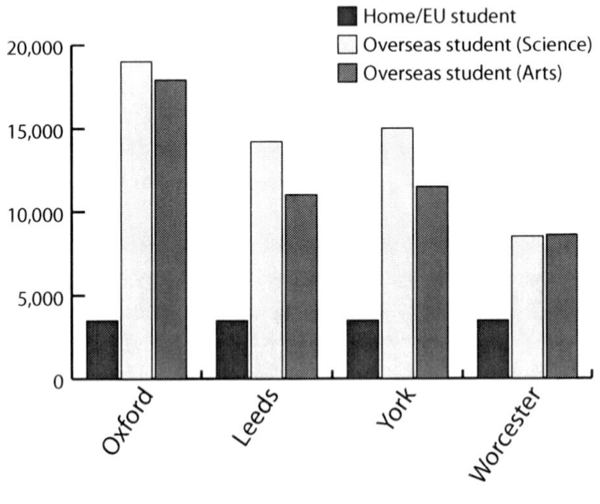

Source: Tuition fees charged to different categories of student in the 2010/11 academic session, across four UK universities. Data is from the *Guardian* website's Data Blog, October 2010

From these figures we can see that, for a reputable non-Oxbridge UK university, the fee requested for a science course is around the £14-15,000 mark, with arts courses significantly cheaper at around £11-12,000. Universities with a lower reputation, such as Worcester, charge lower fees. We can suppose, therefore, that this is what a free market in university fees might look like, with the caveat that overseas student fees at present are probably inflated due to the artificially low cap imposed on UK and EU undergraduate students.

A new university tuition fee policy, therefore, should seek to achieve two things:

Education: Unequal Resources, Social Mobility and Poverty of Aspiration

- End the perceived bias in favour of overseas students at top universities by removing the financial incentive for universities to take on these students over and above UK and EU students;
- Restore aspiration to pupils in the state education sector in the UK, by ensuring that fees are affordable for these students.

With this in mind, I propose the following:

- The cap on undergraduate university tuition fees to be raised to a level reflecting fees charged to overseas students – the level can be closely negotiated with universities, but a preliminary figure could be around £12,000;
- The introduction of a system of non-repayable grants for pupils educated in the state sector, to cover the full cost of their university tuition;
- The introduction of a system of means-tested non-repayable grants for pupils educated in independent schools, to cover the partial or whole cost of their university tuition.

Enrolment of a pupil in an independent school constitutes a conscious, voluntary withdrawal of that pupil from the state education system: it is therefore morally justifiable to delineate between state- and privately-educated pupils when university tuition fees are considered. Furthermore, many of the top private schools charge well over £12,000 per year for tuition; it is therefore obvious that attendees of such schools will be well able to afford the cost of university tuition as well.

For those students who are educated in the independent sector through receipt of grants, or at schools charging significantly less than £12,000, means-tested tuition fee grants should be available to ensure that part or all of the cost of their university education is covered by the state. A "sliding scale" of grants is therefore envisaged, though the vast majority of pupils (those educated in the state sector) would receive the full cost of their tuition, rather than the present situation whereby many pupils – including those from less well-off backgrounds – receive little or no help at all.

This system is redistributive because it ensures that those less able to pay are not required to do so, whereas those who are able to pay more are asked to contribute. Moreover, the university receives exactly the same level of tuition fee regardless of whether the student is educated in the state sector, the private sector or overseas. This should end the present imbalance, where certain categories of student who are asked to pay more are potentially preferentially treated over students whose fee levels are capped.

The system ensures that the state, by funding the studies of a significant number of students, has a stake in higher education provision; but the higher level of fees charged means that the amount of money passed directly to universities in the form of teaching grants can be reduced, while the university suffers little to no net loss in revenue and can therefore continue to provide the same high quality of education.

Furthermore, those students who benefit from an effectively free higher education will repay the state's investment in them in future years, through the extra tax revenue generated by the higher average incomes earned by graduates.

Most significantly, the system completely removes one contributor to the issue of the poverty of aspiration among state-educated pupils, by ensuring that university tuition is no longer unaffordable to them. Though in order to be fully effective, the system needs to be accompanied by improving pupil support and careers advice in state schools, this proposed tuition fee scheme goes some way towards rebalancing higher education in favour of society's less privileged.

The main points of this policy proposal are as follows:

- Students educated in the independent sector are disproportionately more likely to successfully apply to the UK's top universities.
- One of the key factors identified as causing this imbalance is poverty of aspiration among state-educated pupils.
- Universities are also thought to prefer overseas students to UK and EU ones, due to the higher fees they are allowed to charge.
- A solution to these issues is to raise the cap on tuition fees to a level more closely reflecting the cost levied on overseas students; to provide full grants to state-educated pupils attending university; and to provide means-tested provision for some pupils educated in the independent sector.
- These solutions should reduce the poverty of aspiration among state-educated pupils, and also reduce the tendency for preferential treatment of overseas students.

Conclusion

The problem is that Labour has yet to come up with anything radical enough to counteract this problem. Higher education has a real funding crisis and it is simply unsustainable to continue to privatise the costs onto teenagers. During conference Ed Miliband announced that a future Labour government would cap tuition fees at £6,000 but does this go far enough to fix the problem the Coalition has worsened?

---

23 http://mori-ireland.com/Assets/Docs/Publications/sri-young-people-omnibus-sutton-trust-full-report-June-2010.pdf
24 http://www.rsc.org/chemistryworld/News/2011/July/14071103.asp
25 http://www.telegraph.co.uk/education/universityeducation/8191811/Tuition-fees-Q-and-A-what-do-the-proposals-mean.html
26 http://www.ifs.org.uk/conferences/pe2010_wyness.pdf
27 http://www.bbc.co.uk/news/education-15430180
28 http://www.ukpublicspending.co.uk/uk_education_budget_2009_2.html#ukgs30220

Part 4

Labour Left and the Importance of Ethical Economics

Consumer Debt

By Carl Packman

Carl Packman is a Labour Party activist based in Westminster. He is an author in his own right and contributes to various blogs including Left Foot Forward and Liberal Conspiracy. Carl's main interest is developing policy to tackle consumer debt and he is soon to publish his book on illegal loan sharking. Carl also has his own blog at http://thoughcowardsflinch.com/.

Labour Left and the Importance of Ethical Economics

Acknowledging and acting upon the problems inherent to a country in debt is the issue which the political right, as well as the Coalition government, felt they had over the Left, and the preceding Labour government. Earlier this year, an attempt by a fringe group of right libertarians and conservatives to march to parliament, addressed not only debt, but how deep cuts to public services were not being felt hard, and fast enough.

Despite its being organised by some well known bloggers (such as Guido Fawkes), writers (such as Toby Young, who later pulled out) and politicians (Nigel Farage), the event lacked support, and thus failed to throw off its enemy: the 'limp Left', for whom debt is supposedly an aim, not a hindrance to be avoided.

In a very basic sense, debt is something gained in the period of time where something, perhaps money, is acquired, without ownership of it, and where it is returned or paid back. Credit, to use another example, is something which is given to a person. To that person it is not owned but borrowed, on the basis that it is eventually paid back – between which time one is said to be in debt. As the authors of a recent Compass publication put it: 'Access to credit is vital for the functioning of advanced capitalist economies'.

Seemingly, debt is embedded into the political right's economic ideology (particularly the Thatcherite Right, also for which state spending is inextricably linked, believe it or not), every bit as much as they'd suggest it is ours. When somebody like Guido Fawkes cynically refers to how much his daughter is in debt because of New Labour, he might be as well to remember the debt inherent to a capitalist society operating at advanced stages.

To say the Left is comfortable, or at best nonchalant, about debt is tremendously naïve. In the following essay I want to talk about the context of personal debt we find ourselves in today, the ways and means of managing that debt, and some of the solutions in the short/long-term future.

I want to combat the myth that the Left is comfortable with debt, show to what extent debt is very damaging for individuals and communities, the dangers of payday lenders, and what hope we have for other means of selling credit are, such as credit unions. Further, I want to advance some simple solutions for how the government could reduce the dependency on cycles of personal debt, and recommendations for the Left to pursue in reorganising the economy.

Context in numbers

Total UK household, or personal, debt stood at £1.454 trillion in February 2011, a figure which might have been serviceable in better times, but after a recession seems only bleak. Projections by the think tank Compass point out that that figure will likely increase to £2.1 trillion in 2015 – an increase in two-fifths of personal debt, or from 160% to 175% of household income. The average household debt is projected to rise to £81,000 in 2015 from £58,000 in 2010. It is the contention of the think tank that since so much of this debt is against homes, and with households projected as borrowing another £600 billion over five years, that public debt is effectively being privatised. Rather than spending on social housing, if debt against homes is increased, the burden has shifted from the government to the individual, for which s/he will remain in long-term debt (more on housing in a later chapter).

Compass found that a fifth of the 14 million low earners in the UK – of whom more than a third have no savings at all, and one-fifth have less than £1,500 – specify debt as a heavy burden. The National Equality Panel found recently that the poorest 2.4% have no wealth or negative wealth. Social housing tenants represent six in 10 of the financially excluded, and of whom one in six have no bank account (which the think tank asserts should be made a universal right by the government, after the revelation in 2007/8 by the Financial Inclusion Workforce that 690,000 households did not have a basic bank account).

Using such sources as BoE and Credit Action, Compass found that:

- Total lending increased by £2 billion; £1.2 billion secured lending; consumer credit lending £0.8 billion;
- Total secured lending on housing stood at £1,242 billion or 85% of total personal debt;
- Total consumer credit lending stood at £21.2 billion. Annual growth rate of consumer credit rose 0.3% to 1.1%;
- UK banks and building societies wrote off £9.7 billion of loans to individuals in the four quarters to end Q4 2010. In Q4 2010 they wrote off £2.27 billion (£1.18 billion of that was credit card debt). This amounts to a write-off of £24.88 million per day.
- Average household debt (including mortgages) in the UK is £57,697. If the OBR projections are accepted, this will increase by around 40 % to stand at almost £81,000.
- Average household debt (excluding mortgages) in the UK is £8,428

from credit cards, personal loans and other forms of unsecured borrowing. This figure increases to £16,207 if the average is based on the number of households who actually have some form of unsecured loan rather than the total population.
- Average consumer borrowing via credit cards, motor and retail finance deals, overdrafts and unsecured personal loans has risen to £4,363 per average UK adult at the end of February 2011.
- Average owed by every UK adult is £29,871 (including mortgages). This equates to 126% of average (median) earnings. The average outstanding mortgage for the 11.4 million households who currently have mortgages now stands at £109,064 (or two-thirds of the average house price).
- Britain's interest repayments on personal debt were £66.3 billion in the last 12 months (February 2010 to February 2011). The average interest paid by each household on their total debt is approximately £2,629 each year, or one-tenth of average (median) income.

In 2010 the Citizens Advice Bureau reported that 9,000 new debt cases were opening up on a daily basis, while the Department for Communities and Local Government observed that UK banks and building societies had written off more than £3.5 billion in bad debts during the second quarter of 2010, up from £2 billion the previous quarter (equating to a daily write-off rate of more than £38.1 million).

The Institute for Public Policy Research (IPPR), in 2010, found that those most at risk from over-indebtedness were disproportionately represented by single-parent families, and that 11,700 homes were repossessed in the third quarter of 2009 – a 5% increase in the same quarter of 2008.

According to figures published by Working for Walthamstow, Britain's interest repayments on personal debt was £67.8 billion in the last 12 months – averaging at £2,692 on total debt per household, while R3, the insolvency practitioner body, has found that 46% of households struggle to make it to payday, 10% of which cite high cost credit as a reason for this. Personal debt is a dangerously normal phenomenon today, and for many it has simply been incorporated into ones monthly outgoings. But the financial environment does not look to be conducive to this means of personal finance forever. Not only do many people find themselves to be uncreditworthy in a time when credit sellers are more risk averse than they have been in the past, but high cost credit on the high street and online seem to be upping their game – which comes with a great many risks of long debt cycles, insolvency and default.

In 2010 Peter Crook, Chief Executive of doorstep lender Provident Financial, said of the economic downturn: 'We may well see a growth in our target audience'. Now that we have seen the context of debt today in Britain, now we shall turn our attention to the ways and means of how debt is managed today.

Ways and means of managing debt today

Payday lending, while not exclusively the options taken by low-income households seem to represent them disproportionately. The Office of Fair Trading's High-Cost Credit Review found that 10.4% of payday customers have incomes of less than £11,100 per annum, and that 49.1% of all customers have incomes of less than £19,200 per year. A similar figure, according to figures produced by Consumer Focus in August 2010, calculated that 67% of payday loan users earn below the average of £25,000 per annum.

A sample of payday loan users were interviewed for the reasons they used this type of lending over more mainstream forms of credit – many of them cited how easy the loans were to understand, and that instead of being required to work out payback figures from APR percentages, were just given a figure that was added as interest at the end of their borrowing time. Seemingly, it mattered more to some that there was simplicity and transparency for the total cost of credit, rather than potentially paying over the odds for it, or not being able to search for a good deal through a comprehensive guide or comparison site/tool.

How a payday lender works is not complex, but it may be slightly counter-intuitive, and slightly at odds with why many worry about them. For example, the costs associated with loans of, say, £200, are the same with loans of £750 – making excessive profit margins on very small loans is tough. On high fixed cost loans, profit is usually by way of the vast amount of loans sold, not the amount of the individual loan itself. The incentive thus being, not to sell a loan of £1,000, but to sell a loan to a person who will borrow week after week. As Consumer Focus put it: "An individual earns about as much on 100 loans for 100 people as he does 100 loans for 10 people." In their work they also found that "high fixed costs of loans and the fixed price charges per £100 loan means that borrowers of large sums are effectively subsidising those borrowing relatively small amounts, given the marginal cost approach to pricing."

The main criticism against payday lenders today is that they can potentially charge 1000s of % in APR charges – though this in itself may prove alarming at first, it is a figure that is assessed on a loan taken over a year, and though the figure may look large, the actual cost of interest may not be, relatively speaking, depending on how long the loan is taken out for (for example, how quickly it is paid back). As the Campaign for Responsible Credit (CfRC) put it: "APR is an annualised compounded rate and is bound to be higher when tagged to shorter term loans – so is not the best marker to judge how expensive the cost of the total loan will be". What is concerning is how payday companies assess their costs. As Compass, alongside the End the Legal Loansharking Campaign, has made note of, payday lenders are not always transparent with how they assess other factoring costs to loans such as processing fees, early repayment fees and staffing costs – leading some to call for the repeal of usury laws, which the United States employed up until 1980 when Jimmy Carter outlawed them, and the UK hasn't had since the 19th century.

Even if it could be found that all costs were above board, of all the options for sub-prime consumers, payday loans are still far more expensive than other forms of loan, and are therefore unlikely to be a good choice for people. As figures from the CfRC demonstrate a short-term loan of £12 per £100 may still be less expensive than an overdraft, but the high end of the market (£25 per £100) may not be – but it is not always clear for the consumer which option is better for them (hence the campaign by some to introduce credit comparison sites, based by area, in addition to more transparency by lenders).

When door to door lenders were a problem that gained more national press coverage, horror stories of 'heavies' appearing at the door, baseball bats in hand, there were subsequent changes to the lending system. By contrast, legal loan sharks seem tame, trying to shake off the shady image of times past, and justifying their existence in moralistic terms, suggesting that they are only providing a service to stop a consumer's debt from being driven underground, and helping the uncreditworthy – but that in itself is not to say how immoral their pricing methods are, and how dangerous their loans are for individuals, linked, as they are, to poorer mental health and long spells of negative wealth.

Moreover, sometimes payday lenders can be seen using purposefully aspirational language in order to appeal to a certain audience. In 2008 the Advertising Standards Agency (ASA) made a complaint against The Money Shop for advertising high rate, short-term credit juxtaposed with aspirational purchases such as those that would further one's career or education.

This isn't the only complaint case for the ASA against payday lenders. In 2009 it made a complaint against Quickquid for failing to include the APR charge in the advert.

In 2010 a complaint was made against online provider Wonga for showing borrowing in a whimsical fashion, with laughter, neglecting to provide information of more prominence in an advert about short term loans.

In addition to the cost of loans from payday lenders, their dire track record on transparency and their odious advertising methods, they can easily lead to debt cycles – or rolling over debts where loans are taken out to service previous loans – which are extremely dangerous for individuals, who as can be seen from figures above are often in low-paid work, find it difficult to manage through to the end of the month on their wages alone, are mostly women and a fifth of whom are lone parents. Campaigns like End the Legal Loansharking and Stella Creasy's Consumer Credit and Regulation Bill recommend the government place a cap on the total cost of credit to protect consumers (which the government have said they will not agree to, nor to oversee fair rates of APR charges, but instead promote 'transparency and greater corporate and consumer responsibility' – which, though noble, is not a solution to the immediate problem in and of itself) which, if married with a cap on the amount of times an individual can roll over on a loan (a cap of, say, five times), will provide great steps towards the short term solution of bad personal debt.

Solutions in the short/long-term future

To reiterate, the very first steps towards a short-term solution for the government (in spite of its reluctance, and that of the Office for Fair Trading, towards them) would be to:

- Place a cap on the total of cost of credit instead of targeting APR alone;
- Place a cap on the amount of times a person can 'roll over' on a loan (in Washington it is eight but Consumer Focus has recommended five);
- Oblige lenders to be transparent with their costs;
- Commission and run an independent comparison site, based on area, for consumers to see what the best deal for credit is available for them;

- Oblige lenders to provide information on the dangers of debt on their websites and adverts, much in the same way that alcoholic drink manufacturers are with the 'drink-aware' campaign;
- Until such time as a 'roll-over' cap is enforced, introduce a levy on lenders to finance independent advice for those who exceed five loans a year purely in order to service previous debts.

The next stage would be to breathe more life into Credit Unions while simultaneously linking them to the Post Office Network. According to the Association of British Credit Unions Limited, last year "the credit union sector has trebled in size in the last decade and now serves over 860,000 people." They recommend that with capital investment into a Credit Union back office individuals would be able to walk into any of the 11,500 post office branches and join their credit union – which not only would restore the relevance of the Royal Mail in the digital age, but would be a major challenge to high cost creditors, both legal and illegal.

Such plans have already been highlighted by the Department of Business, Innovation and Skills (BIS). In their 2010 report 'Securing the Post Office Network in the Digital Age', they note how timely a merger of services would be. The Post Office, they point out, is one of the fastest growing providers of personal financial services in the UK, and it is estimated that in the last six months almost 80,000 credit union transactions have been carried out in post office branches. Projects of note in South Lanarkshire and Glasgow (where customers can access their credit unions payout technologies) show the way for lowering processing and administrative costs, keeping fees low for those seeking credit.

The case for rolling out credit unions, not just as a means to disincentivise high cost credit and thus crippling debt cycles, but, to all who seek credit, providing alternatives to, say, middle income earners who use overdrafts as a way of seeing themselves through to the end of the month, has been made also. The Joseph Rowntree Foundation in 2006 found that offering credit union services only to those vulnerable communities is a less viable model than rolling them out nationwide, including those communities most at need and more affluent communities. Though the report's conclusions don't state this explicitly, credit unions have the potential to drive out bad eggs in the credit market, as well as traditional places where people have usually fallen back on, like banks, but end up staying in the red for long periods of time – such as the trend of wages being used only to get individuals back up to zero, spending the rest of the month eating away through an overdraft.

Certainly optimistic sounds have been made by the BIS, but the government has been tremendously naïve, or at best careless, on beneficial initiatives for personal finances. Banking crises, growing personal debt problems, and a growth market for irresponsible debt, should set a precedent for the government to act decisively and quickly to the betterment of credit services. But further, should use their initiative to help restore a savings culture back to the UK. As mentioned above, a very high percentage of people in the UK still have trouble getting to the end of the month on wages alone. The government knows this, so it seems extraordinary that one of the first things they did after their election was to scrap the Child Trust Fund and the Savings Gateway. As the authors of the report 'Promoting the Effectiveness and Efficiency of Credit Unions in the UK' put it:

"The policy context now for promoting savings among those who are financially excluded, and those on low incomes more generally, has changed, and the ambitious target that was given in the relatively recent past by the House of Commons Treasury Committee, that Credit Unions double their holdings of members' savings to £1 billion by the end of 2010, is plainly in need of rescheduling. In 2010 the government cancelled the Savings Gateway, a matched funding scheme for those on low incomes that attracted interest from more than 100 Credit Unions, and also announced the ending of the Child Trust Funds, public funding that particularly helped those on lower incomes."

New Labour was an abhorrent flirtation with neo-liberal politics, neo-conservative foreign policy and was absolutely comfortable with consumer debt and thus the growth industry of doorstep lending and legal loansharking. Many on the left of the Labour Party consider Stella Creasy and her Consumer Credit (Consumer and Advice) Bill to be typically New Labour and accepting of debt as a means to an end. I, as a Labour leftwinger and Socialist myself, deny this. Sure, what the bill has done is attempt to patch up the flaws in a capitalist system operating right on course, but the reason we on the Left should support it is because by simply banning, outright, alternative forms of credit will drive the industry underground and empower doorstep lenders and illegal loan sharks who intimidate and pressure the indebted into backstreet practices and false legal compromises.

As we all know the really long-term solution is to find another reliable means of national growth than enterprise zones and consumer spending.

But let's not kid ourselves that this is all the Coalition government's fault: New Labour, during the economic downturn, wanted us to spend more on the high street – clearly the culture needs to change, growth options need to emerge and George Osborne needs to ask his local newsagent if he can have a paper-round (and as a former paperboy myself I'd like to be first to tell him he's got a long way to go before he acquires the skill-set). Empowering credit unions and the Post Office Network is one thing, but the economy already relies too much on commodity fetishism – we need to move swiftly beyond that, and the figures for those who struggle concurs quite clearer. The culture of social housing needs to change, a culture of fair banking, and credit, needs implementing, but also fairness for people needs to be accomplished. There are debt crises, the expense of childcare could make it more cost-effective for some parents to give up work and stay at home, according to insurer Aviva, and high cost lenders are doing all the marketing they can to pounce upon those who are uncreditworthy elsewhere (that's not a point where we say they are the undeserving poor; that's a point where we question the business methods of 'acceptable' money lending).

All which I have presented could be done by any government – most of which patches, not challenges, the capitalist status quo. But I believe that debt does sustain capitalism, and that should give us pause, particularly when we consider how much dangerous and bad debt sustains the normal functioning of an economic system, which many of the richest and most successful consider the most acceptable. In this respect I write as someone who wants to consider both short- and long-term options, but hopes to ultimately see the end of a system which relies so much on an individual's poverty.

A Living Wage

By Teresa Pearce MP

Teresa Pearce MP was born in the northwest and moved to London with her family in the late 1960s. She has lived in the Erith area for around 30 years and has two grown up daughters. Before becoming an MP Teresa worked for the Inland Revenue and as a Senior Manager at PricewaterhouseCoopers specialising in tax investigations. She has extensive knowledge of the UK tax system and is an expert on the National Minimum Wage. Teresa has been a local Councillor for Erith and a school governor at both Castillon Primary in Thamesmead and Townley Grammar in Bexleyheath.

Labour Left and the Importance of Ethical Economics

Imagine if one of the vastly profitable large chains of supermarkets had their electricity bills paid by the taxpayer, or maybe their advertising costs were greatly subsidised by the general public. The same general public that they make their massive profits from.

I would expect a massive public outcry at the unfairness of it. However, week in week out, such companies do get an enormous subsidy to help with one of their major overheads, staffing costs. This is because many employees in these large and successful companies are paid only the minimum wage. And because the current minimum wage is not a living wage, nearly everyone on it has to claim tax credits to be able to make ends meet. Those tax credits are funded by the taxpayer.

That means that the public purse has to subsidise the low paid employees of many of our household name large stores and fast food outlets so they make their high profits rather than paying a living wage.

I believe that everyone should be paid a decent wage for a day's work. It is a simple vision based on fairness and my belief that the national minimum wage needs to be replaced by a realistic living wage. The national minimum wage at the moment is not enough for workers, and especially those with children, to live on. Because of this we have big levels of state subsidy through working and child tax credits to bump up the incomes of people in low-paying jobs. I am not against tax credits, but I think more people need to understand that in many sectors the taxpayer is subsidising the wage bill of some of the biggest employers.

I recently researched job advertisements for some of the big supermarkets, where the hourly pay is below the living wage or London living wage. As an example, I'll use one job I found, advertised at around £6.54 per hour, although that is by no means the lowest hourly rate of the jobs I saw advertised. Many other retail or customer service jobs offer wages at a similar level, with permanent, part time and full-time hours covered.

Say you are employed on a full time wage of £6.54 an hour; then your annual salary works out at £13,603 before tax and £11,676 after tax (tax based on a single adult aged 18-65 working 40 hours per week, 52 weeks a year). There are various scenarios in which this worker and his or her partner will try to make ends meet, but the most common require some level of state subsidy to make up for the fact that the national minimum wage is not enough to live on.

If this supermarket worker has a partner who is not working, they will be in receipt of £4,539 in benefits excluding tax credits. This takes the combined income for the family to £18,100. If they have a child then they are also entitled to a maximum of £4,200 in child tax credits, bringing their pre-tax income to £22,300, around £21,000 after tax. With average housing costs around £8,500 a year, transport costs of £3,000 and fuel, maintenance, electricity and council costs in the combined region of £4,200; life is already a struggle for families on the minimum wage even before childcare, food and clothing costs are taken into account.

We need a national living wage to put an end to this deeply unfair situation where we are all subsidising poverty pay and the profits of big companies. The living wage is currently calculated at £7.20 an hour outside London and £8.30 in London to allow a worker to provide their family with the essentials of life. It should be adopted sooner rather than later. It is not too much to ask that workers at the bottom of the income ladder should at least be able to make ends meet.

I realise that there will be many who object to what I am saying. They will say I am anti-business. I am not. But I am anti-exploitation, and if you are a business that depends on cheap labour whilst making massive profits for your shareholders, then there should be a mechanism whereby the numbers of minimum wage jobs are reported to HMRC and a profit levy is charged via the tax system to refund some of the subsidy. There is an argument for helping small firms or those who provide a public necessary service, but I really do not believe that supermarkets and retail giants, who are making billions a year, deserve or warrant state subsidy.

People will say I am anti-jobs. Nonsense. I would ask you to consider the proposition that the next time one of these firms press releases that they are creating 5,000 jobs, what they really mean is they are creating increased profits whilst you and I pay part of the staffing cost for those 5,000 jobs. If you are operating a business in a modern European democracy, then the people working for you and helping make you that profit should surely be earning enough to be able to live in that modern European democracy without relying on state benefits.

People will say I am anti-free market on the basis that if employers are forced to pay decent wages, they will go out of business. But we don't really have a free market when companies need to be subsidised by the benefits system, and where institutions such as banks are not allowed to fail because of the effect on the UK economy. Or when private companies, contracted by governments to provide services, fail and have to be propped up financially, to ensure essential services are protected. Companies taking the profit without ever bearing the risk. Hardly a free or fair market.

I personally think that profitable employers who can't afford to pay living wages or who depend on cheap labour are not the business model we should be building the recovery on.

We need a proper, clear, informed discussion about this and the public needs to understand the level to which these companies are helped by public funds. Let's stop calling them "wealth creators" and start calling them state subsidised industries. If we are serious about making work pay then the first step is getting those making the profits to pay the wage bill of their own workers. The workers, who are often the true unsung wealth creators.

Tax at the Heart of Labour Left

By Richard Murphy

Richard Murphy is a chartered accountant and economist. He has been described by *The Guardian* as an 'anti-poverty campaigner and tax expert'. Kevin Maguire, associate editor of the *Daily Mirror* has said "it is Murphy who is the heroic figure. Tireless and forensic, driven by an admirable moral fervour, I take my hat off to a campaigner with Duracell batteries".

Copyright notice: This note was written by Richard Murphy for Tax Research LLP © 2011. The contribution of Alex Cobham to the 5 Rs of taxation is gratefully noted.

Tax is at the heart of left-wing thinking. Left-wing politicians believe that government has a fundamental role to play in the economy, society and helping individuals – all individuals – to achieve their full potential, economically or otherwise.

Government of this sort is not possible without taxation: there's no point arguing that point, it's a fact. As a result a left-wing agenda for government cannot be delivered unless the necessary funding is available to sustain it and whilst tax is not the only way to finance government (both borrowing and selectively creating credit through the creation of new money being other options open to any government) tax is undoubtedly at the heart of the economic equation for any left-wing government.

That means Labour Left has to address difficult questions surrounding tax and all that goes with it if it is to succeed in its aims.

It's time for Labour to talk tax

Given the need for urgent change in the UK's social and economic infrastructure it is time Labour began to talk tax, seriously. That does not mean it continues to apologise for tax. It did that in the New Labour era, and that was a serious mistake. It made people lose faith in government and its ability and that of politicians to address the real issues we face with the confidence that people want from their elected politicians. If tax is what funds the type of government we not only want, but so obviously need, then now is the time for Labour to begin talking tax unapologetically and with confidence.

By that I mean Labour needs to begin talking about taxes as if they are a good thing – because that is true. Tax is what pays for so many things in life that we too easily take for granted but which are essential to us all, like the NHS, education, pensions, social welfare, social housing, law and order, job creation, the fire service, defence and so much more. These are things to celebrate. And in that case we should celebrate the tax that pays for them and make clear that Labour does not apologise for tax: it thinks it is a good thing.

Labour can do that, but if it is to do so it has to change a long-held habit of talking about the tax the government manages as if it was someone else's money. Time and again we have heard it said that government 'manages taxpayer's money'. That is not true. Tax belongs to the government, and no one else, and it's a very convenient right wing myth to suggest anything else.

The fact is that even the most hardened right-wingers agree that any government has the duty to defend the state, maintain law and order and to establish and defend property rights, which are the law that lets us work out who owns what.

However, if the government can create the law that says who owns what it can also say that if you do own, earn, buy, sell, gift or use something then you owe tax as a result. In other words, the government can say that your right to own, earn, buy, sell, gift or use things is conditional on you paying the taxes it says are due as a result. That's not to say you cannot do all those things: of course any government wants you to have the freedom to contract for legal activities. That's a right it seeks to uphold on your behalf but what it should also be saying is that you have a duty to pay tax as a result.

To put this way, you don't have a legal right to your income free of tax. You have a legal right to your income after tax. And you don't have a right to buy things without paying VAT when VAT is due: you only have a right to own whatever you bought if the VAT due has been paid.

That might seem like a statement of the obvious, but it is a philosophy very different from that promoted by thinking over the last 30 or so years. That has suggested that your gross income is yours to enjoy and that if you can find a way around paying tax that is a good thing. And that has also suggested that companies that have set up complex schemes, often involving tax havens, to get round VAT being charged, then a blind eye should be turned to them. And it's also true to say that because of the resulting attitude that tax is a bad thing that it is acceptable to get round too little attention has been given to collecting the tax really due in our economy.

Tax: one of the best things ever invented

So a new language of tax is needed: a language that celebrates tax as one of the best things ever invented because it provides opportunity for us all to achieve like nothing else does. Three things follow on as a result.

The first is that it can be said that tax belongs to the government. That means we can stop the stupid comments that have become so prevalent in politics that governments 'spend your money'. No, they don't. They spend their own money that is as rightfully theirs as our net pay is our own. The government just needs to be confident about that fact and then get on and manage its own cash as well as is possible rather than spending all its time looking over its shoulder – especially to big taxpayers – to whom it somehow thinks it is beholden when it isn't, and to whom it has paid attention far too much as a result.

Second, this means that Labour Left – and any government, come to that – can be confident about its right to collect the tax that is due to it. The timidity of successive governments in collecting tax has resulted in massive injustice in the UK tax system where, deadening on the estimates used, between £42 billion and £95 billion of tax is evaded and avoided in the UK economy each year. Arguing the detail is not necessary here: even at the lower end of the estimated range the loss is so big it is obvious that there is a massive crisis in the tax system in the UK that needs to be addressed.

Third, and as important, a government that realises it has the right to tax and to manage its own affairs also realises that it can use tax to achieve its social and economic goals as well as to simply raise revenue. That liberates a whole spectrum of policy tools to empower its intervention in the economy to achieve the common good.

To put it another way, a government that realises tax is a good thing can pursue tax justice.

Tax justice

Tax justice is a broadly based concept. It relates to individuals and all taxable entities. But it also relates to tax systems as a whole. All these ideas are explored in what follows.

Tax compliance – the duty of the taxpayer

For the individual taxpayer (whether a warm blooded human being or a company) tax justice is about tax compliance. This happens when the individual seeks to pay the right amount of tax (but no more) in the right place at the right time where right means that the economic substance of the transactions they undertake coincides with the place and form in which they report them for taxation purposes.

It is the duty of Labour Left to promote and reinforce this idea. But that means three things must happen.

First, tax law must be clear. It must be possible to calculate the right amount of tax.

Second, the UK tax system must be robust against attack from tax havens and the tax systems of other countries that seek to undermine it.

Third, the systems needed to ensure that the government can identify taxable income must be in place.

Each of these ideas is explored in greater depth below.

Tax and society
Tax justice is about much more than the individual though: tax justice is also about the existence of tax systems that promote social well-being within and between societies. It is about the creation of environments in which all people can prosper. That necessarily means that the state institutions and businesses that meet the needs of people can also prosper. But it means yet more than that: it means that those who fail to prosper are protected from misfortune until such time as they can prosper again.

That means tax justice is about four things above and beyond the duty of the individual to be tax compliant. First, it is about understanding why we tax. Second, it is about defining the attributes of a good tax system. Third, it is about defining the process that delivers tax justice and finally it is about understanding transparency – without which tax justice is not possible.

The 5 Rs for taxing
There are five reasons for taxation. Tax is used to:

- Raise revenue;
- Reprice goods and services considered to be incorrectly priced by the market such as tobacco, alcohol, carbon emissions etc.;
- Redistribute income and wealth;
- Raise representation within the democratic process because it has been found that only when an electorate and a government are bound by the common interest of tax does democratic accountability really work; and finally to facilitate:
- Reorganisation of the economy through fiscal policy.

If tax justice is to prevail, taxes must be set taking all these considerations into account.

The 10 Cs of a good tax system
An efficient taxation system has nine attributes with one over-riding characteristic to which they all contribute. An efficient tax system is:

- Comprehensive – in other words, it is broad based;
- Complete – with as few loopholes as possible;
- Comprehensible – it is as certain as is reasonably possible;
- Compassionate – it takes into account the capacity to pay;

- Compact – it is written as straightforwardly as possible;
- Compliant with human rights;
- Compensatory – it is perceived as fair and redistributes income and wealth as necessary to achieve this aim;
- Complementary to social objectives;
- Computable – the liability can be calculated with reasonable accuracy;
All of which facilitate the chance that it will be...
- Competently managed.

In combination these are key attributes of a good tax system.

The 6 steps to tax justice
Tax justice can be defined as a six stage process:

- Define the tax base. This is the first essential step in creating progressive taxation and in promoting the better use of resources within society.
- Find what is to be taxed. If the tax base cannot be accurately located then there is no point trying to tax it.
- Count the tax base. Unless the tax base can be quantified it cannot be taxed.
- Tax the tax base at the right rates of tax. In the process making sure that the inter-relationship between the various tax bases is properly managed to ensure that the essential revenue raising, repricing and redistributive qualities of a just tax system is vital.
- Allocate the resulting revenues efficiently through effective government spending designed to achieve best social effect.
- Report – governments must be accountable for what they do with tax revenues or the democratic principle fails.

The 11 steps to financial transparency
Tax justice cannot happen by chance. To achieve it information is needed. That means all potentially taxable people, whether they are human beings or legal entities created under law, must be transparent about what they do, are and have done.

Financial transparency exists when the following information is readily available to all who might need it to appraise transactions they or others might undertake or have undertaken with another natural or legal person:

- Who that other person is;
- Where the person is;
- What right the person has to enter into a transaction;
- What capacity the person has to enter into a transaction.

And with regard to entities that are not natural persons:

- What the nature of the entity is;
- On whose behalf the entity is managed;
- Who manages the entity;
- What transactions the entity has entered into;
- Where it has entered into those transactions;
- Who has actually benefited from the transactions;
- Whether all obligations arising from the transactions have been properly fulfilled.

What this means is that tax justice is not just about tax, it is also very obviously about the need to create proper systems for accounting to make sure that the right amount of tax (but no more) is paid in the right place at the right time.

Creating tax justice
Tax justice is not simple, as is already apparent. That, however, is not a problem: a great deal of what humans do is not simple, and yet it is achieved nonetheless. Tax justice is possible: that is what is important.

These five criteria, tax compliance on the part of taxpayers and the four sets of attributes on which just tax systems are built, are the foundations of tax justice. Together they create a world in which social justice can prevail for all. That is what tax justice seeks to achieve. That is what Labour Left has to embrace.

What does tax justice look like in practice?
Using the above principles Labour can have a clear set of principles that establish the basis for its tax policies. That is vital. Without such clarity taxpayers do not know what a government is trying to achieve and that benefits no one.

What though does such a policy look like in practice? The following provide some suggestion of what could be done to deliver tax justice:

Our tax system is not progressive: the poor pay a higher part of their income in tax than do the rich. This has to be corrected by:

- Making the 50% tax rate permanent;
- Aligning the income tax and capital gains tax rates as the Tories did in 1988;
- Restricting the maximum amount of tax allowances and reliefs that the rich can claim for offset against their income. Some claim tax reliefs worth hundreds of thousands of pounds a year at present. This would simplify the tax system;
- Ending the tax reliefs given to the rich to encourage them to save when they are already wealthy;
- Reducing the rates of VAT on essential items and increasing them on luxuries, as Thatcher did in 1979;
- Taking steps to prevent the rich hiding their income in companies that reduce their overall tax rates considerably;
- Taking more people on low income out of both tax and national insurance;
- Introducing a much broader introductory tax bracket for those on low income, whilst ensuring the benefit does not go to those on higher incomes;
- Extending national insurance so it applies to all levels of income, but reducing the income tax rate for those earning between about £40,000 and £100,000 to compensate;
- Increasing an investment income surcharge so that those with more than £5,000 of investment income a year (excluding pensioners) pay a charge equivalent to national insurance.

Our tax system does not adequately tax wealth. We need to:

- Increase capital gains tax rates, as noted above;
- Lower inheritance tax thresholds: those with wealth need to make their proper contribution to society;
- Amend or abolish many of the exemptions and allowances for private business owners, agricultural land and other assets in the current tax system that have reinforced the concentration of wealth in the UK;
- Reform local council taxation so that it is progressive and is applied at higher rates on higher value properties that is not the case at present. Provision for the elderly, by letting them defer payment until they or their executors dispose of their properties should be allowed.

Company taxation should be transformed:

- Small limited companies should be re-registered as limited liability partnerships with their members then being taxed on their share of profit as if it was their income, so preventing tax avoidance through such structures;
- A minimum rate of corporation tax due on profits declared in a set of accounts should be set for multinational corporations;
- The UK should embrace European wide unitary taxation for multinational corporations that will help tackle profit shifting and tax rate shopping;
- An aggressive policy for tackling the abuse of tax havens by multinational corporations should be adopted;
- Country-by-country reporting by multinational corporations that would require them to report a profit and loss account for each and every country in which they operate, so showing how much profit and tax they make and pay in each such place should be required, meaning it will be much harder for such companies to hide their profits and tax abuse from view;
- All small companies in the UK should be required to put their full annual accounts on public record and heavy, mandatory fines for the directors of those that do not do so should be introduced. Investment in UK law enforcement on small companies should be made to prevent up to 500,000 disappearing a year without paying their taxes.

Tax abuse should be tackled:

- A general anti-avoidance principle should be introduced into UK tax law to make tax avoidance much harder;
- An aggressive approach to tax havens should be introduced, demanding information on all structures in which UK resident people have an interest with threat that tax will be withheld from all payments made to the jurisdiction in question of cooperation is not offered;
- The UK should promote the extension of the European Union Savings Tax Directive that will dramatically improve tax information exchange in Europe and beyond;
- At least 20,000 new staff need to be engaged at HM Revenue & Customs to tackle the endemic tax evasion that is crippling the UK economy and which is denying a level playing field to honest small

businesses who have to compete against those who persistently cheat on paying their taxes;
- Directors of large companies should be personally liable for at least part the penalties their companies owe for tax misdemeanours including those on failed tax avoidance schemes.

Conclusion

Labour has apologised for tax for too long. Tax works. Tax is a good thing. Tax transforms people's lives. Tax can be legitimately collected. If tax is not collected, when it is due, then injustice results. Labour has to embrace these ideas, and act on them. That is possible. Now is the time to do it.

Private Renters – the Forgotten Millions who Abandoned Labour

By Dr Éoin Clarke

Éoin Clarke is a Labour Party member from Northern Ireland. Having been born into a large impoverished single-parent family, his interests are in solving poverty and promoting the importance of education. Dr Clarke tutors history at Queen's University Belfast. Éoin also works with all the major examination boards in assessing of secondary level qualifications, as well as this he is also a member of the Chartered Institute of Educational Assessors since its founding. For more, email: DrEoinClarke@LabourLeft.co.uk

About 40% of those from the rented sector who voted Labour in 1997 had abandoned them by 2010. Considering that a smaller figure of 27% of those renting social housing deserted Labour, and 26% of mortgage holders deserted Labour, it is possible to observe the effect that this extra financial burden of renting privately has had on people's voting behaviour.

Percentage of householders voting Labour, 1997, 2010

[Bar chart showing Private renting: ~48% voted Labour in 1997, ~29% in 2010; Mortgage holders: ~39% voted Labour in 1997, ~29% in 2010]

Source: Ipsos Mori

According to LSL, the average rental property in the UK costs £720 per month, or £8,640 a year. This is in two thirds of cases for two-bedroom accommodation. More than 70% of private renters work and are in no receipt of Housing Benefit. For them, life is an unbearable tale of poverty.

For someone on the minimum wage that is around 80% of their salary. If only they were a little poorer, perhaps unemployed then fortune might favour them with the granting of social housing. But with the squeeze on middle incomes, they are consigned to a life of cramped and overcrowded misery in shared accommodation.

As private rented accommodation is soon to overtake social housing as the second biggest provider, what hope is there for these people caught on the wrong side of the banking collapse?

This piece examines why things have gone so horribly wrong for those renting privately and how the Tories are making their lives much worse. The final part of this piece lays out some policy suggestions as to how the lives of private renters can be made better by Labour.

Percentage of private renters who voted Labour

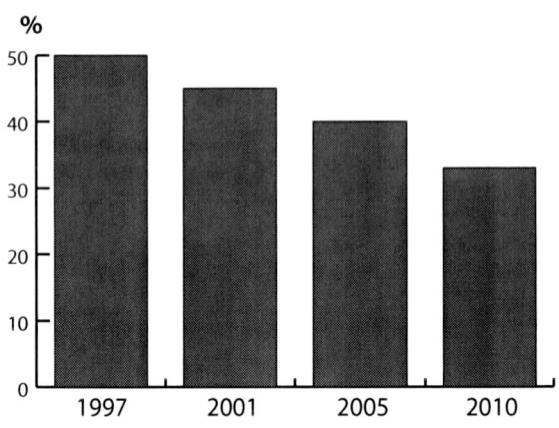

The above graph shows the year-on-year drop in the portion of rental voters choosing Labour. It is interesting that 41% of the private renting voters, who deserted us, did so by 2001 never to return. I argue that it was Labour's continuation of presiding over a dwindling social housing stock that part caused this. To reiterate, 40% of private renting voters deserted Labour. That equates to roughly 630,000 people.

Where Labour's private rental voters deserted to

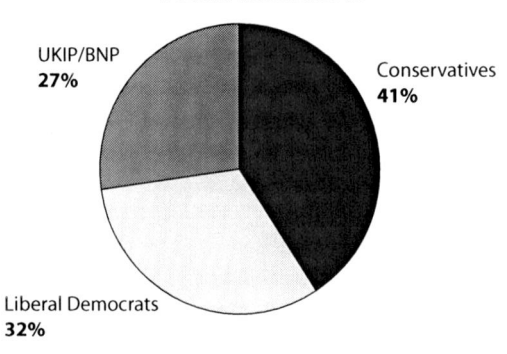

UKIP/BNP 27%
Conservatives 41%
Liberal Democrats 32%

This chart assesses where the voters went to. The 'others' category is the most interesting. The squeeze on available rental accommodation boosted the perception that immigration and over population were causes. Of course, this ignores the depletion in housing stock. But, there has been a 200% increase in the proportion of private rental voters choosing to vote for none of the big three parties in the last 13 years.

How has this happened? How have these people been allowed to hide away in squalor struggling to make ends meet? Why have these voters been abandoned to UKIP and the BNP? Who is to blame for this and how do we fix it? In my view, the problem began when the nation stopped building social housing (see below).

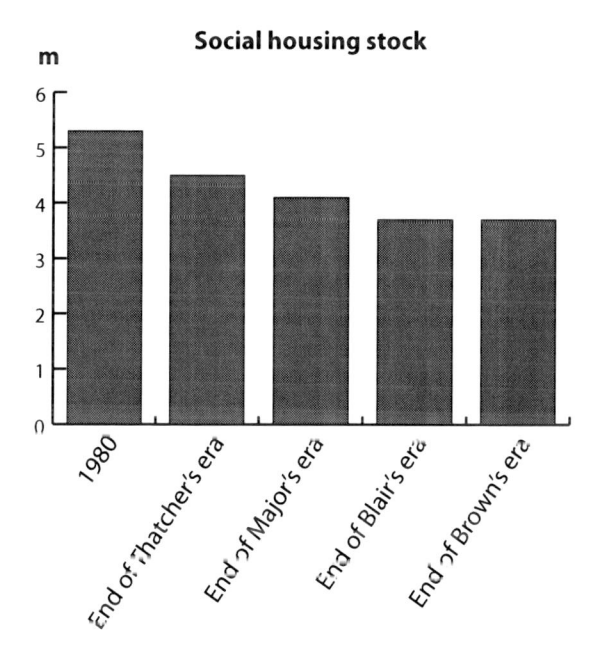

Social housing stock

Period	Millions
1980	5.3
End of Thatcher's era	4.5
End of Major's era	4.1
End of Blair's era	3.7
End of Brown's era	3.7

When Thatcher came to power we had 5.3 million social homes, but today we have just 3.7 million. This has led to a growth in dependency upon the private rental market, where most of the exploitation is taking place. Allowing the nation's housing stock to dwindle at a time of increased demand both fuelled a property boom that catapulted millions into poverty, and condemned a generation trapped between social housing and owning their own homes. That is why I conclude that the problem began with the Right to Buy scheme.

Social housing sales: Total social housing sales to sitting tenants, England

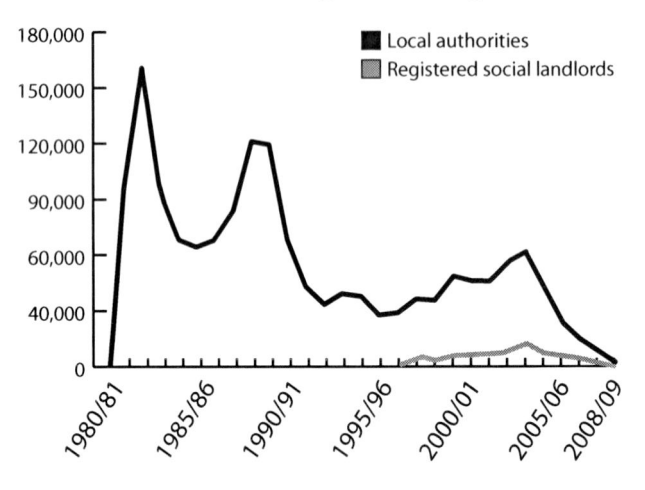

The Right to Buy [RTB] scheme launched by Margaret Thatcher in 1981 was initially a good thing. It enabled people with no stake in society, who had been paying rent faithfully all of their lives to finally get on

Number of social housing units built

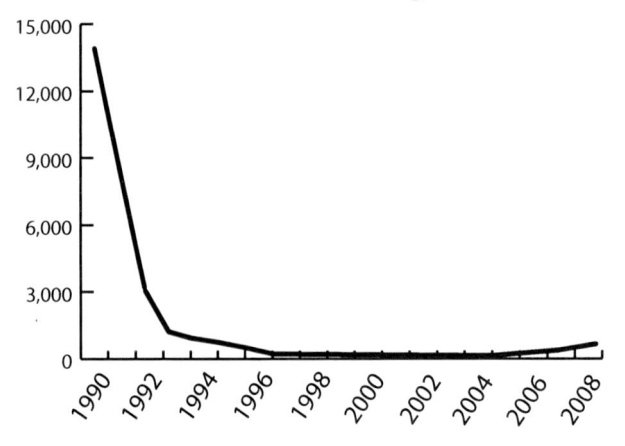

the property ladder and build an inheritance for their children. Although the number of sales declined under John Major, RTB aided social mobility, which is most likely the reason Blair increased the number of sales in 1997. This increase lasted until New Labour's last term in office where it began to tail off. I have no criticisms to make of the main principle of the RTB scheme.

Of course, it only makes sense to inject social mobility into those renting council property if indeed you continue to build house to replace the ones you are selling. That way, future generations who rely on council housing in the same way their parents and grandparents did, will have the same opportunity. Now, Thatcher actually deserves some credit in this instance. One can see from the chart that as she left office in 1990, the number of council homes being built was comparable, in the first few years, to the number of sales. Thatcher did not fall into the trap of selling public housing whilst refusing to replace it. But she did forbid councils from retaining the proceeds from their housing sales. In the long term, this crippled house building and it was a wrong that John Major and Tony Blair never righted.

The number of social houses built under John Major declined steeply, as did the number of council sales. But if one looks closely they can see that sales began to exceed builds under Major. This was an unsustainable path, and meant that it was inevitable council housing shortages would arise. Sadly, Tony Blair only intensified this folly, the number of council sales under Blair dramatically increased and the building of social

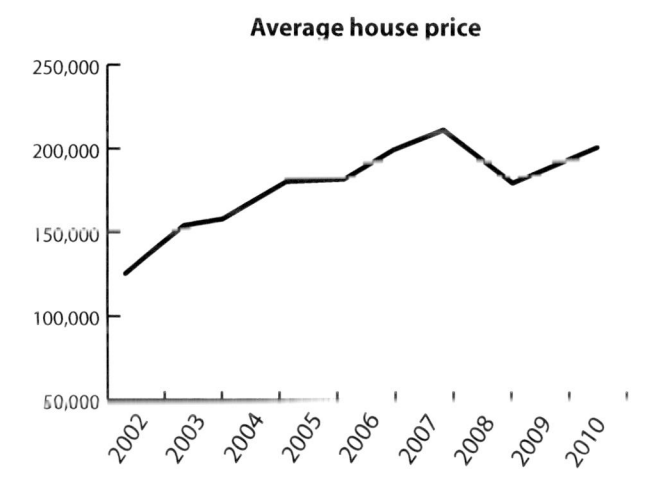

Average house price

housing halted. The UK's population grew 4.41 million under Labour but the number of social homes continued to fall. A socialist PM did not see fit to invest in social housing. Thankfully, when Gordon Brown became PM, social housing sales collapsed, and actual new builds began to climb again. Whilst this is to his partial credit, the number of actual new builds was woefully inadequate at just 400 per year. Under Brown the problem stagnated.

The unsustainability of these neo-liberal antics was compounded by the increase in house prices over this period. As the social housing stock dwindled, the cost of buying your own home rocketed. There was no option for young families who did not have the income to afford a mortgage. Their only option was to rent privately.

This meant that their rent payable was often extortionate, and at the whim of the landlord, subject to rise at any moment. For these people the noughties were a Victorian time warp. The level of disposable income of these families shrank as an increasing percentage of their income was spent on housing costs. That is the legacy of New Labour's handling of housing.

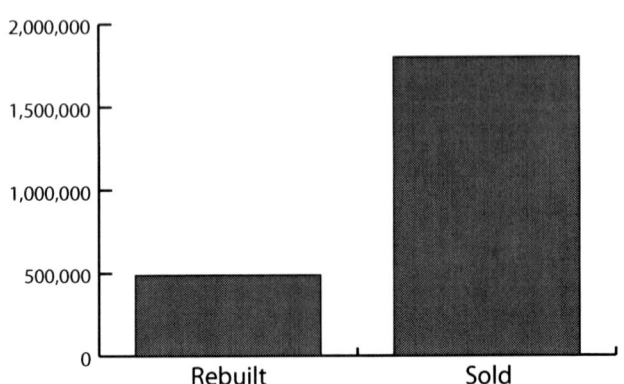

1980-1998: Homes built/sold during RTB

Thus, it is fair to conclude that Margaret Thatcher's Right to Buy scheme was, on balance, a disaster for British housing. The Tories sold 2 million homes (which today would be worth £320 billion) but they only replaced one in four homes sold (or 585,000, to be precise). This meant that from 1980, housing waiting lists have grown. Today, 5 million men, women and children are on housing waiting lists for social homes. 45,000 are homeless and 4 million families struggle with £8,500 private rent bills as a consequence of the Tories' actions. The Tories wrecked British housing, but the sad thing is that Grant Shapps wants to repeat their failings (see below).

The only thing that could possibly be achieved by reinvigorating the RTB scheme would be the injection of neo-liberalism into the very bottom rung of society. But, we don't trust the Tories to build adequate stocks of social homes, because in their last 18 years in power they only built one for every four they sold.

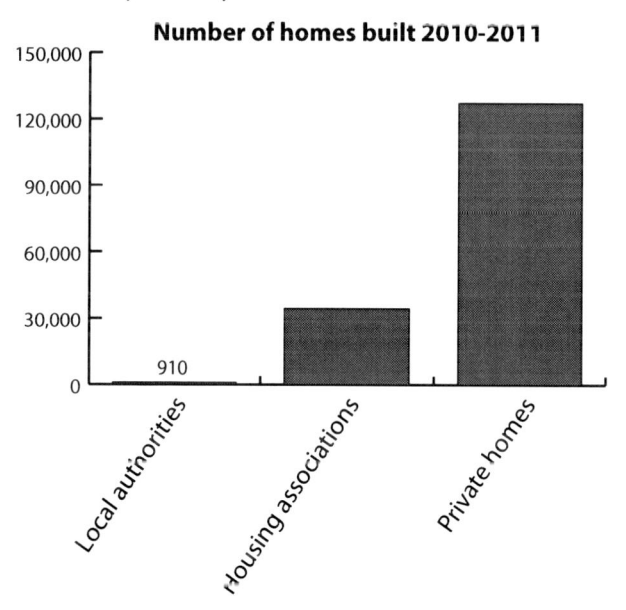

Number of homes built 2010-2011

Local authorities	910
Housing associations	~34,500
Private homes	~125,000

From 1 July 2010 to March 2011, only 910 council homes have been built by local authorities. Just 34,500 homes have been built by housing associations.

Bearing in mind that sales of council homes actually still take place, the overall stock of social homes has barely stood still. The solution for British housing is for the government to build affordable homes for the 5 million waiting on housing lists, for the 40,000 homeless and for the 4 million struggling with private rental bills.

Annual net additional dwellings

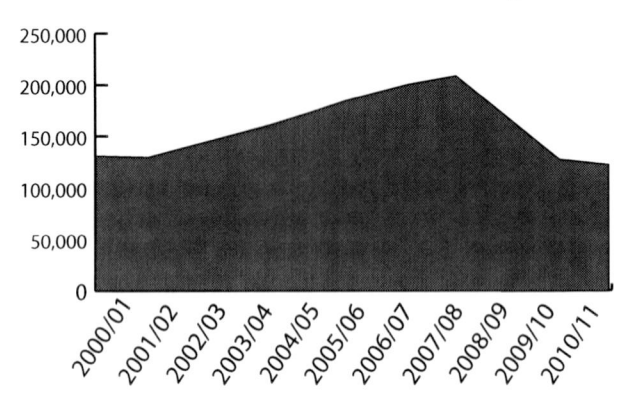

[Graph showing annual net additional dwellings from 2000/01 to 2010/11, ranging from 0 to 250,000, peaking around 2007/08 at over 200,000 and declining to around 125,000 by 2010/11]

The above graph is taken from data released by the ONS on 2 November 2011.[29] It shows that the total number of *net* dwellings added to the UK housing stock is at a 10-year low. This shows that the problem has worsened under the current Tory government. It increases the urgency of housing supply as an issue at the next General Election. Put simply, the problem is getting worse.

Number of households designated as statutorily homeless, by quarter

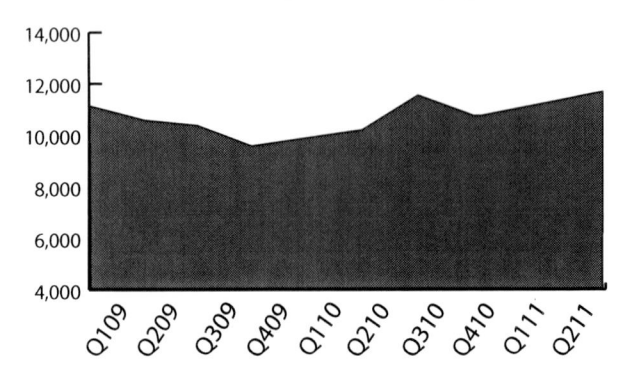

[Graph showing quarterly figures from Q109 to Q211, ranging from 4,000 to 14,000, hovering around 10,000-12,000]

According to the Office of National Statistics, the quarterly figures for those households statutorily homeless are at a 10-quarter high (see graph above).[30] Levels of households being designated as statutorily homeless are 17% higher than they were in Q2 2010, when Labour left office. In the year before Labour left office 40,030 households were designated as homeless, but in the last year that has risen to 45,880. In other news, Shelter claims that up to 35,000 more will experience the loss of their home between now and Christmas.[31] Up to 630 people a day face the threat of losing their home. This is further evidence that homelessness is set to worsen under this Tory government. Repossessions, one would hope, will fall as the recession fully clears but the evidence from recent data suggests that the lack of housing supply will have a direct impact on homelessness.

The average cost to rent a property in England for a year

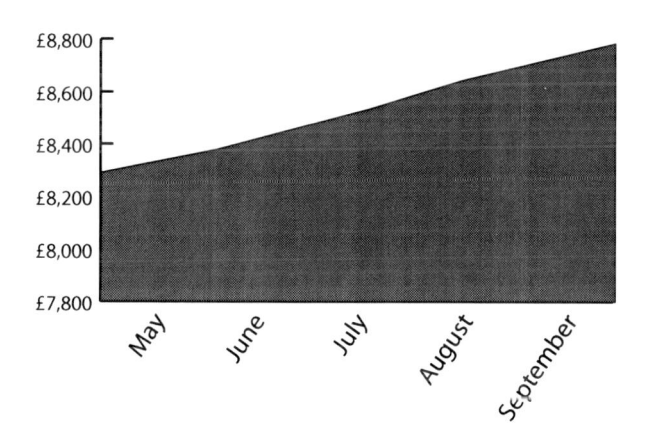

According to LSL property services, average rental prices have reached £8,616 a year. That is a £316 increase in the last four months and it means that rents are growing at an annualised c.£1k a year. The average rental property is a two-bedroom apartment, and three-quarters of private renters receive no help in housing benefit (HB). This is a very real crisis.

- Rental inflation is now growing at 12% on the year;
- Fuel inflation is growing at 17-23%;
- Transport inflation is growing at 8%;
- But wages have only grown £2 per week this year.

This is a crisis that yields a concoction of fuel poverty and health problems related to living in squalid housing. The surging rental prices are a logical consequence of a poor housing supply. As the population is set to hit 70 million by 2030, this problem will only worsen unless we improve the housing supply urgently. Below, I outline the main consequences of the Tory failure to tackle this problem.

The number of 'working poor' has doubled in three years

Snapshot of November 2008 working poor

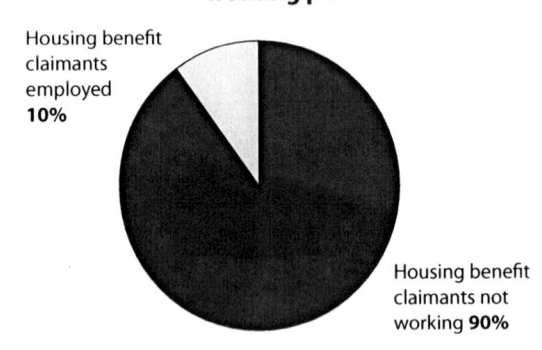

Housing benefit claimants employed **10%**

Housing benefit claimants not working **90%**

The explosion in the 'working poor'

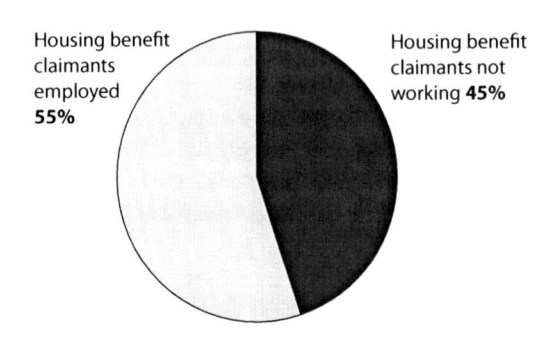

Housing benefit claimants employed **55%**

Housing benefit claimants not working **45%**

In November 2008, just 10% of existing HB recipients were employed. Most HB claimants were unemployed, elderly or disabled. But since that date there has been an explosion in the 'working poor'. By that term, I mean people who, although in employment, cannot afford a roof over their head (see above).

In the last 32 months, the proportion of 'new' HB claimants who are in employment has increased five-fold. There are now more people added to the HB register who are working than who are not. A majority (55%) of new HB claimants are the working poor. A national tragedy is unfolding before our eyes. So how many people are we talking about? (see below).

Persons working but in receipt of housing benefit

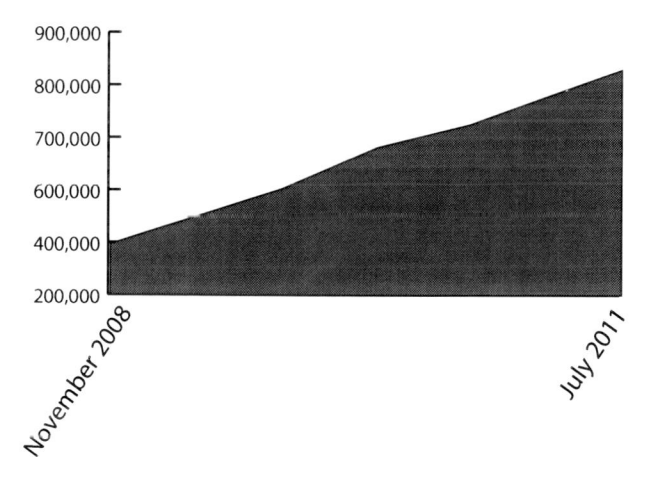

[Chart showing increase from approximately 400,000 in November 2008 to over 800,000 in July 2011]

The numbers of working poor have doubled in less than three years. In November 2008, just over 400,000 workers could not afford a roof over their heads. But by July 2011, that figure had climbed to over 800,000. In the next year it is quite likely the number of working poor will breach 1,000,000.

That landmark will be a sad reflection of the state of UK housing. The only solution to this problem is to build affordable homes that help reduce the annual private rental bill of £8,600 a year.

Private rental and HB are an economic time bomb

In November 2008, we the tax payers paid £5.5 billion a year to private landlords. That's bad, but it could be worse. The private rental sector accounted for 25% of the total HB households back then. It's getting much worse, and I fear this will be an economic drain on the State if it continues at this pace.

Housing benefit recipients by sector, November 2008

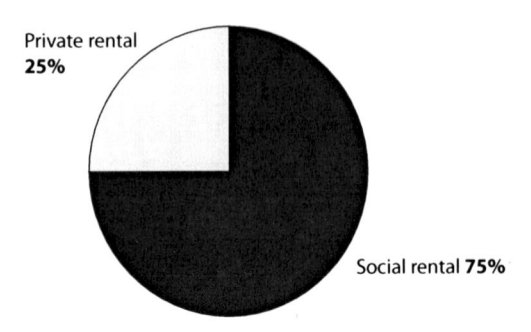

Private rental **25%**
Social rental **75%**

Housing benefit recipients by sector, January 2011

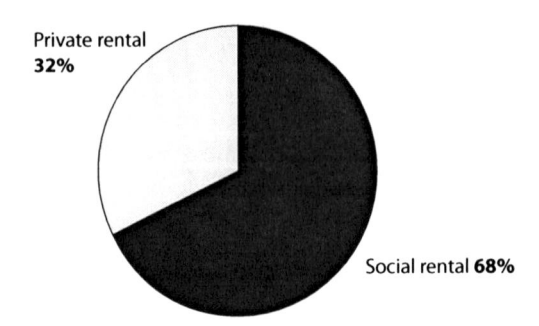

Private rental **32%**
Social rental **68%**

In just over two years the bill has grown a staggering £3.5 billion a year or £17.5 billion extra a parliament. That's 35 years' worth of EMA payments. We are now giving private landlords close to £9,000,000,000 a year. As a portion of HB market, private landlords have grown from constituting a quarter of the market to a third. If it continues to grow at this rate we all will collectively suffer. There is only one viable solution. The State needs to build social housing or not for profit private rental housing. This crisis is a ticking time bomb. It is an even bigger problem when you consider that an average HB payment to the private landlords is £110 a week, whereas the average payment in the social sector is just £76 a week. Thus, whilst the chart above shows the percentage of recipients who are receiving HB in the private sector, when you actually look at the private sector as a proportion of the payments, the problem is even more drastic.

Housing benefit payments per sector, January 2011

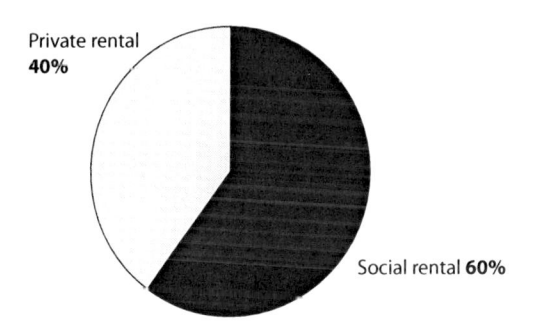

Private rental **40%**

Social rental **60%**

The private rental sector makes up 40% of the HB payments made by the state yearly. This is growing, and in the course of this parliament could well overtake the social sector as a proportion of the payments

The cost of a home is 7 times the annual income of the bottom 8 million families

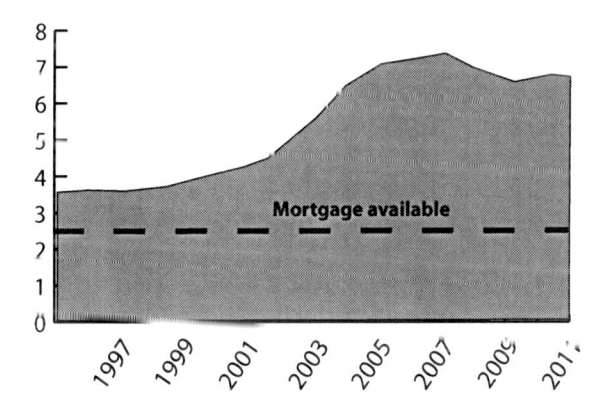

Mortgage available

made. This near £9 billion a year could be better spent investing in social housing. This, in turn, would also create employment and get the economy growing. This is the great 21st century no-brainer of UK politics.

Even if the bottom 8 million families in the UK received a 200% wage increase overnight, they would still not be able to afford to pay for a mortgage on a new home. On rounding, the bottom eight million families annual income is seven times smaller than that of the house price. The white dotted signifies their borrowing potential at 2.5 times their income. You can visualise our own borrowing potential on the graph by simply referring to the left-hand axis. Even if you place the borrowing potential higher at five times their income, the purchase of a home is still beyond their reach. As you can see, the scope for poorer people being able to afford to buy a home has worsened remarkably since 1996. Since 1979, however, we have sold of 1.8 million state homes to private ownership. The housing stock is dwindling, while the demand for a council house is accelerating.

The National Housing Report 2011

The National Housing Report has slammed the government's record on housing in a number of key areas. Eighteen months into an electoral term, the government has been given the red light for failing in four ways. The four key failures are as follows:

1. Housing supply. "Total new housing starts and completions remain at historically low levels, and public investment in new affordable housing has been severely reduced."
2. Help with the housing costs. "Cuts to housing benefit are already impacting on many lower income households, and may have further unintended consequences."
3. Homelessness. "The numbers of households accepted as homeless and in priority need has increased, as has the use of temporary accommodation. A welcome change to the way data is collected means no assessment of rough sleeping is possible at this time."
4. Affordability of the private rented sector. "Increased demand means private rents are high and rising, and it is not yet clear that reductions in Local Housing Allowance rates will reduce rent levels."

The Housing Report was jointly commissioned by the National Housing Federation, the Chartered Institute of Housing, and Shelter and can be read here (http://tinyurl.com/d2jw7qt). It is clear that the current housing strategy is failing and a new direction is needed. Below I outline where I think the solution lies.

Four policy initiatives

Four policy initiatives to tackle the £8,600 average private rents families pay, and the 5 million adults and children on housing waiting lists.

- Build 100,000 co-operative homes (per annum) halving the private rents currently charged by landlords.
- End Council Tax exemptions (and other tax loopholes) for those owning second homes and shortening Council Tax exemption periods for those moving between properties.
- Doubling stamp duty on 'buy to let' home purchases.
- Slum Landlord Exclusion Zones.

100,000 co-operative 2 bedroom rental homes throughout the UK

Herein, I am laying out the case for a not for profit privatised housing scheme. I propose that the government set up an independent co-operative housing body to take responsibility for a share of the privatised rental housing sector. The aim of this scheme is to help the millions who have been struggling to make rental payments in the private sector. These homes would not be for purchase, but instead set rental prices at a fair rate of £4,000 per year rising with inflation. They would only be available for people who were not eligible to receive housing benefit and who had demonstrated a willingness and ability to pay private rental market prices for the previous 12 months.

This scheme would not prejudice any other housing scheme in which the government and social housing sectors participate. It is exclusively for hard working individuals or families who cannot afford to buy their own home. To be eligible the proposed HRP would have to demonstrate that previous rental costs comprised of more that 40% of the household expenditure. They would have to demonstrate that they were ineligible or unable to attain social housing. Frozen out of that sector, and unable to enter the home owning sector it is the state's job to protect them from exploitation in the private rental market.

Year on year the initial start up cost would be repaid. The new body would also be allowed to borrow on the back on its assets and rental income. It is hoped that co-operative housing could become a significant player in the private rental market, and that it would through time pay its initial start up funding back to the government. The plan is to have the body self financing within 10 years.

Costing of 1.8 million homes
It would cost £120,000 to build an affordable home per year. This price includes materials and labour as well as planning costs. The figures are independently supplied by the Home Builders Federation. The HBF also states that each home built creates 1.5 jobs per home and four times that in the wider employment field. Thus to build one home, the HBF calculates that 5.5 jobs are created. In addition, a new housing estate requires a new bus route, a new grocery store, a lollipop lady, a barber, a taxi depot, a fast food outlet, a licensed premises, and so on. 100,000 homes would require new schools, doctors, gas meter readers, newsagents, bookmakers, and so forth. What we are talking about here is the regeneration of entire communities and with it, new employment, spending and growth.

Based upon these figures I have calculated the cost of setting up a co-operating housing body that would build 1.8 million homes making up the shortfall in social housing lost since 1980 and at the same time create 750,000 jobs. Once the 1.8 million homes are completed this plan does not cater for any more being built. The cost to build 100,000 homes every year over 18 years should in theory, on today's prices cost £216 billion. It is planned that the government would commit to paying for half of these costs (£113 billion), while the co-op would be allowed to borrow a further £43 billion over an 18-year period.

The co-op's rental income would make up the shortfall. I calculate that this would in fact result in a net benefit of £40 billion to the Treasury as savings in the benefit system due to increased employment and increased tax take would leave the Treasury £8.5 billion a year better off. Based upon the rental agreement outlined in my previous post namely that £4,000 is generated per home per year, I calculate the net rental benefit to co-op housing to be £66.6 billion at the end of the 18-year period. This excludes running costs of the co-op housing which I estimate to be £100,000,000 per year. Of course, this is an overestimation for the early years, but admin costs later in the programme might well be higher. The generated rental income by 2055 would actually exceed the entire costs of building the homes. Thus the homes would then be net assets to the co-op company. The co-op company would then benefit from a rental income of £7.1 billion per year, and valuing each home at £120,000, the company would also enjoy property assets of £216 billion.

It is proposed that the government pay the initial start up costs of £12 billion to complete the first 100,000 homes. Once completed, they would generate £400 million of rents per year, but £100 million of those would be retained for running costs. To complete the next year's 100,000 homes, it is proposed that the co-op be granted borrowing powers. It would, in this said year, borrow £5.7 billion declining at a rate of £400 million annually thereafter. The government would provide 18 annual £6 billion pound payments until the 1.8 million homes were completed. The co-op would borrow from years 2 to 18, after which it will be no longer necessary for the government to spend or for the co-op to borrow. From this date the £7.1 billion surplus rental income could be used to pay back borrowing. This would not be a PFI initiative. The co-op would, with the aid of the government, be allowed to raise capital on the back of its own assets. Given that the assets grow £12 billion per year, and that the borrowing required would decline every year, there is little

By 2054/55 the 1.8m homes will have paid for themselves

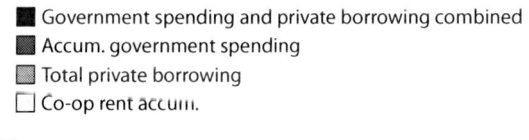

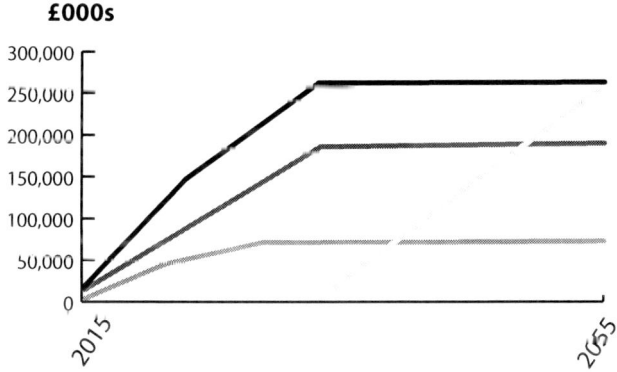

■ Government spending and private borrowing combined
■ Accum. government spending
▨ Total private borrowing
☐ Co-op rent accum.

Note: To view the costing, copy this link into Google Chrome: http://tinyurl.com/d5f956b

doubt that this credit facility for the co-op is achievable. Co-op housing would remain a not for profit organisation. (See above for projections as to when borrowing will be exceeded by rental income (accumulated).)

Benefits to GDP, tax take, and reduced benefit payments
If 750,000 people are employed as a result of this, it means that they do not have to a) claim benefits and b) they can now pay taxes. One unemployed person on average claims £82 a week in housing benefit. They also claim job seekers allowance of £67.50.

Both these are modest estimates. Evidence shows that many claim other benefits in addition. But I have omitted these from my calculations. In terms of Child Tax Credit

I assume that those eligible as unemployed will still be eligible when they get a job, so I have omitted CTC savings. WTC tends to climb in a gradient as the CTC element decreases but if these salaries were over £15k a year, then up to £2.5k in tax credits would be saved from those families who were previously in receipt of WTC. But I have not factored

Yearly benefit of housing plan to the Treasury

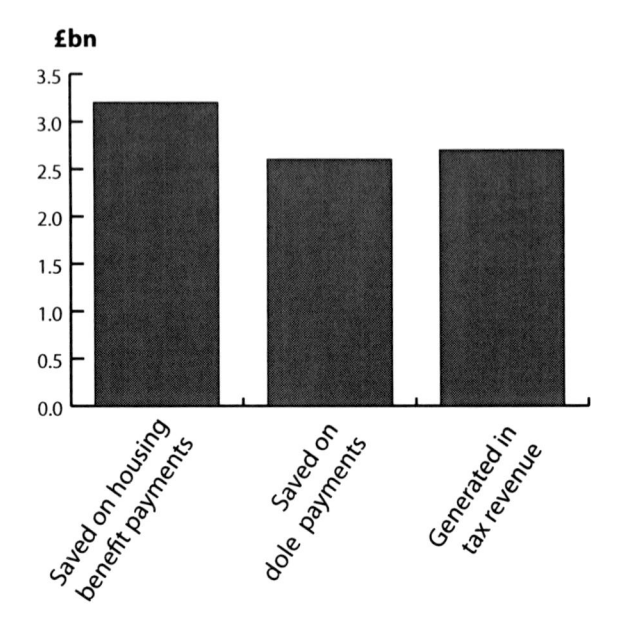

in these savings. Thus, I repeat, these are conservative calculations.

Having explained the caveats, I calculate based upon 2011-2 tax and benefit system that this would save the Treasury £8.5 billion a year in reduced benefit payments and increased tax take. Note that the Treasury would be investing initially £12 billion (year 1) and £6 billion thereafter. Thus, these saving above are not net. In fact from year two, the total savings to the Treasury would be £.25 billion on the year. As I said, house building would cease after year 18. From that point, the net benefit to the Treasury would be £8.5 billion a year as no expenditure would be required.

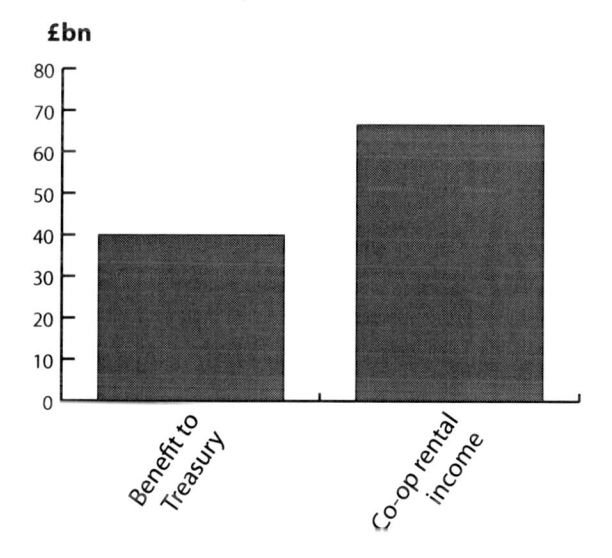

After 18 years and 1.8m homes

£bn

Benefit to Treasury	Co-op rental income
~40	~67

Thus, deducted investment costs from Treasury benefits, and the Treasury would gain c.£40 billion over an 18-year period rising by c.£8.5 billion thereafter. In addition, net rental income from the co-op housing scheme would total £66.6 billion after an 18-year period. All of this would be ploughed back into rebuilding more homes, which would year on year reduce the borrowing costs.

In the end it would be necessary for the government to spend £113 billion on building the 1.8 million homes. But during this period, c.£153 billion would be added to the treasury's coffers though reduced benefit payments and increased tax take.

Once the debts have been paid to private lenders, the co-op could conceivably run at a profit of c.£7.1 billion with assets of c.£216 billion. Since the co-op would by law be forbidden from making a profit, the government, or indeed the co-op, could discuss how to proceed with arrangements thereafter. The stated goal of this policy is to halve the annual rental costs hard working couples, families and individuals on low income are paying in the private rented sector.

A secondary goal is to reduce volatility in the construction sector that forces labourers to live a life of seasonal employment. These plans are at a very early stage and would require a detailed feasibility study to determine exact costs, including recruitment and building costs based upon state bargaining power that may be able to deliver the properties for even cheaper.

Council Tax exemptions for second home owners and empty homes

Business rates/council tax exemptions per parliament

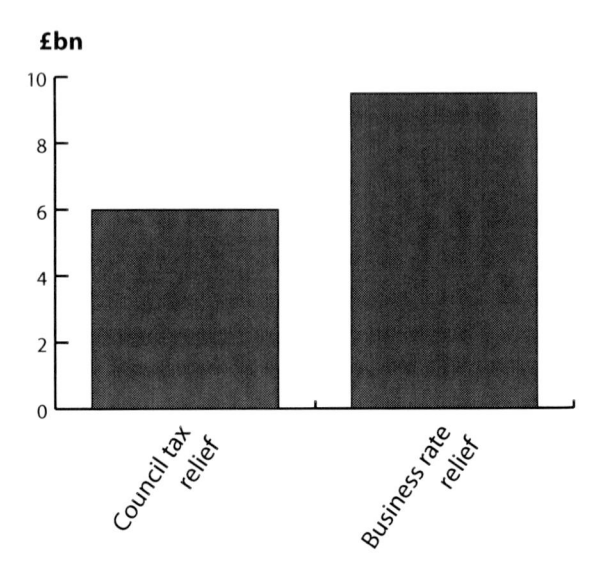

£bn

Category	£bn
Council tax relief	6
Business rate relief	~9.5

The government exempts businesses and home dwellers about £15.5 billion in Business Rate Tax and Council Tax per parliament. In most cases this is for a very good reason. The premises may be unoccupied due to bereavement or insolvency for example, or it may be used for charitable purposes, and so it is right and proper that the owner be exempt from financial punishment.

There are cases, however, where the empty property rate relief or band A/C Council Tax exemptions could be denied. The government itself estimates billions of pounds of fraud take place in this area per parliament.

I am proposing that we significantly alter the rules of Council Tax exemption and Business Rate exemption for unoccupied premises.

There is a moral case for doing this. There are currently c.45,000 homeless in the UK, and 5 million adults and children on housing lists. There is something unethical about hundreds of thousands of homes claiming six months' exemption from fees because they are unoccupied. I would propose reducing the six-month exemption to one month. This gives any new dweller time to move in whilst at the same time punishing a person who may own a second home and simply be trying to fiddle the system. This one move would save the government about £2 billion over five years.

There is also an economic case for looking again at the Empty Property Rate Relief. If you examine by local authority the premises who benefit most from this you will note that Westminster authority, for example, features heavily. Having properties in this areas unoccupied when there is such a high demand for property both for business and domestic purposes is unethical and does not make economic sense. Once again I would propose reducing the three-month exemption window in these cases to just one month. In all you would save about £1.8 billion over the course of parliament.

Buy to let mortgage holders and second home owners

The graph below shows that of the 2.8million second owned homes in the UK, more than 2 million of them are bought to let to tenants. Just 21,000 are leased to university-going children. And 100,000 are awaiting the owner moving in, while c.700, 000 of them are used as second homes by the owner. In view of this, legislative reform of the buy to let (BTL) sector is required.

In areas where there is an acute housing shortage, BTL mortgages should be prevented on new builds. Too often, entire developments are snapped up by speculators and then rented to people who would dearly love to have been able to buy them. Also, those buying second homes, or taking out BTL mortgages should pay double the stamp duty. The revenue raised could be used to permanently exempt first time buyers from paying stamp duty.

Status of 'second' homes in UK

Leasing to tennant	2,065,000
Awaiting removal	105,000
Children	21,000
Personal use	703,000

Slum landlord exclusion zones

I wish to float the idea of nationwide implementation of slum landlord exclusion zones. The purpose behind these would be to tackle the 1 million homes currently being rented that are deemed unfit for human habitation.

Landlords that rent these properties to those claiming housing benefit should be a) denied HB payments and b) be banned from letting out other properties. Follow the link to the example of Newcastle City Council which has already been using the orders to tackle rogue landlords in their areas (see http://tinyurl.com/2vmtq29).

Conclusion

Now, you may not like any of my policy suggestions – that is neither here nor there. The aim of this piece was to convince you that the private rental market in its current form is unsustainable, that the current housing shortage is a national tragedy and that the Tory Party is making things worse. Private renters are a key voting bloc at the next election and they are Labour's to gain.

---

29 Department of Communities and Local Government http://www.communities.gov.uk/publications/corporate/statistics/netsupplyhousing201011
30 Department of Communities and Local Government http://tinyurl.com/29pz3cj
31 Shelter http://tinyurl.com/ctkelfh

Houses not to Blame

By Austin Mitchell MP

Austin Mitchell is the MP for Great Grimsby. In his past life, Austin lectured history at University in New Zealand before working as a journalist for Yorkshire Television. He was elected to parliament in 1977 and has served as Great Grimsby's MP ever since. Austin is a member of the Socialist Campaign Group.

Labour Left and the Importance of Ethical Economics

Housing, once a central commitment for all parties, and a major part of Labour's achievements in government, has suddenly become the elephant in our recession room. It played a big part in boosting Britain's recovery from the great depression in the nineteen thirties and could do so again in recovery from the great recession. It certainly should because all the evidence says a housing crisis is building rapidly and will hit hardest those who can't afford to buy at present prices, and can't get a mortgage in any case. Homelessness increases. Hopeless waiting lists grow to huge levels. The private rented sector is turning nasty and we desperately need to redeem the failures and disinvestment of three decades.

Only a huge house building programme can do all that. Yet neither Party has an adequate housing policy. It's too small a part of Ed Balls's five-point plan for growth and the building numbers he proposes are small compared to the need. As for Grant Shapps, his policies are all public relations rather than bricks and mortar, his programme leads to a two class housing sector with subsidies and support for those who can afford to buy, but blame, higher rents and insecure tenancies for those who can't. Meanwhile, the build declines remorselessly, builders go bust and the provision of new, publicly rented, housing for those who need it most plummets.

Here are the makings of a major crisis and the most depressing housing situation since the War. Instead of building the 'affordable' houses, and the good public housing for rent we need, the politicians shower blame on existing tenants as if they were lepers, subsidised scroungers and personally responsible for the problem. Both parties propose to intensify the pressure on the shrinking stock of council and social housing. The Tories want to turn it into a transit camp for the poor and sell off as much as possible. They'll stimulate the most profitable form of building: bijoux residences on green field sites, helped by a revival of Labour's kick start finance (which the incoming government scuppered) to revive stalled private building schemes, by throwing open government land and by relaxing planning laws. Their Right to Buy at knock-down prices is unlikely to be heavily taken up. Sales are already low and much of what's left is unsalable tower blocks. Yet insofar as the bargain is accepted, its revenues won't be adequate to finance building the one-for-one replacement new houses for every one sold. It will also compound the decline of the estates which Mrs Thatcher began. As for the huge waiting lists, they'll be reduced, not by rehousing, but by a massive pruning exercise to cut out anyone who's not in desperate need.

Housing Revenue Accounts will now be left to the councils and not milked by Treasury as they have been, but the price for this is that councils must take on the historic housing debt (which has in fact already been paid off), plus an extra £7 billion to force them to increase rents. So remaining tenants will face steep rent increases and the shrinking stock will become a transit camp for the needy, as secure tenancies end for new tenants who'll get only limited tenures to ensure that if they get a job, or their income rises, they'll be free to taste the joys of the private rented sector. There rents and tenancies remain unregulated and tenants will face both higher rents and lower housing benefit, resulting in social cleansing by driving the poor out of city centres into cheaper areas, well away from jobs. A new Rachmanism is certain in this sector.

Clever stuff. Yet instead of opposing these prejudiced policies and mobilising tenants against it, Labour has echoed the Tory strategy, suggesting that those in work should be given preference for public housing (an illegal proposal which conflicts with the first duty of local authorities to provide for need) which might provide a profitable future for transport contractors ferrying the employed in and out. We're silent on the pressing need to restore controls on the private rented sector and have flirted with the empty room campaign by proposing that tenants not using their entire space should either move to smaller premises (assumed to be available) or take in lodgers. This may do wonders in turning the pensioner vote against us, but little to ease the crisis.

Neither Party recognises the importance of a mass build of the good, affordable, public housing for rent the nation needs. Only this can provides the basis for better health, by ending overcrowding and poor conditions, open up the benefits of better education by giving kids privacy and building stable, settled communities rather than ghettos where the deprived take their miseries out on each other. Everything proposed so far is better calculated to advance the Thatcher achievement of turning all too much council and social housing into ghetto dumping grounds for the poor and deprived, though they'll now, if Tory fantasies are fulfilled, be shuttled out if they riot or are otherwise naughty, or if they improve themselves by managing to get a job. Two different futures. One common punishment.

This destabilising vindictiveness is an irrelevance in the face of the housing crisis already building. In Labour's years we built fewer houses than at any time since the 1920s, less council housing than Mrs. Thatcher and far less in total than growing needs as households split like amoeba and immigration and population increased. That gap now gapes even wider at over 100,000 houses a year, resulting in a major shortage in the next few years. This will hit the two-fifths who can't afford to buy hardest and is already leading to overcrowding, sofa surfing, staying at home with mum, sharing with mates or struggling on in over-priced and over-crowded private rented accommodation. London MPs are already grappling with the consequences of this for the poor and the rest of us soon will be.

Paradoxically house building offers the best, indeed only, opportunity to generate the growth and jobs Britain needs to escape our Great Recession. Housing boosted recovery from the Great Depression before re-armament kicked in. It sustained growth and jobs in the 1950s,, 60s and 70s. The mini boost to building produced by Labour's death bed repentance in 2008 was too little too late, but still increased employment and produced a short lived recovery which the Tories killed. The big build is even more essential now. We're not like the US where the subprime era led to overbuild, or Ireland with its huge numbers of houses unsold and, in many cases, unfinished. Here by contrast we have not only the opportunity but a pressing need to build to boost our stagnant construction sector, put people back to work and into housing where they will buy the furniture and household goods they need. The market won't do it because so much of the big build, perhaps half, must be public housing for rent, publicly financed and built by councils and housing associations. Only the public sector can do that.

Labour must commit itself to a big building programme but we've been loath to do so because of fear of the inevitable Tory rejoinder "Who's going to pay for it?" In fact, public housing for rent pays for itself with the return in jobs, growth and investment in a revenue producing public asset. Far from being subsidised, tenants have been robbed. Government has already siphoned out £68 billion from council rents and receipts since 1979 and the proposed rent increases will continue that robbery.

There are several ways of financing the build. We could revive Municipal Housing Bonds. We could propose that the next round of quantitative easing, instead of flowing into banks to build reserves, be mandated to building societies, councils and housing associations to build houses and add repossessed properties to their stock. We could set up a National Investment Bank to bring in private capital and invest in SMEs, housing and infrastructure. We could require pension funds to invest in public housing or to finance housing associations which would be as profitable for them as they've been for the banks. As with Roosevelt's New Deal, stimulating a failing economy requires restless experimentation, a readiness to defy convention and sustained inventiveness. This government shows none of that. Labour must if it is to avoid a national tragedy of bumping along the bottom for years while poverty increases and the housing crisis gets worse. Let's show the government what has to be done. Let's campaign for housing.

Labour's Co-operative Future

By James Doran

James Doran is a Co-operative Party member from Darlington. He is interested in how best we re-balance the UK economy in a post neo-liberal age. For James, that means harnessing common endeavour and promoting organisations that manage responsible profit levels and create sustainable employment. Since joining Labour Left, James has a concentrated his efforts on building up grass-roots support for Labour Left and has shown himself an effective organiser and capable speaker. James also blogs at http://hands-of-the-many.blogspot.com/

Labour Left and the Importance of Ethical Economics

After our party's loss of a parliamentary majority in the 2010 election, a debate started on the political economy of last and next Labour government. In contrast to the beginning of previous periods of opposition, it has been without damaging splits and though differences exist, there is much greater common ground. Through the course of the leadership contest and the new leader's first year in office, a consensus seems to have been reached on the successes and failings of the economic model that prevailed before the global financial crisis. The Labour Party can use its strong links with the co-operative movement to regain the trust of voters on the economy.

From New Labour to Next Labour

In the context of the industrial strength of trade unions having been greatly reduced by mass unemployment and restrictive legislation, the Labour Party made a compromise with corporate and financial power that had arisen virtually unchallenged during the years of Tory rule. This allowed the Labour Party, trading as New Labour, to win a large parliamentary majority in 1997, and to sustain a record three full terms of office. The introduction of much-needed social-democratic reforms was welcome, but the compromise with Britain's ruling class prevented the party from articulating a critique of power wielded outside of democratic structures. The dominance of the City meant tax revenues for public spending throughout the UK, but it also led to the delusion that we were heading towards a 'weightless economy', that manufacturing industries did not matter as much as financial services, and the problem of wage stagnation could be solved with increased indebtedness (Turner, 2008).[32]

The global financial crisis shattered the settlement with the British establishment, and some of the illusions about our economy: the banking collapse demonstrated that the state was the last Few in the Labour Party would now disagree that the UK needs an active industrial strategy, a reform of corporate governance in the financial sector, and an emphasis on responsibility throughout society. But as the Tory-led government has embarked on a five year austerity plan, it seems as if the achievements of Labour in office could be wiped away under the guise of creating a 'Big Society' and 'rebalancing the economy'. Vague rhetoric from the Coalition about using co-operatives to empower people is without credibility given the context of 'expansionary fiscal contraction' – an attempt to reduce the deficit with large-scale cuts but without an economic recovery.

And rebalancing is only possible with the policies and funding that they are cutting.

Our economic policies have to offer hope because truth alone does not bring social change. Although industrial activism and corporate governance reform are needed, they do not easily translate into the language of electoral campaigning; so it will not be enough to assert that the Age of Austerity is an attempt to restructure the economy in the interests of the few at the expense of the many. By drawing on our long-standing relationship with the co-operative movement, and our sister the Co-operative Party, we can better communicate our values, particularly in the seats Labour needs to win again and in regions such as the South East and South West of England (Carey-Dawes, 2011).[33]

The potential of co-operation

In the 18th century, men like Robert Owen and William King provided the organisational and ideological impetus to many of the early attempts at co-operative enterprise. The wisdom of crowds has proved greater and more flexible than any Utopian scheme, ensuring the movement's survival.

The co-operative and mutual enterprise (CME) sector has grown in public trust and political support in recent years. In the wake of the banking crisis, mutuals became the business model in finance that attracted the greatest support amongst customers, with record deposits in building societies and the credit crunch has led to greater awareness of credit unions. The shared prosperity of the Co-operative and the John Lewis Partnership has been in stark contrast to the skewed distribution of risk and reward in high finance and big business in recent years. During the global recession, few co-operative banks, building societies, or credit unions, required state bail-outs like the investor-owned financial sector (Birchall & Ketilson, 2009).[34] And research has suggested employee-owned businesses had a competitive advantage over other firms during the recession: the level of trust and motivation generated by the model of ownership (Lampell, Bhalla, & Jha, 2010).[35]

Activists in environmental campaign organisations, such as Friends of the Earth, view co-ops favourably because the economic participation of members of the community demonstrates that sustainable development in food and energy pays dividends. Allotment associations and community-supported agriculture give people access locally-produced fruit and vegetables; and communities involved in co-operative energy generation are better placed to deal with the growing problem of fuel poverty. Labour's current leader was the energy minister in the last government and supported efforts to increase community ownership of energy assets, writing a foreword to the Co-operative Party's policy document on the subject (Erbmann, Goulbourne& Malik, 2009).[36]

What can be done?

Labour should champion co-operation and mutuality as a good way of doing business: policies which promote the development of co-operatives in the private sector will ensure that job creation occurs within communities, and that people can have more power in their daily lives. We are in a good position to do this in parliament now that the shadow cabinet contains a number of Labour and Co-operative MPs, including the shadow chancellor Ed Balls.

Our party could seek to fill the gap in legislation on corporate structures relating to employee ownership, and potential exists for tendering processes for public contracts to give preference to firms owned by their workers (Erdal, 2011).[37] In the longer-term, we should give consideration to how co-operative models could be used to improve customer service in utilities such as water and rail (Birchall, 2002; Wolmar, 2011).[38]

In the broader labour movement, affiliated trade unions could follow the lead of the United Steel Workers in North America, which is working to establish private-sector 'union co-ops' in the US and Canada. In partnership with the Mondragon Co-operative Corporation, the world's largest worker co-op, the USW intends to 'create good jobs, empower workers, and support communities' (Davidson, 2010).[39]

The Coalition's plans for a Green Investment Bank demonstrate that state-backed investment banking is gaining acceptance within the British establishment. Labour could advocate the establishment of state-backed banks for regional economies with co-operative ownership a condition of lending (Zarb-Cousin, 2011).[40] Incidentally, much-needed reform of the banking sector will only work in the long-term if the question of moral hazard is resolved: monetary reform is required to close the loophole allowing private financial institutions to avoid paying the Bank of England for electronically-created credit (Dyson, Greenham, Ryan-Collins & Werner, 2010).[41]

Labour should be vocal about the role of housing co-ops and mutuals in building mixed and resilient communities. European countries with higher levels of equality and well-being than the UK have a much higher percentage of their housing supply owned or controlled by democratic associations (Bliss, 2009).[42] A co-operative housing body could be established to create a more affordable private-rented sector; such a commitment would show voters that Labour is in tune with worries about rising rents and the receding hope of home ownership (Clarke, 2011).[43]

For the next few years Labour will not be in a position to lead at a national level, and if the Coalition lasts until 2015, it will be in local government that the party will be able to prove itself to the electorate. In the local elections on May 5th, Labour performed well, regaining control of a number of councils – but large-scale funding cuts from central government will mean Labour councillors face years of difficult decisions and a struggle to maintain a positive impact with dwindling resources. In response to this, and the rising interest in co-operative enterprise in the wake of the global financial crisis, the Co-operative Councils Network has been established and is being run by the Co-operative Party to enable Labour councils, and Labour Groups in opposition, to share power with people (Grant, 2011).[44]

It seems that across the Labour Party there is enthusiasm for a more co-operative future. But the question must be asked: if CMEs are capable of combining economic efficiency and social justice, why are they not more prevalent? The answer to this is simple: power. And this is why co-operativism is no easy ride: co-operation has always been viewed with suspicion by those with financial and economic power, precisely because democratic member-owned businesses pose the threat of a good example. If we want to put power in the hands of the many, we have to again understand the power possessed by a few.

---

32 Turner, G. (2008) *The Credit Crunch: Housing Bubbles, Globalisation, and the Worldwide Economic Crisis*, Pluto Press.
33 Carey-Dawes, D. (2011) 'Why Co-operative solutions should be at the heart of Labour's revival in the South' [http://www.southernfront.org.uk/2011/07/why-co-operative-solutions-should-be-at.html].
34 Birchall, J., &Ketilson, L. H. (2009) *Resilience of the cooperative business model in times of crisis*, International Labour Organisation.
35 Lampel, J., Bhalla, A., &Jha, P. (2010) *Model Growth: Do Employee-Owned Businesses deliver sustainable performance?*
36 Erbmann, R., Goulbourne, H., & Malik, P. (2009) *Collective Power: Changing the way we consume energy*, The Co-operative Party.
37 Erdal, D. (2011) *Beyond the Corporation: Humanity Working*. The Bodley Head.
38 Wolmar, C. (2011) *Co-operative rail: a radical solution*, Co-operatives UK.
39 Davidson, C. (2010) 'U.S. steelworkers plan to experiment with factory ownership', The CCPA Monitor, Canadian Centre for Policy Alternatives

40 Zarb-Cousin, M. (2011) 'Mutually Beneficial', Progress [http://www.progressonline.org.uk/2011/05/03/mutually-beneficial/]

41 Dyson, B., Greenham, T., Ryan-Collins, J. & Werner, R. A. (2010) *Towards a Twenty-First Century Banking and Monetary System: Submission to the Independent Commission on Banking*, New Economics Foundation & Positive Money.

42 Bliss, N. (ed.) (2009) *Bringing Democracy Home*, The Commission on Co-operative and Mutual Housing.

43 Clarke, E. (2011) 'Co-operative Housing: 100,000 not for profit rental homes a year available to those currently renting privately', The Green Benches [http://eoin-clarke.blogspot.com/2011/05/100k-co-op-homes-over-18-year-period.html].

44 Grant, P. (2011) 'The common endeavour of the Co-operative Councils', The Co-operative Councils Network [http://www.councils.coop/2011/07/26/the-common-endeavour-of-the-co-operative-councils-cllr-paul-brant-liverpool/]

Recession: the Socialist Solution
By Austin Mitchell MP

Austin Mitchell is the MP for Great Grimsby. In his past life, Austin lectured history at University in New Zealand before working as a journalist for Yorkshire Television. He was elected to parliament in 1977 and has served as Great Grimsby's MP ever since. Austin is a member of the Socialist Campaign Group.

Labour Left and the Importance of Ethical Economics

There are no socialist economics, merely good and bad economics. The good economics are socialist in the sense that they use the power of the community and the state to advance the interests of society – the people – by full employment, economic growth and well-being. The bad serve the interests of the plutocracy by deflation, discipline, spending cuts all imposed on the masses to preach tax cuts and the ability to exercise their will for the classes.

"Never let a good recession go to waste" was the axiom which facilitated the introduction of good Keynesian, Left economics in societies which are conservative and slow to change. Recovery from the Great Depression brought Roosevelt and the New Deal, Labour to power in Sweden, New Zealand and, eventually, Britain in 1945. All created welfare states with full employment and demand management, bringing the long decades of prosperity after the War. This happens because recession can't be reversed by the market but requires the use of the state, effective regulation of capitalist excesses, public spending to protect the people and boost demand, and effective management to ensure fairness. Logically, today's Great Recession should have provided the same opportunities and impetus for the Left as the Great Depression of the 1930s.

Yet the Great Recession did not have the same effect. The Left was in power. In Britain it had lost faith in its basic principles and begun to believe that a great financial bubble was in fact a new paradigm. Thus Labour was totally unprepared when the bubble burst, as it was bound to under the old law that if a thing can't go on forever, it probably won't. It didn't and that lost us the election because Labour, as the party in power, was assumed to be responsible for the difficulties arising on their watch as well as being hit by "time for a change". This brought the Right to power and with it neo-liberal economics (aka Thatcherites or monetarists; the different labels described a common religion among ideologues who you can always tell, but not much) As believers in basic right wing objectives of rolling back the state, slashing social spending, freeing markets to do what always turned out to be their worst, and reducing a tax burden assumed, without evidence, to be destroying initiative, enterprise, even capitalism itself, the Tories implemented the lot.

So the people got what they didn't vote for and with it came results which the Tories, in their ignorance, had never expected. In 2008 Labour had been forced to rediscover a Keynesian Labourite approach which it had been frightened to proclaim before. A recovery in employment and growth resulted from its stimulus spending and house building programme. Both were too little too late but each produced glimmers of recovery only to be immediately halted by Tory cuts, tax increases and deflation.

These were based on two fundamental mistakes. George Osborne assumed that what had worked for Thatcher (fighting inflation) would work for him (fighting deflation) He didn't understand that Thatcherism had seemed to work only because North Sea oil rescued her from her own follies. Obsessed by debt he also failed to realise that Britain faced not a debt crisis, but a collapse in demand to which very different remedies were needed. The result of his misjudgments was rising unemployment, which in turn increased a deficit caused by falling public revenues rather than excessive public spending and leading to more of the borrowing the Tories had promised to reduce. Growth stopped. The economy flatlined, heading for a double-dip recession. Spending was desperately brought forward after 18 months – but it was too little, too late. The only thing which really changed was the blame for the failure, which shifted from 'Labour's legacy of debt' to the Euro disaster.

The immediate remedies

What needs to be done in this situation is obvious. Indeed, Labour is already offering it, though it won't have the power to implement it if there is no election before 2015, so the Tories will have to grasp it sooner or later. Only a boost to growth can check the slide down and only growth, with the rising employment it brings, can pay off debt, as Labour did between 1997 and 2000. That growth can only be triggered by a stimulus which requires spending, and preferably spending directed at the poor because they are more likely to spend than save, as the rich do. There are scores of ways of doing this. None are beyond the wit of even Tory governments.

Simon Jenkins has suggested helicopter money dropped on the people from on high. Ed Balls, constrained by Labour's over-zealous commitment to cut debt (though not as fast as the Tories) has provided five ways, including a small house building programme and a temporary cut in VAT. David Blanchflower suggests a two-year suspension of National Insurance for young workers to make their labour cheaper, and the Germans have successfully subsidised firms to pay full wages to workers hit by short-time working. Bob Skidelsky and others urge a National Investment Bank of the type used in many other countries and the government itself is trying to stimulate house building by reviving Labour's successful kick-start funding for stalled projects and offering government land, subsidies and mortgage support for purchases. Yet these are unlikely to be successful because uncertainty has shattered confidence. A big building programmer of public housing for rent, the type most urgently needed by the substantial proportion who can`t afford to buy, is essential. That could easily be financed by Municipal Bonds or by bringing in investment from pension funds but it's not yet on offer.

Long term

All or any of these measures would stimulate growth. The real problem is to sustain it so as to begin to tackle the more deep-seated problems of the British economy. Here stronger measures, more properly described as Socialist, come in because deep seated problems can't be waved away by a Keynesian wand. That is merely a revival of a failing economy. A necessary first step to re-orientating it. If nothing more is done they merely take us back into the old trap when the real need is to use the respite to begin the work of rebuilding which will fall to Labour after the next election.

The first deep problem is that the recession is deeper, harder and more serious in Britain than in any other economy. It will take more time and tougher measures to recover. Where Germany invested, restructured and formed close relationships between capital and labour to keep wages down and investment up, Britain, because of its overblown financial sector, has squandered the good times on a huge debt bubble which leaves everyone – families, companies, government – with a bigger collective debt burden than most.

The second problem is that de-industrialisation and the decline of manufacturing have gone further in Britain than in any other advanced country, leaving us more dependent on imports, less able to pay our way in the world, and with an economy more heavily colonised than any other. The need is to shift the balances from the finance sector, with its wild speculative propensities, to production by restructuring Industries, developing the new and widening and strengthening the industrial base and the suppliers, utilities, design and research and the energy providers it depends on. Then it must make and keep all this super-competitive.

These are basic tasks. All are difficult in a super-competitive globalised World. None of them can be done by markets which compound prevailing trends rather than reverse them. So only the state, the community in action, can do the job and only socialist measures, invoked now as means to a socialist end in the good society built on a mixed economy, steady growth and full employment can sustain it. It is difficult to set out these measures in detail now. Indeed to display the full armoury would be divisive and frightening to a nervous electorate. Yet it is Labour's responsibility to work them out, to plan, prepare and popularise measures which will become more obviously necessary as the scale of the problem is understood. The basic outline of what we need to do is already clear to the rank and file, if not to our nervous leaders.

The first and most basic requirement is an industrial policy. The City as a financial centre can be left to take care of itself, for it is no longer a British institution financing British investment and industry, but now Kong West, a weakly regulated tax haven and a play space for foreign banks and hedge funds, much as foreign stars dominate Wimbledon. The City's preoccupations and its lack of interest in Britain have already shrunk much of our capacity in ship-building, railway rolling stock production, quality textiles and garments, TV and electronics. All have been lost or taken over by foreign concerns because of lack of investment and support from a financial sector which makes more money from closing industries and building shopping centres. Manufacturing must now helped to face the intensifying rigour of the markets by an industrial policy which encourages, provides and sustains investment, research, design and training (rather than training people for jobs that don't exist); which facilitates transport, provides support, advice and market research for exports; and which ensures that British contracts, whether for railway engines, IT or communications, go to British producers, in the way every other country does. The same encouragement and support needs to go to new and fledgling industries which need to be encouraged by a favourable tax regime, investment, and venture capital, both public and private, to allow them to take root and grow.

New Labour was so frightened of its socialist past that the word "nationalisation" never passed its lips until 2008 when the party reluctantly nationalised banks. In the great reconstruction, such fears are irrelevant. The market neither provides nor sustains, but a mixed economy in which, as Gaitskell proposed in 'Industry and Society' in 1959, nationalised industries provide a new element of competition. This is immediately possible in the banking sector where the state owns two banks which should stay as state enterprises bringing a new ethic, new investment and lending strategies and less speculation to the sector. Similarly, where railway franchises have been given up or fall into the state which now already owns Network Rail. This would allow the railways to be run as a unified organisation at a substantially lower cost in subsidies to that required by a whole series of separate companies. Nationalisation should be a reserve power to rebuild failing companies whose failure is reversible, which have a vital role in the market or which are hit by temporary difficulties.

The power of the state to regulate will also be vital. The Tories complain of the cost of EU regulations with which business has to comply, but this is an excuse for failure, not a cause. Regulation is essential, particularly in financial markets to control their built-in drive to speculative excess. It is also necessary to allow industry to compete by conforming to international standards. The problem is not regulation itself, but the way European regulations are dominated by German and French interests and then gold-plated here by application with excessive inflexibility. A British equivalent of the SEC should be set up to regulate financial markets and a Companies Commission to regulate the business sector, and ensure greater shareholder involvement, worker control over top salaries and pay, and worker participation in the Audit Committee to sustain investment. The two-tier board has been successful in Germany by institutionalising the workers' interest in the strength and longevity of the company. So why not introduce it here, and weaken the short-term imperatives of shareholder value which boosts the rewards of top executives. This requires that the external auditors should stop selling services to the companies they audit which brings them into collusion with management. We also need a Chapter 11 bankruptcy provision of the type used in the US to allow companies in difficulties (such as Chevrolet) to restructure and survive.

Britain needs a national investment bank to provide finance for investment in companies, SMEs, government contracts, and housing and other developments which would otherwise be financed by PFIs. The bank will need to be funded partially by government, partly by the private sector – particularly the pension funds. Britain's major industrial weakness has always been investment. Only the state can encourage it and ensure that it is funded.

Finally, government has a crucial responsibility to ensure that the pound is kept competitive and interest rates low. British industry has for too long been shackled and damaged by an uncompetitive exchange rate kept too high, partly by the prolonged 'battle against inflation' and because of the interest of the City in a high and stable exchange rate, the better to transact their business and acquire assets overseas. This overvaluation, sustained by interest rates higher than needed by industry, has been the central reason for the decline of manufacturing. Under Labour it was institutionalised by the requirement on the Bank of England to keep inflation under 2% a year, unbalanced by any requirement to sustain growth or employment. Labour must change the rubric to maintaining growth at over 3% and replace the inflation requirement by one to sustain competiveness.

The Conservatives, coming to power as true believers, believed that all that was necessary to make the economy healthy was to roll back the state, cut spending and borrowing and then the private sector would take up the slack and generate the growth. This religious belief was clearly wrong, given the perilous situation of the British economy. The path ahead is going to be tough, with recovery more difficult and slower, unemployment higher, and life more constrained than in any previous recovery. This is more like an end game rather than another temporary setback. The growing realisation that this is a basic threat to the future of the nation, will create a climate in which Labour's stronger measures become acceptable, even wanted, provided we sell them not as ideology but as national regeneration: the rebuilding of a strong, competitive country whose production base can once again perform its basic function of paying the nation's way in the world, while supporting the super-structures of welfare, education and health appropriate to the good society. Socialism then becomes eminently saleable to a baffled, but proud, electorate. Our party can then come to power, not following the New Labour path of uniting behind vacuity, but by bringing people together to rebuild the nation they love.

Part 5

Can Academic Philosophy Help us to Learn the Lessons of our General Election Defeat?

We apologise in advance to readers who find this section too indulgent of academia and abstract theoretical concepts. Labour Left fully support grassroots activism and realises that the key to electoral success lies not in the pen of academics but in the feet of the activists. These three pieces, however, are a one-off exploration into the world of political philosophy, so that we may contemplate its relevance in our quest to free Labour from neo-liberalism. We beg your patience and hope that the rest of the Red Book contains enough practical consideration of policy to enable this section to add value to the intellectual weight of the book, whilst not detracting from its relevance to mainstream voters.

Part 5 consists of three pieces by academics who are interested in understanding the Tory working classes, and the lumpen-proletariat. The solution, we all agree, lies in counter-hegemonic strategies designed to ensure that no one person ever again gains such a stranglehold over the direction of the Labour Party. If these types of academic pieces bore you, or present themselves as unreadable, then please accept our apologies. As the cost of living spirals and Tory cuts bite we in Labour Left are the first to recognise that no amount of theorising can put food on the table. The reason we went ahead with the three pieces was that we wished to cater for the tastes of some Labour Party members who relish these types of debates. Thank-you for your understanding

Understanding the Psychology of the Working Class Right Wing

By Rhiannon Lockley

Rhiannon Lockley has been a member of Labour Left since its formation. She is a FE lecturer in the West Midlands in Psychology & Sociology. She keeps her own blog at http://onehundredmilesfromthesea.tumblr.com/. Rhiannon's main areas of interests are public policy surrounding gender equality, and creating a more cohesive and egalitarian society. Her areas of expertise include culture and the influence of media. In recent times her analysis of the Norwegian atrocity and the August riots were of great authority. Rhiannon is also the regional women's officer for UCU in the West Midlands.

Can Academic Philosophy Help us to Learn the Lessons of our General Election Defeat?

One of the most difficult problems facing the Left in 21st century Britain is the need to reach and move forward from the understanding that huge numbers of working class voters are psychologically distant from their political objectives. This distance is much more complex than assumed in the traditional model of the unenlightened masses, where the message of socialism is viewed as providing the power to radically transform the workforce – the message is of course out there, but the resistance to it in the minds of the very people who should benefit from it the most is multi-faceted and robust. To understand where this resistance is coming from, the following may be useful.

1. A review of what working class identity means in 21st century Britain: who it includes, what it defines itself as rejecting, and the surprisingly fluid relationship between working class identity as it is experienced by the individual and working class identity in terms of socially engineered consumption.
2. An exploration of the psychological mechanisms which reproduce right-wing working class thoughts and beliefs. These include the concept of cognitive dissonance, the just-world error, and the cognitive outcomes of early socialisation, where early "pink and blue" and "goodies and baddies" thinking may work to restrict the development of higher cognitive processes in the individual, leading to the later rigid classifications relied upon in the process of scapegoating – crucial to the maintenance of a right-wing working class.

In trying to uncover and understand voter behaviour, income and profession have always been the key means of categorising and analysing the role of class. Class is of course multi-faceted, and as with any psychological or sociological point of interest there is always a tension between the detail of working class identity as it is experienced and perceived, and the need to simplify in order to analyse behaviour on a wide scale. If class was as simple as just looking at money and profession, then there would be no clear explanation as to why in an era of mass education our society remains so unequal and divided, why poverty continues to claim our children, or why huge numbers of working class people are prepared to stand back as spectators and watch the dismantling of the very goal of equal access to higher education and the privatisation of the NHS. Money is important, but money alone does not frame working class identity, and it can actually be argued that culturally the concept of "working class" has been ideologically moved from a simple distinction between the "haves" and "have nots" to a resilient position of being defined by what the individual rejects. Working class identity is a position of rejection – rejection of pretentiousness, rejection of a symbolic "other" who occupies a false position above the individual, in whatever capacity the individual understands this.

Traditionally, working class identity is a rejection of elitism and snobbery, not necessarily always a conscious conceptual rejection, but a rejection in terms of what the individual consumes: both real consumption of physical items – food, decor, newspapers, clothes, all of these things could be defined as working class or not – but also the consumption of ideas. Through decades of media transmission, the individually is cognitively primed to receive ideas themselves as either "common sense" or "elitist academia" (clearly not necessarily labelled as this in the mind of the individual) – even though it may be only the terminology and the level of detail which is different between the two. Therefore we have a culture in which Lord Sugar can be identified as working class, whereas a person who is raised on a similar low income level but in a different environment who then goes on to study for a PhD will not be accepted as working class by a hegemonic mainstream in spite of a much lower personal wealth, because they do not occupy the same cultural position of rejection and have moved into the realm of the rejected. Money itself is not universally considered to be elitist in a working class ethos - in reality, for the right-wing working class, money is aspirational, and it is not oppression and unfair work practices of a capitalist elite which trouble them, but the idea of a liberal elite judging their values.

For the right-wing working class, the position of rejection stretches beyond merely the symbolic other above to the others below – it is categorised by a hostility which preserves the psychological esteem of the individual by imagining a binary between the "decent, hard working" self and a variety of others, currently most consistently an underclass which includes the "scroungers" (primarily receivers of benefits, occasionally also those at the top who have received their wealth through inheritance, however), the "feral" (extending to include all perceived to be criminal or anarchic, whether this is the young, children of single parents, addicts, ethnic minorities, rioters, protestors), and also the purposefully destructive: primarily Islam in the 21st century UK. The purposefully destructive are culturally framed as distinct from the feral destruction of the previous category in the right-wing press and the mind of the working class right-wing voter because they are constructed as having specific goals of social destruction and the disintegration of democratic (ironically often liberal) values rather than liking destruction for its own sake. In some cases, and particularly amongst the far right, liberals and Marxists are also put into this category as being either apologists for Islam or enemies of "working people who really want to make something of themselves".

The real elite and the media have done a good job of framing socialist messages as disempowering because they are constructed as stripping away the power from the individual to achieve using their own hard work – socialism is packaged and consumed as a "prizes for all" mentality which replaces what is perceived as a fairer and more meritocratic system in which inequality is the price for some level of justice in terms of economic rewards and punishments. Because the tiny possibility exists for the poorest to transform their lives and wealth, this is falsely magnified into the option for all – if the working class just worked harder, they too could be the occasional (media-prolific) council estate millionaire. They may not choose this option, but through the resolution of cognitive dissonance emphatically consume the ideology that choice is ever present and is equivalent to freedom.

Cognitive dissonance is a psychological concept developed by Festinger (1956) amongst others which has been used to explain why people often react without obvious rationale to the sudden appearance of information which dramatically goes against their prior beliefs. For example, Festinger studied a cult as they went through the day which they believed would be the end of the world, unscathed. He found that rather than abandoning their beliefs, they simply adapted them by coming to the collective agreement that the world not ending was a sign that they were to be given another chance to convert and save more souls.[45] Interestingly, it has also been found that participants in a psychological study given tedious tasks expressed far more dissatisfaction when paid a higher amount of money to do them than participants given a tiny amount (Festinger and Carlsmith, 1959).

This could be seen, in a simplified form, to be representative of the mental processes which surround the level of reaction to social injustice shown by the right-wing working class.[46] The individual wishes to preserve the self-image of happiness, satisfaction and ultimately, faith in a just world which justifies many prejudiced belief systems already internalised, so rejects information which goes against this and actively takes on alternative explanations for the new information. The just world error is fairly universal and in itself psychologically protective, because through the belief that ultimately the self is protected from most ills, it is possible to shut out the realisation that the world is full of risk, and the accompanying destructive anxiety.

Capitalism and consumer society have helped to reframe class into something which is defined by consumption rather than wealth. In 21st century Britain, working class identity cannot be understood by capital and profession alone. It is etched out mainly through consumption, consumption of a media which goes beyond the messages of newspapers, TV and the internet and transmits and transforms through the consumption of day-to-day life: messages are carried in each item consumed, because each item by its availability for consumption carries the message of empowerment through consumer choice central to the maintenance of a working class who believe that uninhibited choice is available to all. She may be in her last days, but Margaret Thatcher's biggest legacy to her party is working class populism.

It may be an engineered populism, reproduced and distributed by the media, but it is perceived as natural and organic to the voter. Capitalists are not oppressive because the workers whose labour they transform into power and luxury choose to work for them. People with depression who take benefits rather than going to work could somehow choose to move beyond their biology and environment if they really wanted to. Third world economies could choose to end poverty if they just looked to see what Westerners are doing right. Immigrants choose to come to the UK, and it is this rather than the global capitalist uneven distribution of wealth which undermines the white workforce in the minds of the right-wing working class.

The system which allows cheap foreign labour to undermine a living wage and mass unemployment benefits the real elite, not the migrant or outsourced worker, but the message of free will and choice discourages wide scale analysis – the immediate belief is common sense, and lengthier consideration is a choice to accept "liberal elitism" over one's own beliefs. 21st century Britain is a place of ever multiplying choice for the working class – multiple TV channels, £1 shops which stock increasingly extensive ranges, an internet where every kind of taste can be cheaply satisfied. It is, of course, illusion. An increased level of choice of consumption does not actually increase power, but it provides the smoke and mirrors to hide increasing levels of poverty and inequality.

Primarily because class identity is now not only about social origin but

CAN ACADEMIC PHILOSOPHY HELP US TO LEARN THE LESSONS OF OUR GENERAL ELECTION DEFEAT?

also a common set of values which reject anything dismissed as pretentious or elitist, the working class now includes comparatively wealthy people (in particular, skilled manual workers, self-employed construction workers, small business owners) who benefit from a conservatism because it provides relative material comfort but also the psychological comfort of an ideology which places them in the imagined position of industrious and empowered consumers.

Contrast this with socialism, which, once it has been filtered through the right-wing media, is a patronising viewpoint, deeply critical of many of the prejudices held dear to the right-wing (fundamental opposition to racism, in particular, is artificially presented as elitist or "do-gooding", ignorant of the realities of "real" working class struggles in the workplace and community – struggles which are ultimately the result of a culture of competition innate to conservative capitalism, of course). Socialists are framed as alien from and unable to engage with the working class as though the ideology exists only within a cultural vacuum of an entirely separate group of thinkers.

The position is made worse by occasional actual liberal and socialist elitist accounts of working class life, in which the working class become an object for discussion rather than active participants in their own lives, and a tendency in the Left to romanticise the working class, where the same process of cognitive dissonance previously described dismisses any information which is not agreeable to a rose-tinted vision of workers happily uniting beneath a red flag, without any consideration for the prejudices that run so very deep the lower down the class structure you go. These prejudices are almost certainly the consequence of tactical scapegoating, but to deny their existence or see them as easily removable through rational discussion greatly underestimates the work they do in maintaining both society and the individual. It is probably worth noting that using scapegoating to portray "enemies" in a simplistic and negative way is not the sole reserve of the right, and similar linguistic tools are used by the Left (for example, descriptions of bankers tend towards a caricature).

Scapegoats carry out three key psychological tasks essential for the maintenance of a hierarchical society. They provide a target for anger which could otherwise be directed upwards. They also keep the worker in a state of psychological uneasiness, and therefore much easier to placate through consumer choice. Finally, they raise self-esteem, providing a negative "other" to define oneself in opposition to – this is heavily written into the messages of the tabloid press, where the "decent" reader is always reminded of the injustice of the scapegoat in question (whether this is a "Jeremy Kyle-doley" living on benefits paid for by the tax payer, or a "lazy manipulative trades unionist" costing hardworking parents their holiday) – the injustice in itself, counter-intuitively, is what provides psychological calm, because it allows for the catharsis of a definite situation or person to blame, sometimes even a "system" which is refined into a tangible and easily changeable process through the scapegoating argument, rather than the troubling realisation that there are no easy answers, there are universal injustices which cannot be easily resolved, and that the individual in fact benefits from many of these.

There are two possible support systems for scapegoating. The first is the media, which repetitively broadcasts the negative images and descriptions to the point where the mind of the individual is cognitively primed to pay attention to information which supports the dominant and negative account of whichever group is being targeted and discard or simply not even give any attention to information which goes against this. This process has been written about extensively – suffice to say, the key achievement of propaganda is to make the belief being transmitted internalised to the point where its origin is lost and it is accepted as natural and self-discovered by the individual – in other words, for propaganda to work, the individual has to believe that the ideas being transmitted have actually come from their own thoughts – logical conclusions drawn from a variety of supporting evidence – rather than external sources. The volume and diversity of negative messages about scapegoated groups in the right-wing media today does much to achieve this, and it is also supported by the factual style of reporting present in the majority of journalism aimed at the working class which presents arguments as definite rather than exploratory. The media is of course chosen for consumption by the individual (as opposed to for example education which is perceived more critically) and therefore carries with it the illusion of choice, free will and conscious decision making in the formation of individual beliefs.

The second support system is the socialisation process. By looking at the very rigid and increasingly separate ways in which childhood is gendered in terms of hegemonic working class consumption, it is possible to see the starting point for the "black and white" thinking process Adorno (1947) saw as key to fascism – but for 21st century children, the thinking is not just black and white but also pink and blue.[47] The Pink Stinks (2011) campaign has done a lot of important research to show how, for

Can Academic Philosophy Help us to Learn the Lessons of our General Election Defeat?

children today, boundaries between male and female are polarised, pointing out how toys and media the market produces for children, far from moving forward with progress towards gender equality, actually seem to be becoming more and more limiting in the horizons they present for children in terms of how the consumed item allows the imagination to develop. It should also be noted that the vast majority of toys and media marketed towards boys involve the social normalisation of violence.[48] Reviews have also shown the extent to which children's media show very distinct divisions between goodies and baddies.

It can be feasibly argued that these ever present and normalised distinctions – both between the genders and between good and evil – not only limit the imagination, with consequences for the child's future achievement, but also play a role in the development of schemata in the individual. A schema is a mental construct – it is argued that as children grow, they develop a schema (a set of knowledge and expectations) for everything they encounter. Logically, a childhood where the divisions between categories are universally presented as wide and impassable may lead to an effect on the process of laying down schema itself, in which all future categorisation processes are done in a more rigid and distinct way, making scapegoating much more likely. Whether capitalism deliberately markets such binaries is open to debate – certainly a neo-liberal economic system benefits from the scapegoating processes of traditional conservatism in that it redirects dissent, but it could also be argued that there is an evolutionary function for binary thinking in weaker groups in that it provides psychological stability and certainty, and it is possible that capitalist industries simply identify and benefit from the tastes this produces.

The education system itself can further this process of shallow but rigid schematic classification, in that the combination of limited resources, demand for assessment, and the laudable goal of mass education has led to a process where analysis is perceived as something which can be condensed, bullet pointed and learnt by transmission (however many different learning styles this transmission takes) rather than an individual process encouraged by exposure to wide ranging and challenging material. It could also be argued that post 9/11 there is an increasing level of "black and white" reporting of conflict by media organizations either directly linked to or involved in funding relationships with the state, which may both influence the process of wider schematic categorization amongst adults as well as children, but also possibly provides a real world "fit" for the values of childhood, further reinforcing the rigidity of classification in the young.

Taking all this into account, I would argue that the psychology of the right-wing working class is one of the biggest obstacles any political goal of reduced inequality can face. There is a necessity to move on from traditional idealised visions of working class identity and engage fully with the reality. There is a necessity to challenge prejudices rather than appeal to them, and while the Left has generally lost out on support by a refusal to appeal to mass ignorance through reinforcing scapegoating, this cannot morally ever be different. The danger, of course, is in combating prejudice through debate, which psychologically actually serves to reinforce the belief system one attempts to challenge, rather than undermining it. A dialectic approach is key, but the right-wing media ensure that however non-confrontational and rational the views expressed are, what is heard or read is filtered through a pre-existing set of beliefs about what liberal or socialist arguments are and the message is often lost in this way. However, while a complete transformation of the existing ideological hegemony is unlikely, this is not to suggest that there is no possible direction forward.

Firstly, transmission of right-wing values from one generation to the next is not inevitable. By identifying and engaging individuals who have come from right-wing working class backgrounds to a left-wing world view, a huge amount about how this psychological process takes place could be learnt. This should be as wide-reaching as possible, and ideally actively involve these individuals in a process of developing successful strategies for challenging the individual thinking processes which come together to do the mass cultural work of reproducing inequality. There is also a possible role for trades unionism here – the STUC has shown in recent times how trades unionism can gain support by increasing the amount of work done in and with communities (for example, support for the Glasgow Mayday march and rally grew from 100s to 1000s between 2010 and 2011, attributed to a keen focus on building community relationships), and this model could be studied and applied elsewhere. There is a definite need for a strong positive image of trades unionism in the collective conscious if dominant right wing media driven narratives about obstructiveness and greed are ever to be surpassed.

Trades unions also need to focus heavily on sweated labour, as this is both one of the biggest venues for the social injustice which feeds capitalism, and also the biggest threat to the UK working class. We need a strong worldwide move to protect the people who suffer the most from globalisation, and discussion about how this can be achieved. There is inspiration in looking to the past to the empowerment of women's trades unionists (women, after all, provided the past venue for sweated labour and threat to the male working class), looking at their unlikely achievements to take hope if not methodology for a very different world. Unless we act to create fair working conditions for all, there will never be great increases in equality. If the spectre of migrant and outsourced labour was gone, there would almost certainly be a transformation of working class psychology, though the shape this would take cannot really be imagined.

Finally, there is a need to look at how the hegemonic value system allows such a gaping disconnection between the working class and the Labour Party. The blame here lies partly with the media once more, but we also need a strong look at what the Labour Party symbolises at the point of contact. We need to open up the channels to get home-grown working class activists into the democratic process as representatives, to increase the identification process, and we also need to look at integrity. Dennis Skinner provides a model for the style of MP who could win back a working class vote: if the Labour party can move forward with a new generation of politicians who come from the same lifestyles as the people they represent, who engage with the working class through real understanding of their experiences, who show solidarity with them in their lifestyles and show integrity in their behaviour, then the right wing would have a much tougher job in scooping up the electorate.

---

[45] Festinger, L. (1956). *When Prophecy Fails: A Social and Psychological Study of A Modern Group that Predicted the Destruction of the World*, by Leon Festinger, Henry Riecken, and Stanley Schachter. Harper-Torchbooks
[46] Festinger, L., &Carlsmith, J.M. (1959). Cognitive consequences of forced compliance *Journal of Abnormal and Social Psychology*, 58(2), 203–210.
[47] Adorno, T. W. (1947) *Wagner, Nietzsche and Hitler* in *Kenyan Review* Vol.ix (1)
[48] Pink Stinks (2011), The campaign for real role models http://www.pinkstinks.co.uk/ accessed 31st August 2011

The Real Lesson of New Labour

By Dr Phil Burton-Cartledge

Phil Burton-Cartledge received his PhD on the life histories of revolutionary socialist activists from Keele University in 2010. Formerly blogging at A Very Public Sociologist, he now divides his time between bag-carrying for Tristram Hunt and Stoke-on-Trent Central Labour Party, co-founding the soon-to-be-launched civic participation think tank, Democratic Futures, and occasionally tending to his Twitter account.

Can Academic Philosophy Help us to Learn the Lessons of our General Election Defeat?

It is a sobering thought that the biggest crisis capitalism has faced since the 1930s has not been accompanied by a corresponding mass radicalisation. True enough, student politics briefly captured the media spotlight at the end of last year, though not always for the right reasons. March 2011 saw a magnificent demonstration organised by the TUC that poured in excess of 500,000 people onto the streets of London. But, sadly, anti-cuts campaigns across the country have not pulled in large numbers and, despite everything, the Conservatives have not dipped beneath the 34-35% polling range since the cuts started to bite.

Labour bears some responsibility for this state of affairs. At the time of writing, it is yet to articulate an alternative to the Tories' vicious attempts to use the economic crisis to reinforce class privilege. From the pledges of Alastair Darling to ram through cuts 'worse than Thatcher's' prior to the general election, to the mantra of cutting 'too far and too fast', Labour's incoherent opposition speaks of a quiet but nevertheless profound existential crisis it is going through. The party wants to oppose the Coalition's reckless cuts programme, but consistently pulled its punches. The party wants to reconnect with 'the base', but is afraid of advocating the sort of policies that could win them back. The party needed a wide-ranging debate about the New Labour years and where it should go next, but instead instituted a top-down consultation exercise.

So as we entered the 2011 conference season, a big question mark hovered over Labour. What does the party think? What is it for? And what should it do?

Political problems of this magnitude require political solutions. In this short essay, rather than proposing a raft of left-wing policies, I suggest the Left is uniquely placed to pursue a strategic activism that can rebuild the party and the movement. This begins with reflecting on Antonio Gramsci's ideas about political organisation.

Gramsci and the working class 'Party'

Gramsci's arguments around hegemony, counter-hegemony, historic blocs, and revolutionary socialist strategy in advanced capitalist states have, ironically, been more influential among various reformist and social democratic currents than the remains of the revolutionary left in Britain today. But, taking the three chief pillars of Gramsci's Selections from the Prison Notebooks, Labourist and 'post-Marxist' intellectuals have embraced his arguments around the importance of 'organic intellectuals' (for example, organisers – a mould they tried to cast themselves in), class alliances and blocs of classes, and hegemony/counter-hegemony. However, in so doing they have, neglected arguments around the Modern Prince, or, revolutionary party.

For political traditions that believe building a socialist society, it is understandable why Gramsci's emphasis on the leading role of the revolutionary party was put to one side. Nevertheless, and perhaps in spite of himself, Gramsci makes an important contribution relevant to our seemingly 'post-class' times.

His arguments about the revolutionary party are predicated on the classical Marxist understanding of socialism and communism. For Marx and Engels, the dictatorship of the proletariat was short hand for a democratic society which was collectively run, organised and planned. It was the rule of the waged workers, of the immense majority by the immense majority. By the same logic Britain and Saudi Arabia are examples of the dictatorship of the bourgeoisie: very different societies, but nevertheless societies where hierarchies and class structures are generated and underpinned by capitalism.

In classical Marxist political theory, socialism requires the successful prosecution by the working class of their interests against the antagonistic interests of the owners and agents of capital. The core of this is the organisation of the entire working class. It requires that the myriad institutions that keep society ticking, from the smallest workplace to the mightiest of public institutions, should be taken over and democratically run by those who work and use them. For this to take place, the working class must either be organised as or led by the revolutionary political party that expresses their interests and has successfully fought the hegemonic battle with capital.

Whilst this has not been borne out in history, and seems unlikely to in advanced capitalist states, Labour Left can take something from Gramsci's reflections on political organisation.

In any given country, Gramsci follows Engels by noting that parties are divided along class lines – ergo a bourgeois party, a workers' party, etc. More often than not the 'fundamental' bourgeois party is split into factions for a variety of reasons. In Britain, capital's political representatives are historically split between the Tories, Liberals/Liberal Democrats and the Labour Party. Each faction is formally independent whilst vigorously and bitterly opposing one another, but at times of crisis the situation brings out their identity of interests. Existing differences are comparatively trivial set against what unites them, at such times of crisis they can and do they form united fronts; becoming the de facto ruling class.

Parties such as the Labour Party, which are formed by cross-class alliances between sections of capital and sections of the labour movement, are, on the whole, beholden to capital. Its leading cadre are consumed by the day-to-day business of running a government or shadowing one so it can present itself as a credible alternative at election time. At the level of local government, the party finds itself managing huge authorities with enormous influence in local economies. Politically, due to the party straddling different, competing interests and depending on the different balance of forces in wider society, it can have a very volatile internal politics. Equally, if capital is hegemonic the party can act as a pacifier in the wider labour movement.

Therefore whilst Gramsci was concerned with the project of building a revolutionary party, he simultaneously allowed for a wider definition of a party through the complex totality of how a class organises politically. Despite the many problems plaguing the labour movement, we still have the advantage that the institutions it has built remains and still organise masses of workers, economically and politically. The trade unions, co-operatives, labour and social democratic parties, community groups, socialist societies; all combing to form a political party for and by the working class.

Unfortunately, this matrix of institutions and parties are not a unified bloc. It expresses the divisions and differences found in the working class. The effects of relative privilege, sectionalism, regionalism, de-industrialisation, and the legacy of prejudice, all of these find their expression in the ideas that circulate around the labour movement. None of this is helped by the separation of the Labour Party, the trade unions and the cooperative movement.

The level of sophistication Gramsci elaborated his theoretical ideas at such as his ideas around intellectuals, hegemony, counter-hegemony, historic blocs, and cultural struggle – have proven immensely influential on all sides of the labour movement. But the vehicle for it, the working class 'party', is divided. How then to make the leap from the status quo to the primary driver of socialist politics we would like it to be?

The new consensus

As the party moved towards the 2005 general election, the Blairite slogan of 'Britain Forward Not Back' was the rallying call to the ever-decreasing faithful. However, for Labour to go forward we must look back to the Kinnock years to the debacle of 1983, and more to the party that emerged out of the struggle for working class political representation. Then, Labour was unambiguously a party of the working class and its traditional middle class allies. Whether one held Labour as the vehicle for building socialism in Britain, as a sociologically proletarian party with a pro-capitalist leadership, or the party of the aspirational and respectable working class, there were clear organic links that bound the party and movement together.

After Kinnock, the relationship became more fractious and confrontational, then under Blair and Brown there was (and still is) a wide perception in the labour movement – that the support it has given Labour has not been reciprocated. Many trade unionists feel that for 13 years their unions were treated as the party's piggy bank. They were an embarrassing relative that our party was happy to ask for money, but little else. Their requests for frequent visits, more conversations and a sympathetic ear went unheeded. Yet, union's leadership continued to give money to the Labour Party with comparatively little to show for it.

Whilst this relationship was extremely unhealthy for the party and the movement, it would be a mistake to blame this entirely on Labour Party's and trade union's leadership. The subservience of the unions to the party happened because it reflected wider changes in the political economy of British capitalism, and particularly the change in the composition of the working class.

Britain's industrial heyday – with communities clustered around factories, workplaces comprising hundreds and sometimes thousands of workers, a sense of class consciousness and pride, a time when everyone knew their place – has long since gone. The industrial worker, fêted and fetishised by many on the Left never formed an absolute majority of the working class; indeed the structure of Britain's division of labour pre-1979 put them in a position of latent power; with the joining-at-the-hip of workplace and community forming a potent combination. The trade unions, and by extension the Labour Party, were constantly nourished by these relationships. Here, union and party were conveyors of social mobility. From the shop floor, a person could reach high office in local and national politics.

This vision of Britain and experience of working class life has, however, largely been swept away. The decline of British manufacturing was underway prior to Thatcher, but the assault her government led on organised labour only served to increase the speed of the process. Closure of

Can Academic Philosophy Help us to Learn the Lessons of our General Election Defeat?

'lame duck' nationalised industries created mass unemployment, which reduced working class leverage in the labour market. The strategic battles with the labour movement, exemplified by the 1984-85 miners' strike, demoralised and defeated a generation of activists, leaving our movement sufficiently weakened so that reams of more repressive anti-trade union laws were allowed to pass. The privatisation agenda of the 1980s, as seen in the selling off of British Gas and British Telecom, promised a popular capitalism all could take part in through cheap stocks and shares. Indeed, in what was perhaps Thatcher's master stroke of domestic policy, the 'right to buy' saw millions of council tenants become home owners in a relatively short period of time. The messy contradictions that resulted were such that many former miners used their redundancy money to buy their council homes, then set up their own businesses to become part of Thatcher's experiment.

The Thatcher government laid the foundation for the political economy of the British working class today. New Labour's opponents like to point to the growth of the public sector under its watch, but it did not attempt to reverse the latent neo-liberalism of British capitalism.

At its best, New Labour's 'Third Way' could be described as a well-meaning attempt to harness the unfettered market for equitable economic reward. In this sense, New Labour itself was an attempted revision of Crosland's own revisionism, which placed emphasis on the state to secure socially just outcomes. As such, it was unashamedly managerialist and authoritarian. At its worst, it was neo-liberal business as usual. New Labour rebuilt x amount of hospitals, y number of schools, poured funds into infrastructure projects, and improved individual rights in the workplace through policies such as the minimum wage. But it continued with the subordination of manufacturing to finance in a pre-crash disregard of Keynesian policies, the failure to build replacement social housing, an erosion of liberty, widening inequalities, the waste of the Private Finance Initiative, unnecessary back-door marketisation of the NHS and other public services, and it rarely deviated from the free market fundamentalist consensus. Every step taken to protect the most vulnerable against the vagaries of capitalism was accompanied by a further commodification of public goods. The studied avoidance of strengthening collective workplace rights left the balance of power in the labour market tipped decidedly in capital's favour.

This was at massive cost to the Labour Party itself. Between 1997 and 2010 it lost nearly five million votes (four million of them under Tony

Blair) and went from 405,000 members to approximately 176,000 – the lowest in our party's history. Clearly continuing in the same vein is not sustainable. In other words not only did New Labour pursue some policies that were antithetical to social democratic traditions, it actively broke up and discouraged the formation of the kinds of social relations needed to sustain itself as an effective mass party of the centre left.

An 'official' response to New Labour

Despite never being expressed in these terms, all too often the post-New Labour response to its problematic character is reduction to a question of authoritarian leadership. Political criticisms are usually given as a failure of communication. On issues such as the Iraq War, the 10p tax debacle, tuition fees and other unpopular, regressive policies, New Labour found itself taken to task for 'not listening' to what the public had to say. It is almost as if the leadership of the party fought shy of a substantive political critique in favour of bland statements against excesses in government.

An inability to face up to what New Labour meant is unsurprising. After all, nearly the majority of the current Opposition front bench played important roles in the last government. But, it does make the road to renewal much harder.

The problematic position of our leadership is encapsulated in the otherwise laudable 'Movement for Change' initiative. Launched by David Miliband during his leadership campaign, Movement for Change has attracted warm words and support from all sides of the party. Its attempt to align the party's organising capacity alongside grassroots, community-focused campaigning is an important step in the right direction; anything that seeks to expand Labour Party activists' repertoire beyond Contact Creator and Voter ID is valuable.

But ultimately it is more an organisational fix rather than a political answer to the quandary Labour is in.

Movement for Change has "[run] campaigns on issues as varied as holding retailers to account for selling alcohol to teenagers, repairing security doors in estates and holding developers to account for road safety plans." This is the sort of bread and butter politics Labour needs to get stuck into. However, effective community organising will eventually run up against complicated and uncomfortable political issues. In Stoke-on-Trent, community campaigning cannot simply dismiss the fact that the Labour-run City Council is being forced by central government to cut £56m from its 2010/11 and 2011/12 budgets. Inevitably, community organising will place demands on local authorities, and for most, it will be very difficult to meet them. Hence what is a promising local initiative could have the unintended consequence of tying local Labour parties in knots. Such is the danger of substituting organisational measures for political solutions.

A touch of class

Labour Left's political answer should begin with the political relationship Labour has with the working class.

We need to remove the image of the industrial worker as the working class writ large from our heads. We also need to stop conflating class with fixed positions in Britain's class structure. Marx was right to treat it as a social relationship, one that on paper seems simple but at the same time grasps the full complexity of class relations.

How class is experienced has changed these last 30 years. The working class is now more amorphous than at any time in the previous century, yet capitalist relations of production have extended their hold over society like never before.

More people than ever are at the mercy of a labour market biased towards employers and the needs of capital. This is due to the growth of part-time work, of all kinds, the flatlining of real wages, the lack of career prospects, the huge numbers of workers who do overtime, insecurity at work, and more point to the continued relevance of class. The 'squeezed middle' to which Ed Miliband seeks to appeal are, for the most part, as subject to the precariousness of class relationships as the minimum wage shop worker. Capital in one sense drives inequality, but as it does so it becomes a great leveller in quite another.

Labour must find its salvation in the people who are subject to these class relationships. I believe there are three ways it can go about it.

1. Class is a dirty word in British politics

The march of consumerism has levelled class cultures to a degree and eroded its popular efficacy as a component of identity. Labour has the mammoth task of articulating policies that speak to the (nevertheless) class-conditioned lives of the overwhelming majority. This is more than presenting Labour as stout defenders of the NHS and the welfare state, but articulating anger of frustrated aspirations, of promoting a real sense of community, of being the party of democracy, and advocating a popular vision of the socialist good society. Labour should always seek to be a credible alternative government; this does not have to mean bowing to the consensus of remote and well-heeled elites.

2. The policies we pursue in the short to medium term need to protect our base as much as possible
This is not only the right thing to do from a moral point of view, it is vital for the party's political health. Many Labour-run local authorities are strictly conditioned by the government's spiteful austerity programme. Whilst cuts will be made, Labour should not allow them to become an opportunity for overzealous employers in local government. For example, too often the conditions of council staff find themselves assaulted by the part or full privatisation of services, or the introduction of (precarious) agency workers, or management attempts to redraw terms and conditions. This is nothing to say of the most vulnerable and disadvantaged who depend on local authorities for care. Labour needs to explain the position government has put our councils in, not collude in the neo-liberal modelling of local government beloved of many a chief executive.

3. Labour needs to organise more cohesively
It may be a banal observation, but it is one that is depressingly true. The three pillars of the movement – the party, the trade unions, and the Co-operative Party – rub together with varying degrees of friction. At times we get along, like the recent love-in Labour is having with the Co-op Party, and at others we are at loggerheads, such as the relationship between the party and the trade unions in recent years. While there will always be friction it can be managed better and more effectively by strengthening and founding new relations between them. Practically, it means encouraging trade unionists to join Labour and, where affiliated, getting their branches to send mandated representatives to CLP meetings. It means encouraging party members to become active in their trade union branches. It means unions and the party becoming enthusiastic supporters of co-ops, and co-ops in turn using the avenues open to them to promote their alternative form of ownership.

Advocating a socialist politics that engages with the contemporary realities of class, protecting and strengthening the social relationships the labour movement rests on, and repositioning Labour as the organiser of the interests of the majority is an answer to our party's existential crisis. But this will not drop from the sky. It is a strategic orientation that has

CAN ACADEMIC PHILOSOPHY HELP US TO LEARN THE LESSONS OF OUR GENERAL ELECTION DEFEAT?

to be fought for. It is however one that I think can engage constructively with some of the measures favoured by the leadership, and other positive ideas coming from other quarters of the labour movement. However, in the main if there is one lesson we should take from New Labour, it is that what passed for its common sense needs turning on its head.

Labour Winning in the South

By Thomas Gann

In 2010, Tom Gann was Labour's Parliamentary candidate in Salisbury and is a party activist in Greenwich. He writes on politics and philosophy at labourpartisan.blogspot.com He also studied Philosophy at Warwick and University College Dublin, and has had work published on Marxism and Modernism, Left-wing Zionism, and council housing.

Can Academic Philosophy Help us to Learn the Lessons of our General Election Defeat?

In the 2005 election, Labour won 45 seats in the South of England: we now hold 10; 70% of the votes we lost between 2005 and 2010 were in the South. By largely ignoring the South, the Labour Left has allowed an electorally impotent and politically and morally suspect analysis to become dominant. The lengthiest and most systematic development of this dominant analysis is Southern Discomfort Again (Radice and Diamond, 2010). The dominant analysis can be summarised briefly:

- The most important reason for Labour's loss of Southern seats was that we appeared out of touch with the sense of 'fairness and responsibility' and the 'anxieties and aspirations' of C1 and C2 swing voters (Bradshaw, 2010; Denham, 2011).
- We can only win in the South by not 'jettisoning the New Labour legacy' (Bradshaw).
- We appeared particularly out of touch on immigration and 'relaxed' about those on benefits 'ripping off our society' (Radice and Diamond, p. 17; Denham).
- Whilst we need to retain the support of our 'core working class' vote, focusing too much on this, 'would give the signal Labour was no longer interested in power' (Radice and Diamond, p. 8).
- We must quickly regain a reputation for economic competence based on a 'credible plan for reducing the deficit' (Radice and Diamond, p. 29).

The dominant analysis has two blind spots: taking 'core' DE voters for granted and failing to distinguish between men and women voters. Ed Miliband, noting the growth in the gap between AB and DE turnout between 1997 and 2010, began to set out some of the conditions of an alternative approach to the South. In contrast to the dominant analysis and its stress on C1 and C2 voters, Miliband noted that had Labour done as well with DE voters in 2010 as in 1997 we would have won 40 more seats including key Southern marginals such as Stroud and Hastings (E. Miliband, 2010, p. 55).

In the South, the gap between DE turnout and the rest may have been greater than the national gap. In Gloucester and Dorset South, in the council elections held on the same day as the General Election, the turnout in wards won by Labour was between 52% and 58%; in those won comfortably by the Tories it was between 74% and 80% (Gloucester City

Council, 2010; Weymouth and Portland Borough Council, 2010).

Radice and Diamond dismiss attention to women, arguing: "No significant gender divide has opened up in voting patterns over the last 13 years" (Radice and Diamond, p. 11). This dismissal is particularly odd as, based on Radice and Diamond's definitions, women are considerably more 'Southern' than men.

Their polling data reveals women are substantially more anxious about their own and their children's futures (59% of men and 49% of women were confident of having enough money to make ends meet in the future; 32% of men and 22% of women were confident that their children would be able to find a home and job in their local area) (YouGov/ Policy Network Results, 2010, p. 21, 25). The data also show that women are less clear about what political parties stand for and sceptical about the ability of parties to solve economic problems (YouGov/ Policy Network, p. 1, 17).

In an important criticism, Don Paskini pointed out: "astonishingly, the Diamond and Radice pamphlet doesn't devote a single sentence to local campaigning ... .Rather than trying to 'triangulate' on pet topics of the right wing press like immigration and welfare reform, personal contact with voters allows Labour to find out which issues really matter to people, and to take up and help sort out problems" (Paskini, 2010).

To put it in Marxist terms, the dominant analysis makes no effort either to interpret or to change the South; the place of theory and practice is taken by an intellectually and morally indolent empathy (reconnecting with the voters). Radice and Diamond's description is not necessarily incorrect, the problem is it is abstract – it is not rooted in the South's social and economic conditions, and static – there is no account either of how the Coalition government's policies will, and Labour action could, transform the politics of the South.

This challenge to the dominant approach demands thinking through what the function of Labour as a political party is and how this relates to other campaigns in the South.

Two observations from Gramsci are pertinent, firstly, the political party synthesises theory and practice and, secondly, that through this the party can raise the disorganised common sense, particularly when it is of a relatively homogenous social group, to philosophy (Gramsci, 1971, p. 335, 325-6). Without acting upon this and responding to Southern common sense we will have no chance of winning on a left platform in the South.

Theory 1: What's squeezing the squeezed middle

The dominant analysis is limited by conceptualising C1 and C2 Southerners as 'middle class' and DE Southerners as 'working class' and presenting their interests and concerns as antagonistic. One solution to this limitation would be, following Maurice Glasman and Tony Judt, to argue the need for Labour to build cross-class solidarity. (Glasman, 2010, p. 37 Judt, 2009). The alternative is to base politics on an expanded conception of the working class which includes C1 and C2 voters, this question is more than academic because of the antagonism and solidarity a broader conception of the working class creates. Ralph Miliband's 'The New Revisionism in Britain' helps with thinking through what constitutes the Southern working class and what politics it requires.

In 1985, Miliband argued: "the working class has experienced in recent years an accelerated process of recomposition, with a decline of the traditional industrial sectors and a considerable further growth of the white-collar, distribution, service and technical sectors." Despite this, he continued, "there has been an increase in the number of wage-earners located in the subordinate levels of the productive process who... in terms of its location in the productive process, it's very limited or non-existent power and responsibility in that process, its near-exclusive reliance on the sale of its labour power for its income, and the level of that income, it remains as much the 'working class' as its predecessors" (R. Miliband, 1985, p. 9). The process Miliband describes has become ever more apparent in the past 25 years and, due to the preponderance of white collar workers within its working class, particularly relevant to an analysis of the South.

The economic forces determining the recomposition of the working class are precisely the forces which are squeezing the Southern squeezed middle. Southern non-industrial capitalism with low levels of public sector employment and competitiveness stemming from high levels of agency working and labour market flexibility is capitalism in a more pure form and closer to that which the Coalition wants for the whole country (Denham, 2007). What Southern competitiveness in the globalised world has meant, however, particularly for the squeezed middle, is stagnant wages, demoralisation, housing pressures, long hours for those in work and ever-increasing personal debt. Median British wages have been stagnant in real terms since the 1980s and have made up a decreasing proportion of GDP from a high of 66% in 1975 to 54% in 2010 (Weldon, 2011). Furthermore, as Weldon argues 'the Coalition's export-led growth model is premised on a further squeeze on living standards.'

The 'purity' of the South's capitalism means its socio-economic problems cannot be explained as a deforming of capitalism's normal functioning demanding precise interventions as has been suggested with the North of England or the very poor. The South demands the forming and organising of an electoral bloc to take control of their own lives rather than 'charitable' interventions within capitalism by elites whether Labour or Conservative.

The appropriateness of an analysis by Gopal Balakrishnan of the chronic problems in global capitalism to the South is suggestive. Balakrishnan explains, "A faltering rate of profit... yielded smaller surpluses for reinvestment, leading to a slow-down in the growth of plant and equipment... this led to either wage stagnation or higher unemployment. Attempting to restore profitability, employers the world over held down wage and benefit levels, while governments reduced the growth of social expenditures. But the consequence of these cutbacks has been a protracted sluggishness in the growth of demand, reinforcing the stagnation stemming from overproduction" (Balakrishnan, 2009, p. 10).

These tendencies in the Southern economy can be drawn together in the concept of 'privatised Keynesianism'. Most people in the South were, at least temporarily, able to evade the consequences of wage stagnation through increased borrowing. The IMF have noted that prior to the crash of 2008 wage inequality grew substantially but consumption inequality did not, a gap bridged by increased personal indebtedness. (Kumhof and R. Ranciere, 2010, p. 28) The same report notes that a lack of trade union militancy was one of the major causes of wage stagnation, given the low levels of trade union membership in the South this is particularly apposite (p. 4).

Indeed, the ability to sustain an increasing standard of living without wage increases partially explains a lack of trade union militancy under Labour. In the boom years, the antagonism that 'privatised Keynesianism' created, which appears in Radice and Diamond as one between C1/C2 Southerners and DE Southerners , was between those without easy access to credit and those able to access it, particularly home owners, whose increasing house prices took the place of substantial annual pay rises. As such easy access to credit declines the Southern political landscape will become transformed as the extent of wage stagnation for the squeezed middle becomes apparent creating new possibilities for solidarity within the expanded Southern working class.

Theory 2: The demoralisation of Southern women

Whilst the stresses produced by Southern capitalism were apparent under Labour, Coalition government policy will intensify them considerably. Indeed, whilst the 'privatised Keynesianism' that defined the South in the boom will no longer be tenable, the government's public spending cuts are certain to increase household debt. The distinction that needs to be made is between pre-crash borrowing for an improved standard of living, and under the Coalition, borrowing to survive.

Through intensifying the transfer of costs and risks from the state, and because of taxation, the wealthy, to households (undermining the collectivisation of costs and risks in the social democratic state), the government is also transferring costs from men to women. 72% of the cuts in the emergency budget are being met from women's income, calculated even before the fact that women make up 65% of public sector workers was considered. (Fawcett, 2010) Diane Elson has written on 'the implications of 'globalisation' and 'flexibilisation' and her analysis can explain why Radice and Diamond found women to be more typically 'southern' in their attitudes (Elson, 1998).

Elson argument is centred on the role of women in the reproduction of the labour force. Her argument is that the domestic sector and its unpaid labour is, like the public and private sectors, productive and needs to be resourced properly. She argues: "the domestic sector produces a labour force; and, more than that, plays a foundational role in the production of people who possess not only the capacity to work but also acquire other more intangible social assets... all of which permit the forming and sustaining of social norms" (Elson, p. 197). Elson also notes, crucially for understanding why a transfer of costs onto the household is a transfer of costs from men to women, that for all the sectors and the circuits between them "modes of operation are built upon the prevailing gender order" and "rules and norms... are predicated upon the assumption that the care and nurture of the labour force on a daily and intergenerational basis is primarily a female task" (p. 197-8).

The shifting of risks and costs onto the domestic has quite clear consequences for Elson because of the need for unpaid domestic labour to be properly resourced and not treated merely as a limitless reserve and shock absorber. Elson argues, "In situations of rapid growth and full employment... [or] situations of strong and extensive citizen entitlements to transfers from the state sector, households can cope with greater risk. But when both these conditions are absent it is over optimistic to expect the domestic sector to be able to absorb all these risks" (p. 205). What Elson is describing is applicable to the situation in the South of England and helps to explain the depth of women's anxieties in the South. Elson then explains the disruptive consequences of under resourcing the domestic and therefore limiting its productiveness, she writes, "it is hard to sustain social norms of ethical behaviour in the demoralisation that comes from realising you are no more than a dispensable, interchangeable unit of labour from the point of view of the private sector; and from realising that the public sector will do little to mitigate or contest this ... Dissonances between the domestic, the political and the economic have repercussions far beyond the domestic sector, undermining the conditions of supply of a productive willing labour force" (p. 205).

Elson provides the opportunity to reorientate radically how we think and act regarding the squeezed middle and irresponsibility. She builds up her argument to critique early family intervention programmes (the ideology of which is clearly inspirational for the dominant analysis of the South). Of interventions to improve the parenting of the 'irresponsible', she writes, "there is no suggestion as to why there has been such a deterioration in parenting at this juncture; no recognition of the likely impact on parenting of the extremely long hours of paid work undertaken by many of those men and women in Britain who do have paid jobs; nor of the impact of insecurity, unemployment and loss of hope and self-respect as whole communities are crushed by the force of the global market" (Elson, 205-6).

In terms of Labour's southern policy, Elson's work suggests an interesting line. Instead of ever more punitive measures to punish the irresponsible at the bottom, we must recognise that instead of causing the pressure on 'hard-working families', the irresponsible are the point at which the same pressure breaks out in public. The obvious, public 'irresponsibility' which is being attacked exists on a continuum with the stresses and demoralisation experienced by the majority of Southern women, 'irresponsibility' and demoralisation are produced by the same knot of social facts.

Labour, the Liberal Democrats and the Conservatives all attack the 'irresponsible', blaming them for the pressures the 'responsible face', we must reverse this. It may sound utopian to argue that the problems facing the squeezed middle can only be addressed through building solidarity between the 'responsible' and 'irresponsible,' but articulating a successful position for Labour in the South requires it.

CAN ACADEMIC PHILOSOPHY HELP US TO LEARN THE
LESSONS OF OUR GENERAL ELECTION DEFEAT?

Practice 1: The Party and collective action against a common enemy

There is a crucial analogy between the dominant analysis's treatment of 'irresponsibility' in welfare, directed particularly at women and its treatment of immigration; once again the dominant analysis is unprincipled, mystifying, static and abstract as a consequence of a lack of attention to theory or practice. On immigration, the poll data shows some strongly anti-immigrant beliefs in the South, particularly among those who voted Labour in 2005 but not in 2010: 68% believed "far too often, immigrants undercut British workers unfairly and drive down wages2, 80% believed "we are too ready to change the rules to suit immigrants, rather than expecting them to follow our rules" and 55% believed "immigration is destroying our culture and way of life" (YouGov/ Policy Network, p. 29).

The dominant analysis responds to these beliefs by arguing that Labour must reconnect with the public on immigration. The concept of 'cold racism' developed by Jacques Ranciere provides a means of understanding what is at stake in 'reconnection'. Ranciere argues, 'our states are less and less able to thwart the destructive effects of the free circulation of capital on the communities under their care – all the less so because they have no desire to do so. They then fall back on what is in their power, the circulation of people' (J. Ranciere, 2010). Ranciere's linking of the state's failure (and unwillingness) to thwart the destructive effects of the free circulation of capital mirrors Elson's account of the demoralising effects of realising one is merely a replaceable unit of labour for the private sector and the public sector will do nothing to mitigate this. Ranciere's conception of 'cold racism' is that the position of elites becomes justified by an appeal to an (imagined) popular racist sentiment which elites understand and respond to, control of the circulation of people 'is increasingly becoming their purpose and means of legitimation.' (J. Ranciere) This is precisely what the dominant analysis attempts, in place of challenging the free circulation of capital, a challenge which requires political mobilisation, it posits maintaining a conservative Labour elite in power as the only means of managing popular anti-immigration sentiment.

What Ranciere's conception of 'cold racism', applied to the dominant analysis, shows is how political mobilisation is opposed by creating policies based on an immediate an unproblematic empathy felt by elites for the prejudices of the ordinary Southerner. Labour's indulgence in a populism that, at times, stigmatised sections of the working class helped to undermine the class solidarity Labour ought to be incarnating. This fragmentation of the working class has been one of the causes of the prejudices which the dominant analysis suggests Labour must continue to indulge, thereby making the situation even worse.

Following Paskini's critique of Radice and Diamond, if this position is to be opposed it is necessary to think through the kind of campaigning that can overcome anti-immigrant feeling. In the South, importantly given the high cost of living means the minimum wage goes even less far than in the rest of country, campaigns for a living wage are vital. What these campaigns mean in terms of the belief that immigrants are undercutting Southern wages is shifting the antagonism from an abstract one between immigrant and non-immigrant worker to a real antagonism between worker, whether immigrant or non-immigrant, and capital. It situates the stagnation of Southern wages within capitalism and within the failures of Southern workers to organise against it rather than in a racist antagonism.

A living wage campaign needs to go beyond party activists talking to voters, it should mobilise those voters as genuine political subjects. Ralph Miliband's analysis of political action in the context of the recomposition of the working class is crucial here and links back to the necessity of a working class politics of the squeezed middle. Miliband argues, "Sectionalism, sexism and racism do exist. Yet… they have on many occasions been at least partially overcome in struggle; that workers in different occupational locations, male and female, black and white, have sometimes fought in solidarity against a common enemy; even that millions of workers, for all their divisions and divergences, have been linked, even if tenuously, by their common support of parties whose stress was not on sectional and other divisions but on class solidarity and commonness of purpose; and that there is no inherent conflict that must for ever separate worker from worker" (Miliband, p. 10). What Miliband's argument means for the South is in mobilising across boundaries of race and sex it begins to overcome the divisions and divergences that make the views the dominant analysis empathises with appealing.

In their conclusion the first point Radice and Diamond make is that "Labour should be a party of power, despite its origins in the 19th century as a party of working-class protest. In order to help people, right injustice and widen opportunity, Labour has to be in government" (p. 29). The point to make against Radice and Diamond is that political action, by bringing working class people together across other boundaries, changes the conditions of politics. As with their opposition between different sections of the working class vote, Radice and Diamond's opposing being a party of power with being a party of working class protest is specious. In order to regain power we need to be a party of working class protest again and being a party of working class protest will enable us to help win some victories even if not in power. Crucially, however, being able to take this role within the struggles against austerity requires the party nationally to adopt policies, for example on tuition fees and welfare, which are genuinely different from those of the government, something which we have, thus far, failed on. A party is not the same as a protest group, which is why Ralph Miliband's emphasises organising against a common enemy and the mass party as a party of class solidarity and common purpose beyond sectional interests. What a party can provide is a means of uniting, within a total and universal antagonism seemingly disparate and unlinked struggles.

Practice 2: Beyond the social democracy of fear

For Tony Judt, "if social democracy is to have a future, it will be as a social democracy of fear... the Left, to be quite blunt about it, has something to conserve... The rise of the social service state, the century-long construction of a public sector whose goods and services illustrate and promote our collective identity and common purposes, the institution of welfare as a matter of right and its provision as a social duty: these were no mean accomplishments." Judt's view of social democracy as purely defensive and linked to cross class solidarity represents the starting point for understanding the importance of political action in the South. However, it is his non-antagonistic conception of class and ignoring of the role of the political party that makes original political creation impossible and, thus, must be overcome.

The government, through policies that dismantle the welfare state and through endorsing and extending unfettered capitalism, are undermining Judt's incarnations of collective purpose.

Despite Labour's complicity in these processes, a complicity which demands policy changes, we are still in a position to work as part of a collective defence of our institutions, most notably because of the involvement of our activists in campaigns to, for example, defend forests, libraries or Sure Start centres, prevent schools becoming academies or against new supermarkets, something that the government's changes to planning law will intensify. Furthermore, these campaigns need to mobilise women to prevent transfers of money and risk from the state to families.

However, Labour needs to go beyond an easy defence of popular local services, most notably by supporting trade union action, including strikes. The first thing to note is that it would be hard to argue that low and moderately paid workers facing pay freezes and increased pension contributions (which amount to a substantial pay cut) in a time of high inflation are not part of 'the squeezed middle'. The intensity of the squeezes on the low and moderately paid in the South makes union struggles of particular relevance.

The problem remains, particularly in the South, where rates of union membership and public sector employment are lower than in the rest of the country, of resisting the government's attempt to shift an antagonism between workers and capital to one between pampered public sector workers and hard-working and pressurised workers in the private sector. The trade union movement has made two important efforts to resist this; the first is to present this as part of a more general struggle against the government to defend the public services which everyone relies on; the second, which is perhaps, in the long term, even more important, is to try to move union struggles beyond sectional interests by offering 50p a week 'community membership' for students, the unemployed and single parents (Guardian, 2011). To this we should add that, due to some particularly unpleasant Conservative councils, some of the most sustained union activism in the country has been in the South. Plymouth City Council refused to negotiate with UNISON and Southampton has seen a series of strikes from council workers encompassing refuse collectors, social workers and parking wardens. What is particularly striking is that by moving beyond sectional and economistic struggles for better wages and conditions, the unions are being forced to take on part of the role of a political party, a role that has become necessary as a consequence of the Labour leadership's failure to situate politics within a total and universal antagonism that links the struggle against the common enemy to collective purpose beyond sectional division. However, there are limits to what this move beyond economism can be expected to achieve.

Marx makes clear what is at stake here for Labour: many of the battles over the next few years will be lost, but organising can transform defeat into victory, in The Communist Manifesto, Marx argued "From time to time the workers are victorious, but only temporarily. The real result of their battles is not some immediate success but a unity amongst workers that gains ever more ground... this unity is all that is needed to centralise

Can Academic Philosophy Help us to Learn the Lessons of our General Election Defeat?

the many local struggles of a generally similar character into a national struggle. Every class struggle is a political struggle ...This organisation of the proletarians into a class, and hence into a political party is disrupted time and again by competition amongst the workers themselves". (Marx, 1996, p. 10-11). It is political action that both reveals the shared context and shared interests of a working class that includes such seemingly disparate jobs as refuse collector and social worker.

Marx's argument points to the absolute necessity of a political party which organises disparate struggles. We need to be making this argument to those involved in protests against the Coalition government. Gramsci argues that a political party is indispensible as 'it is not possible to think of an organised and permanent passion. Permanent passion is a condition of orgasm and spasm, which means operational incapacity' (Gramsci, p.138). Further, Gramsci argues that there is an affinity between the activity of social democrats and the non party Left (in Gramsci's terms syndicalism) in that, in both cases, their political action is merely defensive (as in Judt's 'Social Democracy of Fear' or protests to defend the achievements of the welfare state), whereas the party is capable 'of original creation' (Gramsci, p. 130).

In Gramsci, the political party, as well as generalising struggles is the point where theory and practice are unified and where common sense is raised to philosophy. There is nothing esoteric about what Gramsci means by 'philosophy', he writes, "for a mass of people to be led to think coherently and in the same coherent fashion about the real world, is a 'philosophical' event far more important and 'original' than the discovery by some philosophical 'genius' of a truth which remains the property of small groups of intellectuals" (Gramsci, p. 325).

What the dominant analysis responds to is the diversity and incoherence of Southern common sense as expressed in prejudices and the polling data. However, Southern experience and what determines it is homogenous enough to allow thinking in a coherent and shared fashion amongst the Southern working class. The deep structures determining experience in the South are shared, whether it is the pressure on Southern women's lives, the political response to which is to demonise those women least able to cope with those pressures, or the stressful, badly paid and vulnerable jobs, the political response to which is to demonise those who are often even more exploited and vulnerable. A different Labour politics can overcome them by shifting antagonisms from those between two sections of the Southern working class to a general antagonism.

Gramsci ties this unification of theory and practice in the party to the tense relationship between intellectuals and the mass of party members. Radice and Diamond's affirmation of prejudice serves as an attempt, given the lack of contact between theorists and the party base (which, as has been argued, deforms Radice and Diamond's theory and leaves their argument, paradoxically, all too practical) to cancel the difference by having the centre do what it imagines the undistinguished mass of Southerners want without giving up political power. The alternative is to follow Gramsci's argument that "a human mass does not 'distinguish itself, does not become independent in its own right without, in the widest sense organising itself... the process of development is tied to a dialectic between the intellectuals and the masses... In the process, however, there continually recur moments in which a gap develops between the mass and intellectuals... a loss of contact, and thus the impression that theory is an 'accessory', a 'complement' and something subordinate... One should stress the importance and significance which, in the modern world, political parties have in the elaboration and diffusion of conceptions of the world because essentially what they do is to work out the ethics and politics corresponding to those conceptions and act as it were as their historical laboratory" (Gramsci, p. 334-5).

Part 6

Making Affordable Energy Compatible with Sustainable Energy

Energy Efficiency Provides One of the Keys to Affordable Energy

By Michael McAleer

Michael McAleer is a Chartered Engineer and a member of the Institute of Mechanical Engineers. He holds a Masters of Engineering from Queen's University, Belfast and has a wealth of work experience. After seven years working for Rolls-Royce as a manufacturing engineer all over the world, he turned his attention to the sustainable energy industries. He believes that they will be the fastest growing industries in the UK, across Europe and the rest of the world for the next 20-30 years. He chose a degree in Sustainable Energy and Entrepreneurship so as to be positioned to take advantage of the opportunities these industries will present. Since April 2010 Michael had been working with Rhead Group and National Grid on the Scottish Power-lead Carbon Capture and Storage competition, based out of Longannet.

Making Affordable Energy Compatible with Sustainable Energy

This paper argues that the UK will be able to achieve the target of 80% reduction in GHG emissions and zero emissions from power generation by 2050. Not only achieve it, but do so with no impact on the standard of living of the average UK citizen. Although this transition will be achieved largely by the advancement or rather the implementation of technology in two areas, both efficiency improvements and carbon neutral power generation, this paper focuses upon this first as its theme.

The 1990 levels of GHGs were 772.98 million tonnes CO2 equivalent. In a physical sense, an 80% reduction leaves 154.596 million tonnes CO2 emitted per year. This CO2 allowance will be sold to the highest bidder.

Therefore there are, as I perceive it, three options:

- The lights go out and we stop travelling by car and aeroplane;
- We start to deal with the problem;
- We miss the targets.

Assuming no democratically elected government in the world seeking election would advocate option 1 and that the consequences of option 3 are too catastrophic to contemplate then that leaves option 2.

The practicalities of this option are to decarbonise electricity generation and move as much transport and industrial activity as possible over to electricity.

This paper asserts that, in order to meet the overall 2050 targets, all emitters will be affected, including transport, agriculture, industry, domestic, and commercial. All sectors will have to change by resorting to either electricity or hydrogen.

Electricity, if not directly from the plug then indirectly from hydrogen created from electricity or fossil fuels (so called black hydrogen) where the carbon is captured and stored during the conversion phase. The electricity and hydrogen users will in turn rely on the generators being carbon neutral.

Alternatively if carbon capture proves too expensive the technology already exists to create liquid fuel from electricity by sequestering carbon dioxide, water and hydrogen. Granted, it is only at the demonstration phase, but the capability exists; the only unknown is at what cost (see http://www.airfuelsynthesis.comf or further information).

Let me illustrate this point. Domestic users are unlikely to cut their gas fired central heating GHG emissions unless they switch to electricity; similarly, for transport it is unlikely that cars will come equipped with CO_2 capture technology in the tail pipe. The same is true for all other sectors. It will be cheaper to generate carbon neutral electricity or liquid fuels than to capture the CO_2 released at point of use. From this assertion it becomes clear that the electricity demand in 2050 will be significantly higher than today, presenting an even bigger hurdle to overcome in just 40 years.

Can it be done by 2050?

Yes. This paper suggests that technology will save us. And to clarify, it is not relying on technologies that do not exist yet or at the early stages of development, but technologies that are already demonstrated; some may be at small scale or low penetration, but demonstrated all the same. I will break the technologies into two sections.

- Efficiency. Technologies that reduce electricity demand.
  - Efficient motors. EFF3
  - Efficient lighting. Compact Florescent, LED
  - Technological convergence.
  - Heat recovery systems
  - And so on...

- Zero net carbon energy. Technologies that generate with zero net GHG emissions.
  - Wind turbines
  - Tidal systems
  - Wave systems
  - Carbon capture and storage (CCS)
  - Solar, Thermal & PV

Efficiency savings

Implementation of these technologies will achieve the targets asked of them by 2050. A mere 39 years away!

But therein is the opportunity: 39 years in the life of a consumer device such as a laptop, mobile phone or a washing machine is equivalent to 10 generations; for industrial motors, four generations; for industrial processes, two generations; for transport (not including aircraft), four generations. Imagine what your car will look like in 40 years if the advances in technology continue to accelerate at their current rates.

Making Affordable Energy Compatible with Sustainable Energy

Thirty-nine years allows multiple generations, with each generation comes advances, improvements in efficiencies, in manufacturing methods, in processes and power consumption. The lifetime energy consumption of these high volume items will decrease significantly with each generation.

Take the internet for example. It has recently had its 40th birthday, it permeates every part of our lives and is unrecognisable from its conception. These changes were entirely due to human ingenuity and innovation. The same is true for green technologies.

New houses and retrofitting of current housing stock over the 39-year period with insulation, passive heating, solar thermal, reduced electricity demand appliances and micro generation (non fossil-based) will significantly reduce the carbon intensity of our everyday activities.

Retrofitting every house in the UK will require more than 500,000 homes per year to be refitted. A very large but not insurmountable number, especially if the process is started now instead of 2016, as currently planned.

The technologies listed should only be fitted if they are financially viable with a minimum five-year payback. In addition, all the space heating should be supplied by electrical systems such as storage heating and hot water systems. Installing gas burners may be less carbon intense today than the equivalent electricity consumption, but this position will eventually change, and once installed they become a legacy problem. After all a gas-fired stove will always emit carbon, no matter how efficient it is: electricity doesn't have to.

If the efficiency changes are introduced, then GHG emissions from the home can be reduced to zero very rapidly, but passed on to the electricity generator. This increases the pressure on electricity generators to decarbonising their supply.

However, the target is very large and only 39 years away. The UK needs to start somewhere – so where should it start? For me, by far the biggest opportunity for immediate improvement is in Megawatts/efficiency savings.

Within the first 15 years, before significant transfer of vehicles to electric systems, the UK's electricity capacity can decrease by about 20%, due entirely to two key improvements: 1) the smart grid; and 2) efficiency improvements. Please note that generated electricity may increase but capacity will decrease (see below for clarification) After the 15 years capacity will have to grow rapidly.

The smart grid

The smart grid means that, for the first time, the supply of electricity and demand from consumers can be matched with minimal spillage and predictable dispatching. Also, and very importantly, it will reduce the peak load demand, having the knock-on effect of removing the need for peaking load stations, so reducing overall capacity requirements.

The smart grid works by offsetting the demand in the home to periods of low overall demand. Your smart meter will switch on or off the dish washer, washing machine, AC unit, mobile phone and laptop chargers, fridge and freezer, until a time when the supply in the grid is acceptable, without affecting the user, much in the way that some customers have a cheaper electricity supply at night. They will still wake up in the morning with their dishes and clothes washed, food cold, storage heater fully heated and plenty of hot water. The consumer will want this because it will save them money; the utilities will want this because it evens out their demand.

Energy efficiency improvements across all sectors

Energy efficiency improvements of high volume products such as the humble light bulb, industrial motors, television and computer screens, air conditioning units etc., will play a significant part in reducing overall demand. Taking this in reverse, saving 10 watts of electricity reduces the need to consume 500 watts of fossil fuel, and this is true without taking into account the carbon footprint of getting the fuel to the power station. Do this on a large enough scale and the carbon intensity of our electricity supply soon falls (assuming carbon based dispatching is implemented).

The energy efficiency improvements do not rely on technological advances; they are available off-the-shelf today, at economically viable prices. Take the following three examples:

- Incandescent light bulbs;
- Energy-efficient electric motors;
- TV screens and computer monitors.

Incandescent light bulbs

Replace incandescent 100w blubs (4% efficient) with 11w compact fluorescent (25% efficient) or even 4w LED (50% efficient). Considering lighting accounts for 30% of electricity consumption, it represents a step in the correct efficiency direction. Add to this the reduced replacement

Making Affordable Energy Compatible with Sustainable Energy

costs with LEDs (in industrial and commercial settings) which last 25 years and the case to purchase them is compelling.

Site electricity consumption

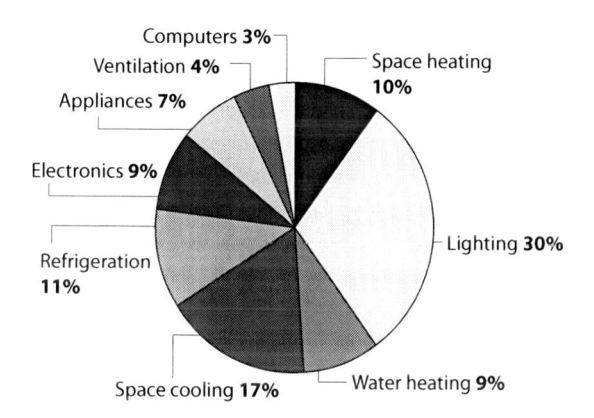

- Computers 3%
- Ventilation 4%
- Appliances 7%
- Electronics 9%
- Refrigeration 11%
- Space cooling 17%
- Water heating 9%
- Lighting 30%
- Space heating 10%

Cost of ownership over 10 years

Light source	Overall efficiency	Lamp life with on/off cycle	Power cost 10 years (43,800 hours)	Replacement cost over 10 years				Total 2000Lm lamp
				Bulb	Qty	Lab	Sub Ttl	
Standard incandescent	2.5-10	500-700	$4.38/Lm	30p	62	£5	£93	£8,853
Tungsten halogen	7-12	1,300-2,600	£3.65/Lm	£5	17	£10	£850	£8,150
Compact fluorescent	10-27	7,000	£1.62/Lm	£6	7	£5	£210	£3,450
Fluorescent (T5 covered)	39-65	10,000-16,000	£0.67/Lm	£9	2.7	£20	£486	£1,826
Mercury vapour	20-40	Up to 20,000	£1.10/Lm	£20	2.2	£20	£880	£3,080
Metal Halide	36-80	7,000-15,000	£0.55/Lm	£10	2.9	£20	£580	£1,680
High-pressure sodium	36-88	Up to 20,000	£0.50/Lm	£10	2.2	£50	£1,100	£2,200
LED	25-60	50,000-100,000	£0.73/Lm	£60	0.4	£10	£240	£1,700

Source: www.ecoledlighting.com, 2006

Energy-efficient electric motors

These account for 65% of industrial electricity us; when replaced with a EFF1 rated energy-efficient motor along with a drive control systems, as much as 8% of the electricity can be saved. Combining this with efficient pipe layout (large bore pipes with smooth redial bends) offering less than half the resistance of today's systems can give an overall systems energy intensity improvement of 50%.

TV screens and computer monitors

Modern flat screen TV and computer monitors consume a fraction of what their CRT (cathose ray tube) predecessors did. By replacing the millions of office and home CRT monitors and TVs, huge amounts of electricity will be saved. Additional savings are yet to be realised; Hitachi has demonstrated a TV that switches off the screen but not the sound when the viewer looks away and instantly turns it back on when the viewer turns back, reducing power consumption by over 90%.

Add to these significant advances in air-conditioning units that freeze large volumes of water during the night and solar thermal collectors that reduce the demand for energy to heat water, and you are left with the consumer not paying any more than they did previously for electricity despite the price having increased. This preserves their standard of living and helps the country go green.

Conclusion

Above I have outlined the various technological innovations that have improved energy efficiencies in recent years. Now consider how these products will continue to develop, Consumer devices are converging; where before there were many devices, there is now only one. Examples include cameras, personal organisers, MP3 players, alarm clocks, phones, video cameras, desktop computers and laptops. It is now possible to replace all these devices with just one. Similarly in the office, photocopiers, faxes, scanners and printers may now be replaced by one device. This reduction in the number of devices uses reduces the demand for electricity.

Financial Benefits of Green Energy Can Help Pay its Price

By Mark Brophy

Mark Brophy is a proud Geordie, Newcastle United fan, and a long-standing campaigner for green energies. Having spent the early part of his career in the nuclear sector, Mark left to pursue a career in ethical energies. Mark is a recent member of Labour Left and is a passionate believer that large scale projects such as wind farms can drive down the cost of renewables and make green energy a more attractive proposition.

Making Affordable Energy Compatible with Sustainable Energy

As stated in the two preceding pieces, there are several key challenges which must be met in order to provide the nation's energy needs in the future. The Climate Change Act 2008 specified that UK greenhouse gas emissions must be reduced by 80% from 1990 levels by 2050.[49] As a major producer of these emissions, the energy generation sector must bear the brunt of a large part of the reduction. Change is required to remove or, at worst, dramatically reduce environmentally unfriendly generation methods in the energy mix. In addition, political instability in several regions of the world which are major suppliers of gas and oil means that energy generation relying on these sources is likely to become more unreliable over time and therefore also more expensive. Security of supply is vital and self-sufficiency in energy sources must be pursued as far as is possible.

About a quarter of current UK generating capacity is due to be closed down in the next decade. In addition, the need to reduce oil and gas combustion for reasons of cost, emissions, and security of supply, means that the method of heating commercial and residential properties is likely to change to use electricity, and road transport will see an increase in use of electric vehicles in place of those powered by internal combustion engines. So demand is likely to rise and generating capacity to fall should nothing be done.

Current UK energy policy is to build eight new nuclear power stations to replace generation plants at the end of their lifespan, and make up the potential future gap between demand and supply of generated electricity. However, a 2003 Parliamentary Office of Science and Technology briefing on nuclear energy options pointed out that "a renaissance of nuclear power in the UK would need the government and industry to address… public acceptability of a long-term strategy to manage radioactive waste", as well as requiring market acceptability that is, financial attractiveness to investors. Yet no strategy for long-term high-activity waste management has been implemented.[50] The Nuclear Decommissioning Authority strategy from April 2011 speaks of using a Geological Disposal Facility for this function, but that it would be "several decades before such a facility will be available to accept waste" and that "development of a Geological Disposal Facility requires both a willing local community and a suitable geology".[51]

No such site has been identified, let alone approved. So the only long-term strategy is that of burying waste for thousands of years in an as-yet unidentified facility somewhere that local people do not object to. New power stations cannot be allowed to recommence adding to our stockpile of this waste while we have no idea what to do with it.

The recent and ongoing disaster at Fukushima, Japan, would almost certainly never be reproduced in the UK, not least because of the lack of earthquake risk. However, the Japanese disaster does show the vulnerability of nuclear power stations to catastrophic events generally. The economic case for nuclear power is no more impressive. What case is generally made relies on the limited liability of energy companies for the consequences of a disaster. From very early in the life of the industry it was realised that "nuclear power makes a valuable contribution to meeting the world's energy demands and that in order for it to continue doing so, individual operator liability had to be curtailed, and beyond a certain level, risk had to be socialized".[52]

Though this is enshrined in law, it does not reduce the actual possible liabilities. If individual operators did not have their liabilities for nuclear accidents limited by a cap, they would have to insure for all possible losses, the costs of which would immediately make the entire industry unsustainable financially. The costs of cleaning up the Fukushima disaster have been estimated by the Japan Centre for Economic Research at up to 20 trillion yen, about £160 billion, over the next 10 years. They also state that nuclear generation costs could treble by 2020 which makes it "difficult to argue that nuclear energy has any cost advantages over renewable forms of energy, such as wind power".[53]

Renewable energy sources provide an opportunity to solve these problems. Replacing dirty energy generation methods with renewables of course takes the associated greenhouse gases out of the total produced. Renewables also remove the need for insecure and unstable fuel supply channels. The renewable natural processes of wave, wind, sun, tide and others could be used for generation in the seas surrounding the UK, on hills and moors, on rooftops and in reservoirs all around the nation. No fuel need be transported from abroad, no remote pipelines vulnerable to sabotage are required.

The intermittent, volatile nature of processes like wind and sun means other energy sources are required, whose output can be controlled to fulfil demand on cold, sunless, windless days when energy generation reliant on these processes will not be operating at full capacity. Hydroelectric, implicitly a storage as well as generation method, cannot provide enough of either in the UK to meet our back-up needs. Such back-up energy generation is generally assumed to involve nuclear or fossil fuels. However, without these, this function could be met also by the use of energy storage methods (such as load levelling), waste-to-energy and other carbon-neutral biofuel generation, the particular advantage of waste-to-energy being that it does not require energy crops to be grown specifically for this purpose, and possibly endangering food security. There are other options for back-up of intermittent primary generation. Although the transmission of solar-generated power from areas of highly reliable sunshine (by schemes such as the Desertec project), while a good match for local wind generation, would introduce vulnerability of supply and undermine the goal of self-sufficiency, Norwegian excess hydro resources could be similarly used to balance demand here.[54] Clean coal technology, and carbon capture and storage generally, could allow the tailing-off of fossil fuel use in a low-carbon way until more long-term solutions kicked in if necessary.

The use of renewables on the scale proposed does have the drawback of the large capital costs involved. A 2010 Department of Energy and Climate Change cost assessment found that onshore wind, currently the lowest-cost major renewable, had capital costs around $2,500/kW, or £1,500/kW, and offshore wind about double that. The report assumed that costs would fall by 2020 due to economies of scale, technology breakthroughs and improvements in production techniques, to about £1,200/kW and £2,400/kW respectively. At some point, however, onshore wind will no longer be able to be expanded or at least will become more expensive due to the finite number of suitable sites. Greenpeace estimates that to provide 30% of total UK electricity supply by offshore wind requires a rate of increase in capacity of 5GW/year by 2020.[55] By 2020 the capital cost just of offshore wind could be £12 billion/year.

The burden of such costs, however, could be mitigated by the economic benefits associated with large-scale development of renewable energy. Such a programme would provide an unmissable opportunity to grow a renewables manufacturing industry. Seeding such growth in regions currently struggling to provide enough jobs but traditionally containing a manufacturing skills base would cut unemployment rates and boost local economics. Co operative onshore wind projects, as well as being funded by communities, would both increase the likelihood of planning permission being granted due to local support, and again boost local economies by channelling profits into the communities hosting the projects.[56]

It has been estimated that efforts to reduce greenhouse gas output in all climate change related industries could create 1 million jobs in the UK, saving the government £13,000 for each job in taxes and benefits, around £13 billion/year.[57] With this industry in place, worldwide requirements for renewables technology as all nations strive to meet 2050 treaty agreements would provide further opportunity for exports, global spending on renewables possibly reaching $2.3 trillion, roughly £1.5 trillion by 2020.[58] Capturing just 1% of this spend, for instance, would provide £15 billion of sales. Virtually limitless demand is therefore projected to exist for a world-leading industry as could be created here.

North Sea offshore wind is possibly the most valuable renewable resource in Europe. Large-scale implementation of generation plant to take advantage of this would necessarily involve building over-capacity to cover peaks and troughs in the range of generation methods. Offshore wind generating at full capacity in this scenario would be likely to provide unneeded energy. After possible storage of some, the sale of energy to other nations without the good fortune to possess access to this resource could pay back some of the initial capital costs. The European Wind Energy Association suggests a feasible target of 50% of EU electricity could be supplied by wind by 2050, of which some 350GW of a renewables total of 600GW would come from offshore in the North Sea.[59] This suggests any unneeded energy generated could be disposed of on a European energy market. The Offshore Valuation Group, 'an informal collaboration of government and industry organisations', set up to value UK offshore resources, describes a scenario with £443 billion capital costs (roughly in line with the yearly estimate mentioned earlier) up to 2050 on building offshore wind, wave and tidal projects which would be providing £62 billion of revenue and £16 billion of profits per year by then, and make the UK a net electricity exporter.[60]

In addition, if the capital costs can be considered to be paid back over time through these general economic movements, operating costs for renewables are relatively low, especially in respect to the currently growing costs of oil and gas generation. This provides another opportunity – comparatively low-cost energy to the consumer in the UK which would take millions of people out of fuel poverty. The health benefits associated with this and with increased prosperity in some of the UK's poorest regions would mean savings in health budgets. A 2011 report on the costs of fuel poverty to the NHS quotes costs of £145 million for the 656,000 privately rented dwellings with these problems, or £221 per dwelling. Extrapolating these costs to the total number of dwellings with these problems, about 3.6m, gives costs to the NHS per annum of £796 million.[61]

Renewables possess an irrefutable environmental, and some would also say moral case for their use. Arguments against rely in part on certain practical difficulties which could be overcome with the application of some political will, but mainly on financial grounds. It is futile to attempt to specify exactly how much energy will need to be generated by which method in 2050, as decisions will be influenced by open market electricity prices, technology developments, the political landscape – in fact, many unforeseeable factors. It can be seen, however, that it is perfectly possible to make a case for a switch to an energy generation mix, based primarily on renewable methods, which would pay for at the very least – a large proportion of the costs through the general economic benefits which would accrue to the nation from that switch.

---

[49] Climate Change Act 2008: http://www.decc.gov.uk/en/content/cms/legislation/cc_act_08/cc_act_08.aspx

[50] *The nuclear energy option in the UK* http://www.parliament.uk/documents/post/postpn208.pdf

[51] Nuclear Decommissioning Authority Strategy Document (April 2011) http://www.nda.gov.uk/documents/upload/NDA-Strategy-Effective-from-April-2011-print-friendly-version.pdf

[52] *Civil Liability for Nuclear Damage* http://www.world-nuclear.org/info/inf67.html FY2020 Nuclear Generating Cost Treble Pre-Accident Level

[53] http://www.jcer.or.jp/eng/research/pdf/pe(kobayashi20110719)e.pdf. Desertec Foundation http://www.desertec.org/

[54] UK Electricity Generation Costs Update June 2010 http://www.decc.gov.uk/assets/decc/statistics/projections/71-uk-electricity-generation-costs-update-.pdf

[55] http://www.greenpeace.org.uk/MultimediaFiles/Live/FullReport/6702.pdf Energy4All http://www.energy4all.co.uk/

[56] *One Million Climate Jobs, Solving the economic and environmental crises* http://www.climate-change-jobs.org/sites/default/files/1MillionClimateJobs_2010.PDF

[57] *Pew Reports on Potential $2.3 Trillion Clean Power Investment by 2020* http://www.energyboom.com/finance/pew-reports-potential-23-trillion-clean-power-investment-2020

[58] *Powering Europe: wind energy and the electricity grid* European Wind Energy Association Nov 2010 http://www.ewea.org/fileadmin/ewea_documents/documents/publications/reports/Grids_Report_2010.pdf

[59] *The Offshore Valuation: A valuation of the UK's offshore renewable energy resource* http://www.offshorevaluation.org/downloads/offshore_vaulation_full.pdf

[60] *The Offshore Valuation: A valuation of the UK's offshore renewable energy resource* http://www.offshorevaluation.org/downloads/offshore_vaulation_full.pdf

[61] *The Health Costs of cold dwellings*, Buildings Research Establishment http://www.foe.co.uk/resource/reports/warm_homes_nhs_costs.pdf

Making the Case for Opening New Coal Mines

By Ian Lavery MP and Michael McAleer

As an active member, Ian Lavery rose through the ranks and in 1992 was elected to the post of General Secretary of the National Union of Mineworkers, Northumberland Area. In August 2002 he was elected as President of the National Union of Mineworkers and he served in that position until 2010. In 2010, he became the Labour MP for Wansbeck. Ian Lavery MP brings a wealth of experience to the topic. Having worked in the coal mines of the Lynemouth from 1980, Ian sees a strong future for clean coal technology in the UK. With the high levels of deprivation and worklessness that exist in the North East, he believes that the time has come to reopen the coal mines.

Making Affordable Energy Compatible with Sustainable Energy

Here Ian Lavery MP makes the case for investing in clean coal technology, carbon capture storage and state investment in opening new coal mines in the UK and building coal power stations on site. This piece argues that:

- CCS (carbon capture and storage) coal-fired power stations can reduce overall targeted emissions by up to 20%;
- CCS on-site coal stations can cut the costs of transport coal from mines to plant;
- More use of domestic coal can shield the UK from the volatility of the global energy market;
- Coal consumption in China and the USA is set to soar in coming decades;
- Investment in CCS technology has been rising worldwide and Green Watch and the *New Scientist* both judge it to be a crucial part of the energy mix;
- Investment in clean coal can help rejuvenate former coal mining regions, reducing unemployment; and
- If the UK leads the world in CCS technology, this can become a key component of UK exports for years to come.

CCS: the scientific argument

As Stuart Hazseldine recently stated in an article in the *New Scientist*, 'CCS is no panacea but it could provide a major contribution to emissions reduction'.[62] The section below explores post, pre and oxyfuel combustion by outlining clearly the advanced nature of current CCS technology.

If by 2050 all the homes and transport systems are run off electricity, then demand is sure to increase. That will mean building more capacity. But, unless this capacity is zero net carbon emissions for the first time round the 2050 target will be missed. The UK is lucky in that all their current thermal plant is old, and will, over the next 39 years, be replaced. So, new and up-to-date generation of industrial generation plants must be constructed – be that super critical coal-fired power stations with incorporated CCS or megawatt scale wind turbines.

By 2050 power generation will go through at least one generation and similarly to consumer goods and housing improvements, there will be benefits in the purchase, installation, operation and maintenance costs along the way. One possible technical solution is CCS retrofitted to existing plants and incorporated into new ones. Old coal powered stations will need to be replaced by more efficient super critical stations with integrated CCS. During this period, technological advances and wider use of new technologies such as CCS, CHP (combined heat and power) and distributed heating, to name a few, will drive down the carbon cost per kW of electricity.

As Stuart Hazseldine recently estimated, CCS technology could account for 20% of the required reduction in CO_2 emissions.[63] All new coal-fired power stations will be designed to easily retrofit carbon capture with easy access to the stack. This technology is already proven and is

Country CCS projects ranking

Country	Count	%	Cum %
United States	87	45%	45%
Canada	19	10%	55%
Australia	15	8%	63%
United Kingdom	12	6%	69%
Germany	9	5%	74%
Norway	8	4%	78%
Japan	8	4%	82%
China	8	4%	86%
Netherlands	6	3%	90%
Italy	4	2%	92%
France	3	2%	93%
Denmark	2	1%	94%
Poland	2	1%	95%
Czech Republic	2	1%	96%
Algeria	2	1%	97%
Malaysia	1	1%	98%
United Arab Emirates	1	1%	98%
Bulgaria	1	1%	99%
Romania	1	1%	99%
Ireland	1	1%	100%
Grand Total	192	100%	

Source: National Energy Technology Laboratory, 2009

Making Affordable Energy Compatible with Sustainable Energy

possible, but the only question that remains is at what price. Ideally, clean coal should be used for CCS through the sequestration and liquidification process which works as follows. Amines are sprayed into the stack absorbing CO_2. This CO_2 rich amines are then heated to release the 'pure' CO_2 to be compressed into a liquid, ready for transportation away from the site. Once the amines cool they are then recycled back around the capture system to be used over again.

This is probably the best understood carbon capture technology, as the basic techniques have been used for many years to capture CO_2 for the fizzy drinks industry, and industry has been working with amine solvents for over 60 years. The challenge is in the scaling up of the techniques and processes involved in handling the vast quantities of CO_2 produced by an industrial power station.

The table on the previous page shows the country rankings for number of CCS projects. It indicates quite clearly where competition lies for the UK's industries and shows the investment each relevant country is making in CCS. So, despite the UK's smaller number of projects, the government has committed by far the largest amount of funds. This is likely to put the UK CCS industry ahead of the world in terms of development and opportunity.

The reasons for UK involvement in the exploration of clean coal technology are evident. We in the UK have 17,000,000,000 tonnes of clean coal underground. As coal production worldwide is set to soar in forthcoming years, has the time come for Britain to invest heavily in coal technology? This could provide the economic growth and regeneration, dependent upon it, that is much needed for the former coal-mining areas of Britain. Despite the ending of the Longannet project, the £1 billion investment from the government remains on the table, so the race is on to identify a new site that may be feasible for such a project.

Other countries continue to view coal as an essential part of their energy portfolio. China and the USA, the world's two biggest greenhouse gas producers, both rely heavily on coal. China, which burnt 2.74 billion tons in 2008, obtains 80% of its electricity from coal, while the US derives 65%.[64] As you can see in the chart on the following page, the UK lags far behind. It should be said that China and the USA are the two economic powerhouses of the world, but they are also responsible for some of the world's most horrific CO_2 emissions. Admittedly, the problems hitherto have lain in coal but now coal can provide one of the solutions.

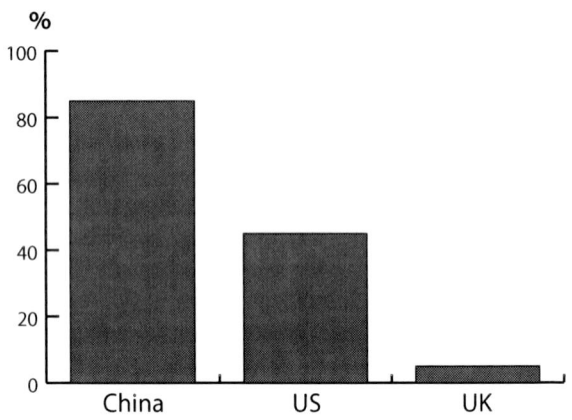

The percentage of electricity derived from coal by country

In fairness to the USA and China, they have both been investing recently in CCS technology. Currently, 30 projects worldwide are investigating CCS and there have been some notable successes. See the CSL Forum for CO_2 carbon capture projects that have been successfully implemented or are currently in progress.[65] If one takes the time to browse the CSL Forum information it is notable that CCS is quite advanced, especially through sequestration, and that the UK has had a prominent part to play in its research and development.

Thus, the conclusions are clear: the race is on to demonstrate industrial scale CCS, with the prize for doing so a chance to become the national and possibly the world leader in what is predicted to be a $100 billion industry by 2020 and up to $2,000 billion by 2050 (Watt, 2010, p. 15). Within the UK, the prize for being selected as the competition winner is a substantial head-start with capital and operational expenses taken care of by the UK tax payer for the first 10 to 15 years of operation.[66] But this does not just benefit the winning consortia as it also benefits the industry as a whole. Jobs can be created in UK exports if we can lead the world with CCS technology.

By building CCS coal power stations on the site of UK mines we can minimise the transport costs and use UK coal to provide our electricity. If CCS technology is funded and developed correctly it can help account for a reduction in 20% of the emissions targets we have to meet by 2050. This is too big an opportunity to turn down.

CCS: The economic argument

There are other reasons why CCS/clean coal and the opening of new coal mines on which we could build new clean coal stations that can provide a stop-gap in our energy mix until renewable energy is able to fully meet the UK's energy needs:

- Employment lost as a result of the closing of the pits in the 1980s was never replenished, and as a result high levels of worklessness exist in the coal mining regions of the UK today;
- The rising prices of oil and gas mean that the competitive advantage over coal that they offer to the consumer in comparison to the 1980s has been reversed;
- The depleting resources of oil and gas coupled with the increased usage of coal by the world's economic superpowers mean that the UK would be unwise not to exploit its own resource potential.

Employment

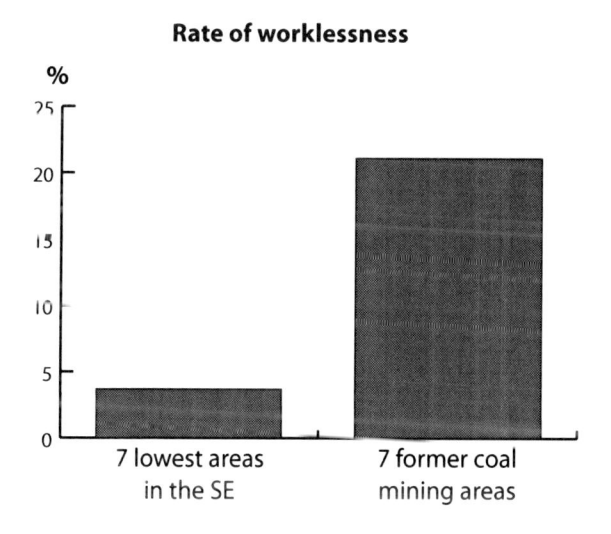

Rate of worklessness

(Bar chart: 7 lowest areas in the SE ≈ 3%; 7 former coal mining areas ≈ 21%)

The above graph shows the 2009 average rate of worklessness in seven former coal mining regions and a comparison with the seven lowest areas of the South East. I hope it reinforces the point that under-employment is rife in the former coal mining regions of the North East. In the latest 2010 data, evidence suggests that worklessness in former coal mining regions is growing faster than other areas of the UK. In Wansbeck, Easington, Sedgefield, Selby, and Hartlepool unemployment is now at crisis levels. It is in the interests of all political parties to intervene in the coal mining regions to provide investment and jobs to reverse these appalling high levels of worklessness. In the 1980s, when the UK was more reliant on coal, employment in the energy sector was four times higher than it is today (see the graph below).

Number of UK-based workers employed in energy

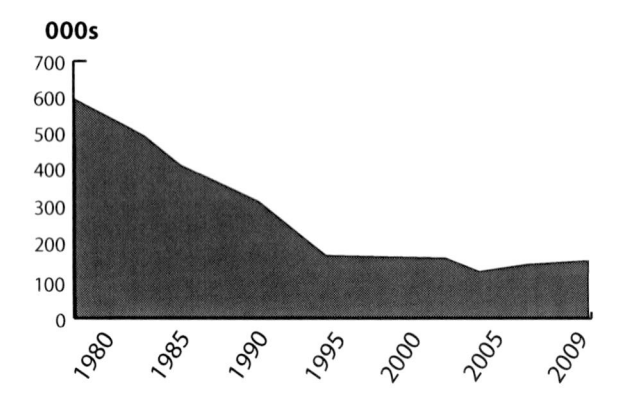

000s
700
600
500
400
300
200
100
0
1980 1985 1990 1995 2000 2005 2009

The number of UK-based workers in the energy sector has declined dramatically throughout this generation. In the last 30 years, three-quarters of the workforce have lost their jobs and today the energy sector employs just a quarter of what it did in 1980. Crucially, only 20% of employees in the energy sector work with oil and gas companies. According to the Office of National Statistics (ONS), the industry only employs 30,000 people in the UK, comprising of less than 2% of our GDP[67]; yet in 2011 Q3 Royal Dutch Shell PLC and BP made £7.7 billion profits between them.[68] The oil industry takes much in terms of resources and profits but it gives little back in return. It was not always this way. Renewable energies as well as CCS offer much greater potential for job creation; they also offer greater value to the customer.

Rising oil and gas prices

A key reason for investing in CCS technology is that the rising prices in oil and gas are quite simply unsustainable (see below).

Cost in pence per Kw for energy supply (2001-2010)

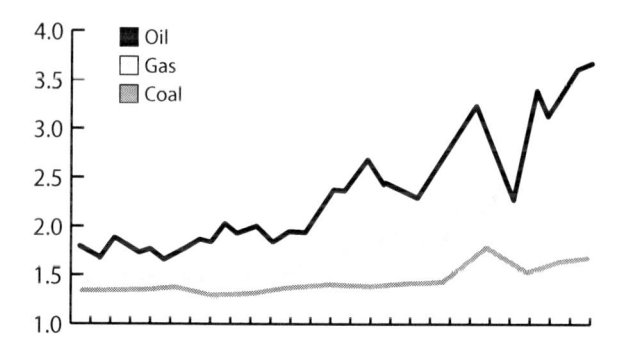

The graph above shows the cost at the point of supply [not retail] of coal, gas and oil per Kilowatt over the last ten years (2000-2011 (Q1)).

Oil: This graph tells us a few things. First, the almost quadrupling of oil costs is unsustainable, and second our dependency on that resource is making our economy much more volatile than it should in terms of inflation and transport/distribution costs. Oil as a home heating fuel and method of transport is simply unsustainable. Whilst only a tiny portion of our generators use oil, the future will see electric cars replace the petrol engines in our car production. And so this increased usage of electricity will require more generators including CCS coal plants.

Gas: The UK's position in terms of gas supply is somewhat better than our European counterparts. You can see that gas prices have 'only' doubled in the last decade, meaning that it is reasonable that gas should feature as part of our energy portfolio in the medium term. But, gas-fired power stations cannot be sustained in the long term. Besides, the volatility of the wholesale prices mean that the inflationary impact of gas prices on our economy has a detrimental effect on sustainable economic development.

Coal: When one glances at coal prices they are struck by just how economical they have remained. In light of this, one is inclined to be rueful at the premature closing of the UK's coal mines. Clean coal technology, smokeless fuel as well as CCS, are not ideal but they are nonetheless expedient methods by which to break our dependency on oil. The liquidification of coal means that it could be used for transport as well as home heating. The potential reduction of overall emissions offered by clean coal is potentially 20% of that which is required.

There is no reason why this investment in renewable energy could not be centred on former coal mining areas. These people have in the past demonstrated great dedication and skills to the energy sector – it is time to unleash their potential once more. The graph below also shows how economical coal is for domestic usage in comparison to gas and oil, and so although the focus is on opening sites and building coal-fired power plants, it should not go without saying that coal production offers increasing value to domestic customers. The graph below shows that the largest domestic price rises (unadjusted) in recent years have occurred in the provision of gas and oil to customers. Coal has remained relatively stable.

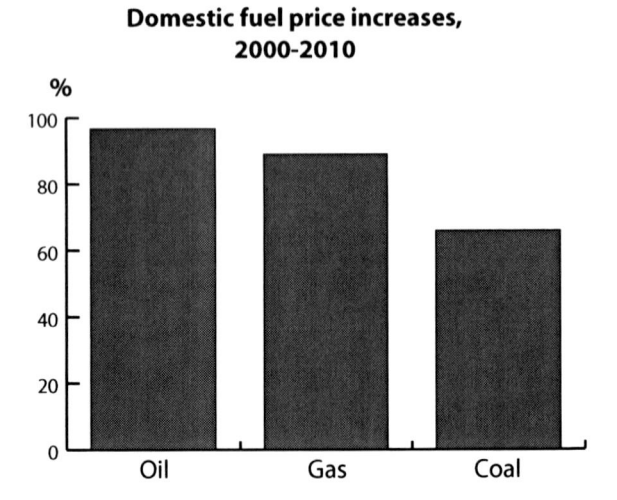

Domestic fuel price increases, 2000-2010

A further key reason for building UK CCS coal power stations on the site of UK coal mines is that it provides maximum security against the volatility of the energy sector. Oil and gas are running out and it is not clear that there are sufficient alternatives in place to meet the demand when oil and gas expire. Take, for example, the case of Yemen (see below).

Yemen's oil production (barrels per day)

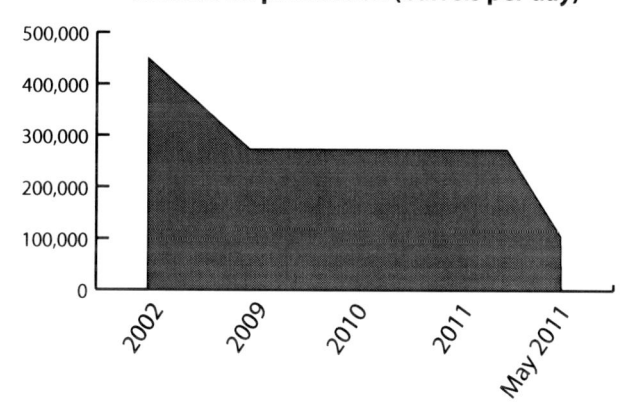

[Chart showing Yemen's oil production declining from approximately 450,000 in 2002 to 290,000 in 2009, holding through 2010 and 2011, then dropping near 0 by May 2011]

Yemen is the 32nd largest supplier of oil in the world. It has c.0.2% of world reserves and at its peak c.0.4% of world production. Oil revenue amounts to 75% of the nation's income. At its height, it produced more than 450,000 barrels per day (bpd), but by 2009 that had fallen to 290,000.

Thanks to the attacks on pipelines and the government halting production, Yemen now produces anything from 0-100,000 barrels per day. The Royal Institute for International Affairs in a report covered by the BBC suggested that Yemen's oil reserves could run out by 2017.[69]

Some reports suggest it could be even earlier – perhaps 2015. Our own conservative estimate is that Yemen will run out of oil in 2034. But we are all agreed on one thing, Yemen's oil will most certainly run out. Globally, our oil supplies might not last long after 2040, and some say by then we will be producing only 20% of the oil we currently do. There is centuries' worth of coal as yet untapped in Yorkshire, the Midlands and the North East of England. One might ponder, if Yemen had coal, would it dig? Establishing CCS stations on the sites of UK mines can protect the UK from the ever increasing global turmoil

Conclusion

The Scottish Power Consortium was, until October 2011, operating a carbon capture test rig at its power station at Longannet in Fife, Scotland.[70] The scheme involved pumping carbon emissions from the station into deep underground coal seams to drive out methane gas which can then be used as a fuel, with the carbon emissions remaining trapped in the coal seams. As you can see, the technology can be easily integrated. The transportation and storage elements have also been demonstrated on many oil and gas rigs where CO_2 is used to aid recovery.

Longannet's rig was installed in May 2009 and ran continuously for 2,000 hours. It was the only energy company in the UK which was operating a carbon capture unit on a working coal-fired power station. The same technology can be retrofitted to the tens of thousands of coal-fired power stations worldwide. The plant's close proximity to the potentially huge undersea storage sites offered by the Central North Sea, we thought, made it ideally placed to kick-start an entirely new industry based on CO_2 reduction. Sadly, concerns over its commercial viability, in terms of cost and installing a pipeline, has led to the project being scrapped. A decision was made to end the project because the pipe needed was too long for the budget that was available. The government has kept the offer of £1 billion funding on the table for another project, but in this case Scottish Power needed more investment than the government was prepared to give. WWF Scotland has commented that it has set CCS and climate change in Scotland back years. We await a decision as to the chosen site to recommence exploration into CCS in the UK. Sites such as Ryhope or Peterhead are probably ideal. The entire industry now waits with bated breath for a new site to be located so that this essential part of our future energy mix can get back on track. In the meantime, other parts of the world will continue to develop their CCS technology and the UK may fall further behind.

---

62 *New Scientist*, April 2011, http://tinyurl.com/cogp4pm
63 *New Scientist*, April 2011, http://tinyurl.com/cogp4pm
64 *Telegraph*, http://tinyurl.com/m94x28
65 CSL Forum, http://tinyurl.com/3wjqr6a
66 Through a tariff on electricity consumption
67 ONS, http://tinyurl.com/cvqpxmc
68 Reuters http://tinyurl.com/bu9fv5r , AP http://tinyurl.com/cbbtpog
69 BBC, http://news.bbc.co.uk/1/hi/7739402.stm
70 Scottish Power http://tinyurl.com/bvxh7ff

Part 7

Labour Left and Issues Beyond Class

This section tackles the very complex topics of gender, sexuality and religious identity. The reality is that identity politics are fraught with contradictions. One identity's advancement is viewed as another's demise, especially in the areas of women's empowerment. But of course that need not be the case. Gender equality is crucial not just to Labour's prospects of re-election but the advancement of the UK as a civilised society. Modernising influences in the area of equalities are of fundamental importance to our society's progression, but that is sometimes viewed as contradictory to our traditional elements of society, especially religion. This section attempts the very difficult task of marrying these competing influences. It does so in the spirit of tolerance and frank debate which we hope that you as a reader can appreciate.

LGB&T and the Next Generation of Reforms

By Dr Mike Homfray

Dr Mike Homfray lives in Crosby, Liverpool and is a member of Bootle CLP. He is active in both Labour and LGBT politics and currently chairs a local LGBT forum and a police liaison group. He works as a part-time lecturer and online tutor and gained his PhD from the University of Liverpool in 2005. Looking at the lesbian and gay community in the North West of England, and the influence of communitarian ideas in understanding a community of interest working for equality, it was published as 'Provincial Queens' by Peter Lang in 2007.

There can be no doubt that the Labour governments of 1997-2010 delivered considerable change in the area of lesbian, gay, bisexual and transgender (LGB&T) rights. Indeed, the changes were far greater than many realistically expected. The initial caution of the government was transformed into a pragmatic approach which blended responding to European directives, developing legislative programs in conjunction with Stonewall, and amending existing legislation in order to remove its homophobic content. European legislation inspired the measures aimed at removing discrimination in employment, the civil partnership legislation mirrored closely Stonewall's ongoing work in the area, and the review of the Sexual Offences legislation largely revolved around ensuring there was no difference in the treatment of offences, no matter which gender the participants were. Legal recognition of transgender status was also established in the Labour years.

It is easy to be critical in hindsight, irrespective of what may need further attention or amendment; the achievements of the Labour governments were considerable. Remembering that the previous Tory regimes' contribution to LGB&T equality was section 28 of the Local Government Act 1988, the change in both political climate and actual legislative direction was radically different. The vast majority of Labour MPs supported the changes with a relatively small number of MPs voting against or abstaining on religious grounds. The Conservative voting profile was far less impressive, with every change being actively opposed by the majority of parliamentary Tories, even during the early part of the Cameron era when a far more sympathetic stance was deliberately taken. However, one notable achievement of the Labour changes was the creation of a situation where these issues are no longer used as a way of attempting to smear Labour local authorities or the Labour Party. Conservatives display no wish to revisit the days of Section 28, and whilst there are individuals within the LGB&T communities who remain suspicious of the Tory transformation, the selection of a number of openly gay or lesbian Tory MPs has changed the dynamic of the debate. It would be hard to imagine the hysterical bile of those who eagerly promoted Section 28 being repeated or left unchallenged when those they condemn are openly sitting on the Conservative benches in the House of Commons.

The changes have made their mark not only on the Labour Party, but also on the British polity, meaning that there has been a significant shift in the attitude towards LGB&T rights. Theresa May is advocating measures related to equality which she nor any other Conservative Home

Secretary would not have done until relatively recently, awkward though she may appear in doing so. My own research, published in 2005, suggested that the Labour government had, in conjunction with Stonewall, adopted an essentially communitarian approach to LGB rights, which emphasised 'rights and responsibilities' and stressed the incorporation of gay and lesbian people within mainstream British institutions such as the workplace, the military, and the family (Homfray 2005). This essential approach is, at the time of writing, being given a further airing in the wake of the August 2011 riots. Amitai Etzioni (1997) and his theories encourage the matching of rights and responsibilities, similar to that espoused by Tony Blair in the early days of Labour's first term, have been a notable part of most political responses. But, whereas ethnicity, race, class and age can quite easily be incorporated within these current discourses, sexual orientation has played no part. Boris Johnson advocates gay marriage for Londoners at the same time as he urges a return to the short, sharp shock for London's young criminals. The sense of 'otherness' with which LGB&T people were regarded no longer appears to apply in the same simplistic, exclusionary way, and there is a strong case for arguing that Labour's legislative changes did have a strong influence on altering the national climate.

It can be argued that this displayed a very clear acceptance of an inclusive ethic in relation to sexual orientation. Previous attempts to enact reform in these areas often fell at the hurdle of 'protecting the family'. The 'familial ideology', where the view held of the family was the 'conventional' nuclear one of the opposite-sex married couple with requisite 2.4 children (Abbott and Wallace 1997) has largely been replaced by a broader and more inclusive view of 'family'. Looking at legislation in a wider scope, the recent changes altered the breadth of the way that public and social policy applies to LGB&T people. Familial ideology developed most strongly in the immediate post-war period, where the welfare state required repopulation of the country when gay male relationships and all other sexual activity were illegal. Whilst this did not apply in the same way to lesbians, their invisibility led to much the same outcome. With the active promotion of heterosexuality, a group of people either branded as illegal outcasts, or invisible, were not going to be considered in terms of the way that social policy affected them, so the 'jewel in the crown' of Labour, the welfare state, was set and developed in a way which actively discriminated against sexual minorities. It is important to recognise this link between familial ideology and the Labour tradition, as it may help to explain why the moves towards equality were slow and cumbersome, and why the early support for legal change did not necessarily come from the Left.

Through making this shift towards a pro-LGB&T stance, Labour did make a significant move towards a more progressive position which in many ways belied the influence of familial ideology. But, it does raise some cogent issues for the Left and for the ethical socialist stance. The Blair government made most of the changes and, in doing so, showed that LGB&T rights had become the mainstream view of all wings of the Labour Party. The initial change of approach has its genesis in the work of the GLC and a select number of left-wing local Labour authorities. Yet, this work was seen at the time as being so much on the fringe that it inspired overt anti-gay legislation from the Conservative government in the form of Section 28, and even Labour's opposition to these measures was cautious, as it did not wish to be seen to 'promote' homosexuality. It could be argued that the religious roots of the ethical socialist approach did not sit well with the seemingly individualist and libertarian approach of LGB&T rights, and as someone active during those times, I recall a somewhat awkward, frosty approach to the issue from some people who would have been expected to be sympathetic. There was a Labour Party and Council in Yorkshire and Humberside who decided not to include sexuality along with race, gender and disability in its equal opportunities strategy simply because 'we are not quite ready for it yet' was actually far more the norm than the initiatives of those few councils who did actively incorporate the sexuality agenda. The moves towards inclusion mean that the underlying ethic of the party in this area has significantly shifted.

As someone involved with working for change before and throughout the Labour period of government, there is a sense of both relief that through perseverance much of the hard work has been done successfully, but there is also awareness that achieving legal change is only the first step in the process of gaining genuine social equality. It is quite possible for legal change to cause little in the way of shifting social attitudes, certainly in societies where religious or other traditions have been strongly hostile or where changes have been enforced from above without any local enthusiasm or organised social movement to bolster the change. Social attitudes in the UK are, however, moving in a pro-LGB&T direction. The latest British Social Attitudes Survey (2010) indicates that 36% of people thought sexual relations between two adults of the same sex were 'always or mostly' wrong, down from 62% in 1983, with this number falling. A larger number believe they are not wrong at all (39%) and the figures become more pro-LGB&T the younger the group questioned. This is not to imply that homophobia has been eradicated: rather that the direction of travel is clear and this needs to be borne in mind when we look not only towards the application and implementation of existing legislation, but to how we may need to tackle ongoing social concerns affecting the LGB&T population.

Looking to the future

It is reasonable to start by acknowledging that with so much change having taken place under the Labour government, the current agenda of LGB&T issues will be as much about implementation of current legislation as the introduction of new measures. This, and the place of the EHRC, will be discussed first here.

The others include same-sex marriage, immigration and asylum, the ongoing debate between religion and sexual orientation as protected areas, the development of LGB&T communities of interest in a time of reduced public spending, the importance of education and young people, and the continuing lack of specific emphasis on the needs of trans people.

This article does not suggest specific policy proposals, but indicates issues of ongoing concern which the next Labour government may still need to act upon when it comes to office. Further discussion and consultation is likely and should be encouraged.

Implementation and the EHRC

The large amount of legislation which brought greater equality for LGB&T people took place before any government body had been set up with the explicit role of protecting the rights introduced by that legislation. The existing commissions looking after disability, gender and race had no competence in the case of sexual orientation, and given the impractical unwieldy nature of six or seven separate commissions to deal with each protected status, the general view from within LGB&T community groups was to offer a cautious welcome to the move towards a more integrated approach.

Part of the justification for this was the promise of legislative interpretation which would cross categories to ensure that there was not a hierarchy of inequalities. This meant that equality legislation would be applied in a way which did not suggest that any one form of discrimination was more or less deserving of action than another. The Equality Act was generally supported, as was a unified and integrated Equality Commission. However, LGB&T groups have found that the current arrangements have some limitations. The Equality Act retained some aspects of inequality between categorisation.

So, for example, there are specific offences of hate crime related to race and religion. For sexual orientation, however, there is no specific legislation, but judges are able to take a homophobic motive into account when setting the level of tariff for a custodial sentence.

Having no specific legislation has made it less easy to take action, with cases related to homophobic and transphobic hate crime occurring which have largely been regarded as not leading to a just outcome by local LGB&T communities. Trans does not formally exist as a hate crime category at all; trans people often have to see their cases being listed as 'homophobic' crime rather than specifically acknowledged as transphobic crime.

On top of this, the EHRC has had a faltering start. It is a hybrid body of three existing organisations, and its apparent expertise appears limited both in amount and scope with regard to LGB&T issues. No initial work was carried out on trans issues at all. It is only in the past year that trans issues have been spoken about as a distinct category. At present no trans person sits on the Commission, and, following resignations, LGB interests are represented by a single Commissioner.

It is also the case that many equalities issues have become blurred by the somewhat hysterical climate of discussion surrounding the Human Rights Act. It is beyond the scope of this piece to look at this in depth, but it is important that any change in the application of the HRA, or, for that matter, the structure or management of the EHRC, do not negatively affect the implementation of the Equality Act.

The court cases which have highlighted anti-gay discrimination have shown clearly that there are service providers as well as employers prepared to discriminate. Indeed, the need for an effective, focused body – to bring cases where appropriate – that also offers advice and support to organisations or individuals is beyond question.

To ensure the legislation can be used effectively requires an EHRC which has credibility and can be respected; at present this is not the case, and the EHRC cannot be said to be fulfilling these criteria. Labour needs to be a critical friend to the EHRC, which will mean some significant reform.

Same-sex marriage

Civil partnerships were introduced at the end of 2005. They were essentially the brainchild of Stonewall and the Labour government, which established a means of recognition of same-sex partnerships based on the template of civil marriage, but there were some specific small differences. The tactical reasoning for this was to establish civil and legal parity without using the word 'marriage' itself. This, in turn, has led to claims that the status of civil partnership is something which is still not absolutely equal to marriage. It is likely that an attempt to introduce same sex marriage in one piece of legislation would have been strongly opposed in the Lords and by hostile forces such as the major churches. On top of which it can be fairly argued that the use of civil partnerships as a term nullified much of the active opposition. Indeed, it was remarkable how little controversy it caused, and it was also notable that the Conservative leadership was keen to support the measure.

Five years on, the colloquial use of 'gay marriage' is widespread, there even appears to be little reason to maintain the distinction between the two named forms of partnership recognition. The 'Equal Love' campaign is calling for the retention of both civil marriage and partnership to open up both of those options to couples irrespective of sexual orientation. Another option would be to have a single category of civil marriage and to transfer all civil partnerships carried out until the establishment of this category to become civil marriages. This is a debate which will take place in the near future, with the government proposing to carry out a consultation on same-sex marriage in the Autumn of 2011. Ed Miliband has clearly stated his support for equality; given that the legislation would be very simple to draw up and introduce given the use of the civil marriage template for civil partnerships, it could be voted on before the next election.

It is therefore important that Labour is seen to speak clearly on this issue. It needs to be remembered that civil and religious marriages have always been separated (hence the ban on religious symbolism and content within non-church weddings); to enable a single civil marriage category has no bearing on what religious organisations choose to do. Some – the Liberal and Reform Jewish Community, the Unitarian Church and the Quakers – have already expressed their wish to allow their premises to be used for civil partnerships, and it seems likely that they would also welcome extension of marriage to same-sex couples. However, there has never been any intention of forcing any religious organisation to provide this service. Given that this is the case, is it not reasonable that Labour MPs should be expected to vote in favour of this measure. Religious marriage will not be affected unless the religious organisation concerned wishes to make a change, and so, any reform will be purely related to the secular law. Should a free vote be allowed, how could this be justified other than as an acceptance of discrimination? Labour should support whatever measures emerge from the consultation which do most to promote equality and remove discriminatory practice in this area.

Immigration and asylum

There are many countries where LGB&T people face not only discrimination, but outright persecution, and where gay people can be imprisoned or even put to death. It should come as no surprise that a number of people in this position have sought political asylum in the UK. The approach of the Home Office has left a lot to be desired, tending towards the view that if the individual was 'discreet' after having been returned to their country there would be no danger of persecution. Effectively, this was an overt indication to LGB&T people to not draw attention to themselves by remaining in the closet or birth gender. The Supreme Court struck down this 'discretion test' in July 2010. The Home Secretary stated that "... asylum decisions will be considered under the new rules and the judgment gives an immediate legal basis for us to reframe our guidance for assessing claims based on sexuality, taking into account relevant country guidance and the merits of each individual case".

Despite this welcome change, campaign groups working in this field have seen little practical change. The UK Lesbian and Gay Immigration Group reported, in April 2010, that the Border Agency was refusing 96-98% of cases where sexual orientation was cited as a reason for seeking asylum, as a direct result of lack of knowledge and training by Home Office officials. The 'Country Guidance' which explains the risk to individuals has been found to be out of date or does not include material on sexuality. The 'discretion test' remains in use, with the cases which eventually do reach court often being thrown out because of the refusal of the judge to believe that the individual concerned is gay or lesbian.

It is of little credit to us that many of these practices were established under the Labour government: looking forward, the Home Office have just started collecting the much-needed statistics on sexuality-based asylum claims. However, the cuts in legal aid and collapse of many specialist services in this area may have a disproportionate effect on LGB&T

people seeking asylum. The next Labour government should aim to work with UKLGIG, Stonewall and other relevant agencies to design a fair and transparent system which is not based on the whims of individuals making decisions about the sexual orientation of others. It cannot be acceptable that individuals are being returned to countries such as Uganda and Jamaica where there is more than adequate evidence of persecution. Unless British judges have been equipped with universal 'gaydar' overnight, their ability to judge someone's sexual orientation appears to have little basis in evidence.

Religion and sexual orientation

Both religion and sexual orientation, as well as transgender status, are protected categories under the Equality Act. It is reasonable to see the clash between the beliefs of people of faith and the case for equality for LGB&T people to have been something which could have been predicted, with the emergent court cases being similarly predictable. The outcome of these early cases has been almost entirely favourable to the gay and lesbian people who took up the cases of discrimination, particularly by service providers all of whom had Christian religious affiliation. This is largely because the demands of the Christian groups to have the right to actively discriminate against LGB&T people on the grounds that it was a part of their religious beliefs.

This was recognised by government in the allowing of a very limited number of 'exempt' posts within religious organisations, effectively to protect the paid clergy. This allows the Church of England not to open their priesthood to gay and lesbian people in active relationships, for example, and not face prosecution as a result. They have found that this limited exemption cannot be extended to other workers such as youth leaders, and cases have not supported the arguments for discrimination – with notable examples being *Ladele v. The London Borough of Islington* and the Chymorvah Hotel in Cornwall.

Labour must stand for religious freedom, whilst also remaining a secular party. One of the major critiques of the 'Blue Labour' thinking of Glasman was its social conservatism and reliance on an essentially religious world-view. Whilst it was never clarified, many LGB&T people within the Party were sceptical of a movement which appeared to have as its aims a return to the social morality of the 1950s. Legislation as it stands gives protection to people who are discriminated against because of their religious affiliation, but it does not protect the content of any one religion. Indeed, without becoming a mono-religious confessional state, it would not be possible to do so without acknowledging a multiplicity of diametrically opposed religious 'truths' eligible for legal protection. LGB&T people are not calling for the right to discriminate against Christians or any other religious group, and this is the clear problem with the demands of the Christian activists. It is worth remembering that not all Christians have taken this line, with evangelical groups such as Faithworks supporting the equality legislation from within a similar theological perspective as those seeking exemption from the law.

The consistent outcome of the legal cases brought forward and the indications that the outcomes were becoming progressively more unfavourable to the Christian cause has led to a slowdown in the number of new cases. Alongside which there was the 'leaking' of a suggestion that the EHRC would intervene in favour of the Christian case in the previously mentioned Ladele case, and that of McFarlane, where a Relate counsellor and sex therapist was dismissed upon refusing to work with same sex-couples. However, Labour needs to emphasise that it has have no intention of 'watering down' this legislation, especially given the fact that individuals within the Conservative Party have indicated that they would be minded to do so, and it is important that there should be a clear party line in this instance.

Another area which may need intervention is the activity of 'counsellors' whose aim is the 'alteration' of sexual orientation. Despite this view being rejected outright by psychological and psychiatric opinion, the lack of regulation of counsellors means that individuals are at liberty to set practice with the explicit aim of using therapeutic methods to alter people's sexual orientation. The evidence suggests that this is largely unsuccessful and fortunately, the take-up in the UK remains very low. Psychological effects on the victims can be severe, and the entire lack of regulation of counselling in the UK is something which Labour should commit itself to challenging.

Community development and LGB&T needs

Many major cities now have designated commercial districts where the gay presence is an accepted part of the city's make-up. Manchester's Gay Village is, for example, a well known and established part of the city. Often these areas can be a magnet for tourism and in the eyes of some social commentators such as Richard Florida, can be a positive part of a creative and innovative city.

Despite this, the evidence of local spending cuts is that the LGB&T sector is very weak. The myth of the hundreds of local councils with paid officers campaigning for gay rights has never existed, and in reality many projects providing services for the community were reliant on AIDS prevention funding. Many small projects have disappeared as the ringfence for that funding was removed, and there are areas where no-one at all within the public sector outside the NHS is paid to provide specific services to LGB&T people. The network of helplines and social groups which once existed across the country is weaker than before. It could be argued that in a more accepting and liberal society, the need for these organisations has lessened, and this may be true. However, by assuming that the commercial sector will be able to provide all that is needed, it assumes that there are no provisions which the LGB&T communities should have as a right of citizenship.

Labour should carry out an audit of the social and community development needs of the LGB&T people across the country, and look towards funding and developing a network of core services including local helplines, non-commercial support groups, and ensuring that the LGB&T voice is enabled to participate within local service planning alongside other minority communities of interests. This is often left to a fast burning-out number of unpaid activists whose work is not supported or helped in any obvious practical way other than whatever piecemeal activity can be organised by equally poorly resourced capacity-building groups.

Education and young people

It was no coincidence that Section 28 concentrated its restrictions on the activity of maintained schools and the way that LGB&T people are presented within the school environment.

Despite the evidence which shows that younger people are more accepting overall of sexual difference, there is still recorded evidence of school bullying and use of the term 'gay' as a casual insult. During his time as Education Secretary, Alan Johnson indicated that the issue of homophobic bullying be taken more seriously, but later legislation blurred the picture by unclear direction as to the content of sex education lessons in this area. This is a particular concern not only because of the presence of a large number of 'faith schools' run within the State system by the traditional churches, which may choose to present a less than positive view of same-sex relationships or transgender identity, but also the growth of academies and the participation of evangelical business men in their administration.

Labour will face a particular challenge: the decimation of local education authorities will make it difficult to enforce schools which operate virtually independently and without any degree of accountability to the locality. However, there is nothing to prevent a future Labour government from altering the balance of power to ensure that the free-standing academy cannot opt out of equalities initiatives at whim, and to ensure that young people in faith schools should be entitled to the same fair and frank sex and relationship education as those in the mainstream maintained sector.

A further issue is the continuing marginalisation of youth services, which have never been a core area of service provision and so local authorities have no duty to ensure their existence. Youth groups organised for LGB&T young people appear to have been hit particularly hard – never well-funded, and not requiring the cachet of an impressive building, they are a relatively cheap facility which can make a significant contribution towards the lives of a marginalised and often vulnerable group of young people.

Space for trans issues

Most of the examples I have given have related to LGB people and those in same-sex relationships. I will not apologise for this, given my own knowledge and experience. The '&T' at the end of the LGB is not just a tokenistic addition, but an acknowledgment that transgendered people make up part of the larger family of sexual minorities. However, the reality is that trans people remain particularly marginalised. The relatively small numbers mean that their needs can often be overlooked or not dealt with: having given equalities training, my own impression is that the trans issue is where LGB matters were back in the 1980s, with widespread misunderstanding, fear and misapprehension.

The Labour government introduced the Gender Recognition Act, which "enabled transgender people to change their birth certificates and marry in their acquired gender". Whilst the Act was largely welcomed, the categorisations used gave only the option of a 'male' or 'female' categorisation, which is not how some trans people choose to define themselves. Most controversial was the requirement for a trans person who wished to change gender registration to divorce a long-standing partner, on the grounds that otherwise, same-sex marriage would have existed specifically for this group. In the proposed changes to enable same-sex marriage, trans people are calling for the right to stay married to their partners. At present, they have to re-register as civil partners after divorce and the change of gender recognition. Research such as that carried out by Whittle, Turner and Al-Alami (2007) suggests that discrimination against trans people is still apparent in most areas of life, and the indication that the EHRC has failed to give sufficient emphasis to the issues faced by trans people. Labour needs to listen to and communicate with its transgender members and supporters and devise a comprehensive programme to respond to their needs.

This short article has aimed to ensure that as Labour, in opposition, reconsiders and reviews many of the stances which it held during its last period in government, and that LGB&T issues remain central to the ethics and mission of the Left. It is probably an aspect of the last government's policy programme which ethical socialists and the Left of the party can be happy with. I recall from my youth, the redoubtable and uncompromising MP for Barking, Jo Richardson, one of the most doughty and consistent supporters of gay equality when it was certainly not fashionable to be so, speaking at a Labour conference. The debate was little more than half an hour and (in)conveniently timed to ensure low television viewing. I can think of no better way to end the chapter than remembering Jo speaking from the platform and stating categorically that "there can be no lesbian and gay equality without socialism – and no socialism without lesbian and gay equality."

What now for Gender Equality?

By Sophie Bryce

Sophie Bryce is an active member of the Labour Party in Blackpool North and Cleveleys constituency. The main focuses of her university education were Sociology and Gender Studies. Sophie has past worked as an intern at a Labour constituency office, and has specialised in marketing and campaigns. She has brought these skills to Labour Left where she has designed our ephemera.

Gender equality as a broad objective did improve under the Labour government of 1997-2010, there's no doubt about it. However, there is plenty of evidence to prove that gender inequality still exists, and that whilst the position of women improved dramatically under the last New Labour government, there is still a way to go in order to achieve full equality. Labour's record on gender is one to be proud of, but there is the belief that the feminist section in the Labour Party comprises those that are already likely to do well due to their class. Throughout this chapter I hope to provide some analysis of the Labour Party's record and why we're the party capable of achieving equality and of understanding the triple jeopardy that people face due to their class, gender and race – but mostly gender.

New Labour and neo-liberalism

It has been repeatedly said of New Labour that it was simply a continuation of the neo-liberal narrative. This is a generally accepted belief by Labourites. The enacting of legislation to advance the position of women has only been met within the neo-liberal aspects of consumerism. New Labour encouraged aspiration and equality, often through means of capital. Within the Party we saw the introduction of All Women Shortlists (AWS), increasing the number of female MPs and creating a Women's Unit (later the Women and Equality Unit), all aimed at advancing the position of women.

These were attempts to feminise politics, but their efforts to create equal opportunities for women were constructed within the framework of patriarchal institutions. What it is important to highlight here is that New Labour operated its feminist goals within a neo-liberal economic paradigm. New Labour failed to recognise that by working within this paradigm they were too focused on competition and individualism as a way of seeking gender equality. This focus on achieving equality and advancing women through capitalist means and labour activation continued neo-liberal philosophies from the Thatcher/Major era, thus leading to the creation of what Angela McRobbie has called the "Post-Feminist Masquerade", a middle-class inspired idea that has led to the belief that feminism can trickle down from the middle classes to those less fortunate. This simply isn't the case.

Neo-liberalism is a political and economic ideology, ergo it is necessary to look at what occurs when a government which claims to be 'the most feminist government ever' tries to enact feminist agendas through the neo-liberal consortia. The Labour government of 1997-2010 had the most female MPs of any government ever. They aimed to achieve a more equal society by highlighting women's issues through having women represented in parliament. Even in 2010 when the Labour Party went into opposition, the party still had more female MPs than the Conservative-Liberal Coalition government.

Many women had high hopes for this supposedly feminist government, but 13 years in power has left many with the belief that New Labour was more concerned with labour market activation and the economic reasons for getting women into employment, not creating a more equal society. The conclusion reached by many is that by operating in a neo-liberal economic paradigm, they fail to recognise that this itself creates and sustains gender inequality.

The Party membership should be hugely proud of the fact that we enabled many mothers to get back into work by helping with childcare and creating Sure Start centres. The introduction of a national minimum wage was a pay rise for 1.4 million people (the majority of which were women). We gave part-time workers the same statutory employment rights as those who work full-time (again, the majority of part-time work is done by women).

The introduction of Working Tax Credit and Pension Credit lifted many women out of poverty and helped pay for childcare. Women under Labour saw a government that understood the fears of domestic violence and rape more than any government preceding it. We introduced Domestic Violence Courts and Sexual Assault Referral Centres that have helped the hundreds of thousands of women (and men) who have been subjected to such attacks.

The problem neo-liberalism creates

The post-feminist masquerade – a concept created by Angela McRobbie – is something which "creates a habitus for women who have marked out the masculine domains of employment, work and public life". The post-feminist masquerade is a show that allows women to pretend they do not need feminism, because if one separates oneself from a collective moment, it feels to them, as though they have achieved individual independence.

This isn't only important as a point for feminism, but also the wider movement of the Left. On the reverse of our Labour Party membership card it reads "by the strength of our common endeavour we achieve more than we achieve alone". This is so important to remember and it is a belief that has been watered down by neo-liberalism in both wider society and the Labour Party.

Feminism did not aim for women to only have access to independence achieved through consumerist means: this is not freedom; it is simply redefining independence and freedom. Women who act out the post-feminist masquerade are never truly independent as they remain attached to the gender roles they have been prescribed as women. Some women may be uncomfortable with the power they hold within a society that values competition and individual success, and feel that it diminishes their femininity (as power/competitiveness are so often masculine coded); therefore they engage with the post-feminist masquerade which involves them fearing being mistaken for a feminist by embracing their femininity.

This is just a redefined version of the female caring role; neo-liberalism has brought consumer capitalism to the forefront, and by giving women the chance to purchase their freedom, they must then care for this freedom by attending to the materials that supply it. It is like a mothering role towards capitalism, as capitalism is nurtured by the woman who believes it is her route to independence, when actually it is the very thing inhibiting it, as it keeps her in her place.

There are two conflicting lifestyles: freedom through either conforming or consuming, both of which perpetuate neo-liberal desires for women. This neo-liberal aspiration is as seen in Goldman's idea of commodity feminism – sign-objects are thus made to stand for, and made equivalent to, feminist goals of independence and professional success. Personality can be represented, relationships achieved and resources acquired through personal consumer choice.

Neo-liberalism has changed the definition of feminism to suit capitalist desires; women can fulfil their lives as consumers without the guilt or punishment of not being feminists. By altering feminism to make its goals achievable through purchasing power, feminism is made almost redundant. Feminism, which was once about a collective movement for rights and freedoms, has been usurped by the desire for individual choices and freedoms that can be bought, rather than granted by human right. Not only are women purchasing their freedoms, but they're purchasing a male created definition of what is female and what is acceptable. Basically, it is a further expansion of the consumption-to-liberate ethos perpetuated by neo-liberalism.

The new traditionalism
The combination of commodity feminism, post-feminist masquerade and 'feminist' policies through a neo-liberal paradigm has fused into the creation of what is called the 'new traditionalism'. This new traditionalism sells women an old lifestyle, it is a conservative approach. This lifestyle pulls from the issues above. This regressive state comes under the guise of a post-feminist society: a society currently emphasising our own enlightenment, which is then used to argue that decisions women make are 'out of choice'. The new traditionalism appeals to those who feel as though feminism has robbed them of being able to behave in a certain manner. It appeals to women in a comforting way, as it is – as Darnovsky notes – "a recruiting agent coaxing women who are struggling to challenge received gender-roles to relax and enjoy them instead". It encourages passivity, status quo and patriarchal dominance.

The new traditionalism causes women's bodies to become a site of conflict as the new traditionalism says to women that their concerns should be family and the home; this plays on women's guilt, as no woman wants to be seen as selfish and uncaring. It appeals to the new traditionalist in all women, showing how difficult life may be as a feminist in a neo-liberal society, it offers a chance to give up that 'hardship' and revert to a time when things were easier. The new traditionalism plays up to Geoffrey Pearson's idea that we look back to the past as though it were a problem-free golden age, when this past is actually an imagined one. Again, this post-feminist creation is an example of complying with the weaker aspects of feminism by asserting the woman's ability to make choices and priding her self-confidence; however, it actually reinforces consumer capitalism, heteronormativity and old-fashioned gender roles.

The new traditionalist is a sight of embarrassment for feminists, as it reminds them that they have not had the life of social transformation that they had wished for. What this concept shows is how neo-liberalism's breakdown of the social fabric has consequently broken down social movements; this is then picked up by concepts such as the new traditionalism. Whilst this concept does not expect women in their hordes to suddenly become housewives, it plays on doubts and dissatisfactions that women have with feminism and their social situation.

Childcare and families
The problem of good reliable childcare is one that many people face. All families could be more productive in the workplace, and better off, with

a sensible childcare and pre-school education policy. The Labour Party created Sure Start centres that would be targeted at those living in the most deprived areas of the UK. Sure Start centres have proved invaluable to many families and are a great credit to the Labour Party, but they need to go further. Many families find that often one salary goes entirely on childcare. This doesn't make work pay. The creation of a not for profit childcare system would be in the interests of all parents and children. The existing childcare system is only really available to households where both parents are working full time. Studies have shown that families with younger children where both parents are working are at a greater risk of living in poverty, with the Institute for Fiscal Studies (IFS) predicting a sharp rise in child poverty in the next few years. By providing affordable childcare and better pre-school education policies, we would be able to combat child poverty and work towards our Millennium Development Goal of eradicating it.

Getting better representation in politics

It is not in our interests to have unrepresentative democratic institutions in our country. It is in our best interests for the House of Commons to represent the people as best it can. This means getting more women, working class people and those from ethnic minorities into Parliament to pursue a progressive and equality-driven agenda. Representation alone does not create equality, but pursuit of that equality with the right people to represent it will.

The Fawcett Society identified four factors that can prevent women from standing for parliament. These four factors – dubbed the 'four Cs' – are culture, childcare, cash and confidence. Standing for Parliament is expensive and very time-consuming and this is a problem that, despite lots of discussion, is yet to be solved. The Labour Party has succeeded in its efforts to have more LBGT (Lesbian, Bisexual, Gay and Transgender) Members of Parliament and the introduction of BAME (Black, Asian and Minority Ethnic) shortlists and AWS are continuing to improve our record on race and gender representation; however, the issue of class is one that still lingers. Whilst we may be increasing the representation of different groups in society there is still an overwhelming shortage of working class people. This is a point that has been put across by various groups for years and it's a problem that is just getting worse. (Just for clarification, I am defining working class in this context as those who are earning less than the average income).

The problem is that standing for a seat is a long, time-consuming and expensive process. The only people who can really afford it are generally from the middle classes. Whilst efforts have been made to get more working class people into politics, the number is declining. With each new cohort of MPs the numbers from the working class falls. I know many may say that politics is a middle class career and that it always has been, but that shouldn't be the case for our party. We are the party of the working class; we're supposed to represent the working class; how do we do that with only 9% of our current MPs from a manual working background? This problem further escalates when trying to encourage working class women to get into politics. Emily's List UK was set up in 1993 to help women get into politics. It provides women with grants in order to pay for the things they need so they may stand for election.

Help for ethnic minorities is also essential; black, Asian and ethnic minority women are the least likely to hold political office. Racism may not be the issue it once was, but it still exists in much of our culture. Cultural stereotyping is still rife in this country, and if these cultural stereotypes are to be broken we need people from all backgrounds in important occupations. Having more BAME people in politics, especially from working class backgrounds is important to our future generations. When Barack Obama announced his candidacy he said "The day I take the oath of office, the world will look at us differently. And millions of kids across this country will look at themselves differently. That alone is something." Whilst Obama may be a middle class Harvard graduate, he has achieved something remarkable on account of his race. The next step is to encourage those who are working class to achieve what many thought would be out of their reach. This country needs those from ethnic minority backgrounds to be seen in positive roles to encourage political and civic engagement and to counter Islamophobia and the politics of extremism and terrorism.

The next step to increase the percentage of working class people would, realistically, have to be a low-income shortlist. I already sense that this is an idea that would be lambasted by many, just as AWS and BAME shortlists have been. However, as with all these diversity shortlists, they're only temporary. We have to remember that with almost every election since Attlee's government the percentage of working class MPs has fallen and so too has our vote from the working classes. We must represent those we wish to reflect the interests of, and a low-income shortlist would help us to do this.

Shortlists and grants for those who are not in the position to achieve office with their own funds need to exist. If anything, more things like this need to exist, they need to be farther reaching and people need to know that help – albeit very limited help – does exist. Alongside this there should be a guaranteed percentage of donations to the Labour Party spent on equality and diversity within our party. This is essential if we are to be the true party of equality.

Gender equality needs to lie at the heart of Labour election victory (and subsequent government) if we believe we are the party of true equality. A person's gender, sexuality, ethnicity, (dis)ability or age should never inhibit anyone from doing anything. Gender equality has been on the political agenda for many years and it's vital that a political party, the Labour Party, continues the struggle to make sure that full gender equality exists, through legislative changes and subsequent societal change. What is vital for Ed Miliband's Labour Party to realise, is that the neo-liberal economic paradigm we had before us did not work in the way we had hoped. We have to move on from that. Freedom through consumerist capitalist means is not freedom; it just reinforced gender inequality and pre-existing stereotypes.

Harsh Lessons for Labour if They Wish to Recapture the Christian Vote

By Graham Burnby-Crouch

Graham is a founding member of Labour Left and a long-standing Labour supporter. Professionally, Graham graduated from the LSE in Economics and has been teaching in Lincolnshire since. Graham's personal interests are in finding peaceful solutions to international conflict, as well as non-proliferation and nuclear disarmament. Graham is a proud Christian Socialist who blends social conservatism with a strong interest in the redistribution of wealth.

Labour Left and Issues beyond Class

This chapter aims to look at the relationship between the Labour Party and the substantial vote of those who associate themselves with the Church in Great Britain. I fully accept that some of the points conflict with what many good Labour Party members hold dear as their Labour principles, and I respect that.

This account is full, frank and honest and it is intended to make uncomfortable reading. This is because I am a very proud Labour supporter and wish to explain candidly why Christians increasingly struggled to identify with 'New' Labour. Ed Miliband has already corrected much of these wrongs, but nonetheless the piece is essential. I hope you as readers can take it in the spirit it is intended. I ask for patience, tolerance and an understanding of difference.

Percentage vote of Church of England identifiers

Year	Labour	Conservative	Lib Dem	Other/ refused
1992	38	40		
1997	39	39		
2001	41	34	17	8
2005	33	43	19	5
2010	26	45	16	13

Percentage vote of Catholic Church identifiers

Year	Labour	Conservative	Lib Dem	Other/ refused
1992	46	22		
1997	43	28		
2001	66	20	9	5
2005	61	11	18	10
2010	40	23	19	8

As the above tables – and the one on the following page – show, the British Electoral Survey found that since a high point of 2001 the Labour vote amongst Catholics and Anglican identifying people dropped sharply, much sharper indeed than amongst the population as a whole.

Many in the Labour movement may say 'so what?' due to a perceived strong anti-religious streak in the Party; however, this is a constituency

Percentage vote of other Christian identifiers

Year	Labour	Conservative	Lib Dem	Other/ refused
1992				
1997				
2001	41	26	16	17
2005	44	21	15	20
2010	38	21	13	28

that is willing to vote Labour in the right conditions and tend to have very high turnouts come election day. According to the British Electoral Survey, turnout among Church of England voters is around 94%, with the Catholics only slightly less than 90%. Nearly 9% of Great Britain is Roman Catholic and they are reluctant to vote Tory even if they desert Labour, suggesting that this section of the electorate could easily be won back. It is worth noting that the Liberal Democrat appeal among Roman Catholics grew 250% between 1992 and 2010. I suspect that this last trend will be reversed by 2015, as this denomination punishes the Liberal Democrats for entering the Coalition. In my view and experience of talking to Christians, there are several possible reasons for this flow away from the Labour Party. They include things such as:

- Liberal interventionism;
- Big Society;
- The wealth gap;
- Perceived sleaze;
- Challenge to the Protestant work ethic;
- Broken Britain;
- Issues surrounding 'aggressive secularism'.

Each issue would not affect each individual, but most would be affected by a combination of more than one factor. I will deal with these one by one and look at the possible remedies from a Labour Party perspective.

Liberal interventionism

Many Christians are uneasy about gung-ho military intervention around the globe, especially in relation to Iraq and its legality, alongside Tony

Blair's other wars. There has always been a strong pacifist tendency in Christianity, for instance the Catholic organisation Pax Christi. This may explain why there was a 250% increase in Catholic voters moving to the Liberal Democrats, whose party policy was to oppose the Iraq war.

In this case steps have already been taken towards healing the situation, with Ed Miliband's apology for the Iraq war. However, a stronger line against the Libyan intervention would have been preferred. In the original Commons debate, the government assured MPs that regime change was not on the agenda, but events have clearly shown that was not true. It was disappointing that Ed Miliband did not seek a further debate to hold the Conservative-led government to account for this.

Big Society

This concept is appealing to Christians, who look beyond individualism and operate in organisations that intervene to provide services through the voluntary sector. Labour needs to develop a policy with a positive attitude towards the voluntary sector, seeing it as a valuable partner in the provision of social care. Certainly working with some organisations that prefer to remain detached from the state because of their rules and regulations could mean that a less centralised approach may actually benefit the party.

The wealth gap

Contrary to popular belief, the Bible, though not despising wealth in and of itself, it is very much against financial injustice: the poor are to be supported and not exploited. The parable of the rich man and Lazarus is indicative of God's attitude to wealth. Here the rich man finds himself in Hell after death, with no solace being found for him due to his lack of help for the poor. Wealth, according to the Bible, is not to be hoarded but rather used for social good. Many Christians are not comfortable with few people holding vast wealth whilst others live in poverty. New Labour did not do enough to arrest the increasing inequality in Britain, and indeed some have stated that the situation got worse, not better, under the Blair/Brown leadership.

To appeal to those Christians concerned about this, Labour needs to reject the neo-liberal consensus and no longer be outrageously comfortable with the 'filthy' rich. A wealth tax would help to reduce the gap between the rich and poor. Measures to address inequality in wages and also the idea of equitable economic reward need to be looked into. One possible policy would be an excess profit tax where firms are taxed if their profit goes above a certain percentage of turnover. This would reduce the reward of capital and could make some firms pay higher wages, as in so doing they would reduce their profit to below this new tax's threshold.

Of course, poverty is not just the preserve of the UK; indeed the current Conservative-led government has done one thing right in keeping the foreign aid budget. However, a review of how to target this to tackle overseas poverty would be useful.

Perceived sleaze

This has been brought to a head by the phone hacking scandal, but is also exemplified by the expenses scandal. Other scandals such as cash for honours meant that brown paper envelopes became no longer the preserve of the money-orientated Tory Party.

It is arguable that Gordon Brown attempted to reverse this. One of his first acts was to scrap the super casinos, a symbol of moral decay where money is king. However, it was a case of too little, too late.

Ed Miliband has led the response to the hacking scandal extremely well and seems to have set the Party on a good course. The pursuit of sound ethics in policy and in conduct is essential.

No more cosying up to the elite, being in the pocket of big business or vested interests. Reversing the trend of deregulation is not red tape for red tape's sake, but a necessary step in protecting society from exploitation in one way or another.

Perceived challenge to work ethic

Perhaps unfairly, the last Labour government became associated with encouraging a culture of worklessness, with people being better off on benefits than working. This offends many Christians and again has its roots in Thatcherism, whose agenda during the 1980s recession helped to rip the heart out of communities and destroyed the hopes of an entire generation.

Labour need to ensure that work pays, not by penalising those who are on benefits but by ensuring that workers are paid well through a living wage, and looking at the taper of benefits, so the effective marginal rates of taxation as people move from and back into work is moderate. Increasing the income tax threshold would be beneficial in this aim.

Ed Miliband's language is positive in this area, but we need that language to be reflected in policy making. We also need to see a return to the concept of full employment rather than using people as mere economic pawns, thus ensuring that there is work available for all.

Broken Britain
In today's society one readily finds people exercising freedoms, but potentially without responsibility. For example, super casinos in poor districts, 24-hour licensing and other excessively liberal measures all in the name of wealth creation, have occurred under Labour's watch. Sexual promiscuity is considered normal, often among those of younger ages, and this has led to an explosion in sexually transmitted diseases, often among those who are not yet old enough to fully grasp the potential harm they are causing themselves.

Towns and cities across Britain are littered at weekends with the effects of 24-hour licensed binge drinking, as people of all ages consume alcohol, seeking to escape the consumer society that offers no real solutions to the needs of humanity. The causes of this include low pay and income inequality which is greater than any time since the 1920s. When looking at what can be seen around us the claim of 'broken Britain' is perhaps not so far wide of the mark.

The ethos of neo-liberalism has much to answer for this, but the perceived breakdown of morality has occurred under the watch of the 'New' Labour Party, albeit with the prefix 'New'. Christians look around at society and do not like what they see.

So what can the Labour Party do? The key is to abandon neo-liberalism, restoring the party to ethical policies with care for people by the people, bringing security into the lives of individuals and families. People are happier when they feel secure; neo-liberalism undermines security and produces desperate people. Ed Miliband's conference speech sets the right tone here and the principles he spoke of need to be pursued into policy.

Issues surrounding 'aggressive secularism'
This is admittedly the most controversial area to be considered. Many on the evangelical and Pentecostal wings of the Church are feeling increasingly beleaguered. Many see that their beliefs in the area of personal morality have become marginalised – especially by the liberal Left. Indeed, the current consensus in some areas has become very liberal, standing in complete contradiction to biblical teaching, thus allowing for the growth in hostility to views that run contrary to that consensus. I have been

in meetings where it has seemed that everything is tolerated apart from Christianity.

The Pentecostal vote has traditionally been pro-Labour, probably because of the high degree of ethnic minorities represented, yet news about couples being refused to foster because of their faith has alienated many Christians. On a personal note, about ten years ago my wife and I were refused permission to foster under-10s, basically because of our faith. In the interview the social worker, once we mentioned that we were strongly committed Christians, recommended we were not fit for fostering.

The Labour Party needs to pursue its adoption policy with some sensitivity. Rather than simply allowing antagonism, <u>mediation</u> may be a far better and more tolerant approach. There needs to be recognition that many caring, naturally left-wing Christians have strongly held beliefs that clash with the liberal agenda, but despite this they would make excellent parents.

To summarise, as Dr. Éoin Clarke often says, Labour would never have won one election without the Christian Socialist vote. Indeed, Keir Hardie himself was a strong Christian and said that his politics was influenced more by Jesus Christ than by Karl Marx. Christianity and Socialism have many similarities;, both have philosophies opposed to selfishness, both abhor poverty, oppression, exploitation and injustice and both have a similar ethical basis. The Labour movement has risked alienating much of this vote and it would be in its interest to change tack.

A New Ethical Foreign Policy for Labour

By Mark Seddon

Labour's historic record

Throughout most of the 20th century, the Labour Party's foreign policy was heavily influenced by competing demands, alliances, and by the ethical, moral and ideological influences that drove them.

From its inception, the Labour Party was an internationalist party. It developed strong links with other members of the Socialist International, was an enthusiastic supporter of the United Nations and was the driving force in the transformation of the British Empire into the Commonwealth of Nations. The Labour Party in office tended to support moves to closer relations with Europe, while playing its part in the development of Nato and in the deployment of global UN peacekeeping operations.

Labour, as a movement, historically sided with the oppressed and the dispossessed. The Party supported the democratic forces in Spain against fascism, and played a central role on the Second World War Coalition government in the fight against Nazi Germany. The post-war Labour government oversaw the ending of colonial rule in India, and the Labour movement supported the various campaigns for colonial freedom in the rapidly unravelling Empire in the post-war period. Labour was opposed to the disastrous Suez intervention by the Eden government, and it condemned the Warsaw Pact interventions, first in Hungary and then Czechoslovakia. Throughout, Labour stood firmly against the Stalinist regimes created by the Soviet Union in much of Central and Eastern Europe.

The Labour movement offered help and support to emerging political and trade union movements in countries under British rule, while later taking a strong stand against the illegal declaration of independence by white settlers in Southern Rhodesia and supporting the campaign against apartheid in South Africa with calls from boycotts and trade sanctions.

Much of the Labour movement was also opposed to American military involvement in Vietnam and South East Asia, although the Party's role in government in the post war period in the Middle East, and particularly what was then Palestine and Trans-Jordan, was much more controversial. Labour in office retained the close military and foreign policy links with the United States, which have tended to define Britain's role in the world in the post-war period and up until the present.

From the mid-1960s, Labour's 'East of Suez' policy saw a substantial drawdown of military resources and overseas bases, from Singapore to Simonstown and the military withdrawal from Aden.

Britain's entry into the then Common Market in the early 1970s substantially altered the country's relations both with the existing Common Market and with the Commonwealth. It was a Labour government in 1975 that allowed the British people to decide, by holding a referendum on Britain's membership of the Common Market.

Making policy, not tea

Throughout Labour's history, foreign policy was as much influenced by the demands and pressures of office – when the Party had it – and by the democratic policy making structure of the Labour and trade union movement. If defence, or in particular, nuclear weapons, can be viewed as an element of foreign policy, then the very real debate and division over this issue during the 1950s demonstrated the considerable influence of the grass roots of the party, who by and large were opposed to a) German rearmament and b) the 'H' bomb.

Right up until the early 1990s, the Labour Party's ruling National Executive Committee and its component policy making committees and the party conference were hugely influential, particularly when Labour was not in government. The Party and the unions were often able to keep a Labour government on its toes, restraining or cajoling where and when it believed it necessary.

This influence was largely lost with the adoption of what was known as 'Partnership in Power' in the mid-1990s, a process which removed policy making from the NEC and its relevant committees, reduced the influence of the party conference, and centralised policy making to all practical intents and purposes in the hands of select ministers and government departments. Labour's foreign policy goals arguably became more influenced by think-tanks and lobby groups, as well as strong financial interests.

Labour's ethical foreign policy

Labour's 1997 General Election landslide heralded the introduction of an 'ethical foreign policy', a concept rooted in Labour tradition, but also copied in part from the ethical foreign policy commitments of the US Democratic Party when it won office under both Jimmy Carter and Bill Clinton.

Labour's ethical policy was particularly associated with the new government's Foreign Secretary, Robin Cook and the party's International Development Minister, Clare Short. Broadly, it identified Labour in government with the key UN Millennium Goals, new targets for aid and child poverty targets, as well as some of the broader aims of the UN; namely, the extension of the International Criminal Court and Responsibility to Protect (R2P).

In office, Labour worked closely with sister parties in the Party of European Socialists and pushing for a progressive foreign policy agenda. Labour in office restored the nationality rights of those in a dozen or so dependent territories, including Gibraltar and St Helena. The actions of the Labour government in both Sierra Leone and Kosovo were broadly seen as a successful operation to halt widespread violence and massacre, and compensation for the failure of the international community to act in Srebrenica and Rwanda.

While the military action in Kosovo proved controversial to some on the Left, others believed that this policy was based on a practical new UN principle of Responsibility to Protect. Attempting to use RP2 over what was to follow in Iraq proved much more elastic and ultimately untenable to a majority in Britain and abroad.

The end of Labour's ethical foreign policy

The resignation of Robin Cook as Foreign Secretary, and the support of a Labour government for military action in Iraq, despite the failure to achieve the backing of the United Nations, effectively ended Labour's attempts to promulgate an ethical foreign policy. With the Party's policy making processes neutered and opposition to the proposed war confined to the margins of the Parliamentary Labour Party and the NEC – despite popular public opposition – the war went ahead.

The war in Iraq over a contested weapons of mass destruction programme by the Iraqis which proved to be a fantasy, ultimately paved the way for a loss in confidence in Labour. Arguably, it led to the eventual resignation of Tony Blair as Labour leader, and the election of Gordon Brown to replace him.

Had the historic checks and balances still existed within the Labour Party, it is possible that war could have been averted. But under the new 'command and control' system in place in both the Parliamentary party and the party in the country, foreign policy had increasingly become the preserve of the Prime Minister and his supporters. Labour, while more often than not an Atlanticist party, with close ties to the US, established even closer bonds with an American administration, described by many as 'neo-conservative'. British support for US military and political objectives from Afghanistan to Iraq and beyond became unquestioning, and to such an extent that British ministers were linked to illegal and extraordinary rendition and torture of terror suspects.

A new Labour foreign policy

The time has now come to restore democracy and accountability to the Labour Party and in the process restore confidence and support for Labour's broader foreign policy aims and commitments.

Foreign policy must never again be the sole preserve of the Prime Minister or the Foreign Secretary or a combination of them both. The checks and balances that allowed ordinary party members and trade unionists to have some say over Labour's foreign policy has to be restored as a matter of extreme urgency. The coruscating experience of Iraq, when MPs and Party members were lied to in order to garner their support, must never be allowed to happen again.

It follows that if foreign policy is made by elites and elitist groups, it will not be representative or fair. Which is why Labour needs the broadest possible input and support for a new foreign policy based on justice, sustainable development and fairness.

The United Nations

Britain's standing in the world is arguably much reduced because there is a belief that a) foreign policy is largely directed by American interest, that it is b) unilateralist and informed by self-interest, and that c) it is elitist. By and large Britain tends to vote with the United States in the UN Security Council over Israel/Palestine, frequently finding itself at odds with progressive and democratic global opinion.

Labour needs to restate without equivocation its belief in the rule of international law and its support for the United Nations, in all its multifaceted forms. Labour should support moves to reform the United Nations, particularly the power structure which diminishes the UN General Assembly while preserving in aspic the post-war structure of the UN Security Council. Britain and France should agree to share their permanent membership of the Security Council on a rotating basis with other European countries, while supporting the entry of countries such as India, Brazil and South Africa.

Human rights

Labour should put the support for human rights at the centre of its foreign policy commitments, at the UN and in other international bodies of which Britain is a member. Labour should argue for the strengthening of the International Criminal Court and that, as part of Responsibility to Protect, a rapid reaction UN Humanitarian Intervention Force be created. Labour in power should lobby to ensure that the UN Human Rights Council comprises member states that observe them.

Democracy

The global financial crisis, coupled with the rise of state authoritarianism is a real threat to democracy, but Labour should support democratic struggle wherever it takes place, without fear or favour. Britain needs to be seen as an honest broker again, prepared to stand up for the rights of Palestinians, for the Burmese and other oppressed people around the world. If that means occasionally falling out with friends, so be it.

North Africa and the Middle East

Labour should support the democratic struggle that has broken like a wave over North Africa and the wider Middle East. It should work with sister parties to help and advise new democratic parties and movements, while advocating strong international action against serial human rights abusing regimes.

Labour should advocate selective sanctions against Israel, should Palestinian rights continue to be undermined. There should be no backtracking on the internationally agreed 1967 borders between Israel and Palestine, and Labour should advocate immediate recognition of the Palestinian state.

Labour should advocate a withdrawal of British military forces from Afghanistan within 12 months.

The Commonwealth

Labour should become a much more effective advocate for the Commonwealth, comprising at it does member states from every continent. While advocating the rule of democracy and law throughout all Commonwealth countries, Labour should develop links with sister parties in member states. In doing so, Labour would also recognise the potential for mutually beneficial trade and other relations with older Commonwealth nations and newer emerging economies in the Commonwealth.

Labour should seek to resolve the historical disputes surrounding the Falkland Islands/Islas Malvinas and Gibraltar, while ensuring that the citizens of both have the final say. Labour should advocate a renegotiation of the leasing agreement with the United States in Diego Garcia, (British Indian Ocean Territory), allowing the indigenous inhabitants to return to their homeland and thus correcting an historic injustice.

The European Union

By the time of the next General Election, the European Union will be a thoroughly transformed organisation, effectively comprising of two zones – a core Euro zone, with tight central political and financial rules to govern it, and the rest of the non Euro zone EU, including Britain.

While recognising the value of working together for a progressive cross-European social policy, Labour should advocate strong supra-national links with our European partners and friends. However, Labour will need to recognise that the European Union is and will be a substantially altered entity, and that public support must be forthcoming for whatever the European Union is to become. To that end, Labour should advocate a national referendum on any new EU Treaty that envisages further powers being transferred to the centre.

While it is important for Labour to advocate Britain retaining an independent ethical foreign policy, there will be many occasions, either through the UN, the EU or Commonwealth, where common decisions are arrived at. However, there should not be an automatic resort to 'common decision making', as this all too frequently results in slow, ineffective decision making.

Conflict resolution

Labour should advocate and train a new 'Peace Corps'; dedicated specialists in conflict resolution, that can be deployed around the world where necessary to help defuse and prevent conflict.

Labour Must Champion the Cause of the 'Working Poor' if We Want to Win the 2015 General Election

By Dr Éoin Clarke

Labour Left and Issues beyond Class

The 2015 General Election was always going to be an extremely difficult election to win, regardless of who won the Labour leadership election in September 2010. In this piece I wish to lay out first why the odds are stacked so heavily against a Labour victory in 2015, and also offer some assessment of how Labour can put itself in the best possible position in time for the May 2015 ballot. My own verdict is that much of what is necessary might not be place by 2015, and that a General Election victory may evade us this time. This gives me no pleasure to write but I offer my views in the hope that they may be of some use now in averting a disaster later. The piece reads at first quite despairing, but I am optimistic that there is a path to re-election for Labour in 2015. If Ed Miliband's words during the leadership election are anything to go by, then I have faith that Ed too sees that path.

One of the main problems Labour has in facing the Tories in 2015 is that about 10 million UK voters, who are actually willing to turn out and vote, are broadly satisfied with the direction of travel David Cameron and George Osborne have taken. Although promises have been broken on the NHS, EMA and winter fuel payments, these voters I speak of do not hold the government to account for that. YouGov measures the 'voter retention' of all three main parties. Whilst the Lib Dems have been shedding votes, the Tories have hung onto the vast majority of the voters who chose them in 2010. Even among those who say they would not vote again for the party, more than half switch to UKIP – not Labour. I expect voter retention may decrease in mid-term but that misses the point. The voter retention levels of a party which has hiked VAT and announced the worse fiscal austerity package for an age is impressive. Roy Hattersley said it best when surveying the Tory's performance in the 2011 Council Elections. He said that there were millions of people in the UK who loved the pain and austerity George Osborne was inflicting upon the country. Indeed, YouGov shows the Tories far ahead in voters' perception of which party is willing to make the tough choices.

All is not lost for Labour, since there are 36 million other voters that might not agree with the Tory government's approach. In terms of counteracting the solidity of the Tory voter, there may be strategic benefit for Labour in a depressed turnout of Tory voters due to UKIP festering alienation among Tory voters over immigration and the EU. But broadly speaking, we can expect 10 million voters to turn out for the Tories in 2015.

Other issues work against Labour's success at the next General

Election. For example, there is also an incumbency factor that will work in favour of the Tories in the final year of this parliamentary cycle. Opinion polls mid-term are not a real choice of who forms the next government, they are more a referendum on the governing party. Inevitably, some voters return to that party as an election becomes a real choice. Analysis of polling from 1983-2010 shows that the incumbent party improved its position vis a vis the main opposition in the final year before the election. Thus, a constant 10% lead in the polls for Labour in 2013 could be easily overcome in the final months of the parliamentary cycle. This is especially depressing news since it means that government popularity now, although seemingly low, is nowhere near low enough for me to have confidence that the Tories will be removed from office in 2015.

Of course, it might be said that in the past the government enjoyed a choice over which date to call an election, but this ignores the advanced briefing to media or indeed pundit speculation that gives voters the heads up when parties with strong majorities call elections after four years. Four year terms are never the surprise to voters that one would have you believe. The conclusion is that Labour would have to enjoy a period of significant polling leads over the Tories to be confident of sustaining a polling lead in the home straight and in the polling booths on Election Day.

The other issue regarding the voter retention of the Tory Party is the likelihood that the Lib Dems will be made to suffer by voters at the next election. In effect, the Lib Dems will be the scapegoats for most of the Coalition's unpopular decisions. This does not mean that I think the Lib Dems will score lows of 10-12% at the polls; in fact I suspect they'll make a modest recovery on current polling. But it does mean that leakage from Tory to Labour will be much less than those who hope to win from the Blairite centre ground would hope for. Long-term analysis of Lib Dem voting numbers shows that they tend to prosper when Labour is in office but weaken when the Tories are in power as anti-Tory sentiment tends to congregate around the Labour Party (with the obvious exception of 1983). Trending in shows that the Lib Dems are on course to lose 2 million votes at the next election but it cannot be assumed that they will overwhelmingly go to Labour. It must also be said that nothing in politics is inevitable; I remind readers that this is simply my analysis. If word count permitted I would explore how it might be beneficial for some Labour supporters to still vote tactically for the Liberal Democrats in some parts of the South of England. I might also explore how unlikely it seems that the Lib Dems will ever recover in the North of England. But both of these debates are topics in their own right and ones I do not wish to go into for the purposes of this chapter.

Speaking of a modest recovery in Lib Dem fortunes, it is worth noting that on every occasion the Lib Dems have shown a flurried recovery since the General Election, it is almost always met by a Labour dip in the polls. This has led me to coin the phrase, 'yellows recover at red expense'. I suspect that if the Liberal Democrats were to record 15-18% at the next General Election, it would be at Labour's expense in terms of the scores Labour has been achieving mid-term. On occasions when Labour have reached 43%+ in the polls, the Lib Dems have been very low, but as the Lib Dems recover the Labour score is dragged back to c.40%. A sustained recovery by the Lib Dems would almost certainly see Labour's share of the vote dip to sub-40s. That said, the last two elections have seen neither of the main two parties record 40%+, so it is not automatic that Labour need do so again.

The other very important reason why it looks especially difficult for Labour to win the next election is that Ipsos-Mori issue polling shows that health and education are much less likely to play a part in the election than the 1997 or 2001 elections. As health and education are issues where Labour traditionally dominates, it is crucial that they become more important political issues in time for 2015. The depressing news from a Labour point of view is that, in the midst of Lansley's reforms or indeed Michael Gove's introduction of Free Schools, the actual interest generating in health and education issues was at best short-lived and at worse non-existent. The reason for this is that the Tories are perceived to have broadly retained a commitment to funding these departments. Unfortunately for Labour, crime and immigration play quite important roles in shaping the outcome of recent elections and this has the result of depressing Labour turnout as well as benefitting the Tories in terms of floating voters. I have very little hope that this will change significantly or sufficiently to alter the outcome of the next election. It is why, however much you disagree with the emphasis of approach by Blue Labour, and it is unwise to dismiss entirely their focus upon this matter.

That does not mean that all hope is lost, since it is possible to attract voter interest in other issues such as unemployment. Although it must be said that unemployment was very high in 1983 as an issue of voter concern, but it was insufficient to shape the General Election outcome. Labour Left often makes the point that new issues have been coming to the fore as concerns among voters. Issues relating to poverty, low wages, and morality in public life have all significantly increased in importance. I broadly categorise these issues as ethical ones, and I see a good future for any party that seeks to champion ethical policies relating to poverty, pay and morality. The general point is this, the electoral landscape is not in Labour's favour, but as Ed Balls argued in his Bloomberg speech, we must seek to reshape a new type of politics if we are to capture the imagination of voters at the next election. Ed Miliband has shown plenty of signs that he gets this with his recent focus on good capitalism versus bad capitalism.

The biggest danger for Labour at the next General Election is that the campaign becomes a referendum on George Osborne's deficit reduction. I have written on this many, many times but I'll recap. When the national deficit entered the zeitgeist of the UK public in winter 2008, it was based upon the belief that by April 2009 it would show a deficit of £175 billion. Today, we can be fairly sure that the deficit will finish the year c.£122 billion and it will fall even further by the time of the next election. In short, George Osborne will succeed in cutting the deficit. Every time Labour raises the stakes on the outcome of deficit reduction they play into Osborne's hands. This is because to the ordinary voter deficit reduction will seem like a bigger achievement than it really is because we in Labour hyped up its difficulties. It is true that stagnation depresses tax receipts, but the Tories have covered for this eventuality by clobbering us with VAT, NICs and other indirect taxes. Now it is, of course, possible to shape the debate so that it becomes more about stagnant growth and wages or about rising inflation, indebtedness or unemployment, but this task becomes harder every day that Osborne is allowed to concentrate the voters' minds on the deficit. Recently, Ed Balls has made significant ground in shifting the debate to 'growth' and this is to his credit. I am more hopeful at the time of print than I was when Alan Johnson was Chancellor that Labour has taken sufficient steps to mitigate against this.

The other fairly monumental problem for Labour is that rapidly decreasing numbers of working class people vote for Labour. Interestingly, the Tories enjoy a significant lead over Labour in attracting the votes of C2 social grade women. Generally, the leakage of C1/C2 voters to the Tories at the last election was quite significant, whilst the leakage of AB voters was negligible. Of the 5 million voters lost by Labour since 1997, 80% of them were working class. Of those voters lost by Labour since

1997, 80% were lost by 2005. It is especially worth noting that since Gordon Brown came to power, Labour retained its middle class voters, but continued to leak working class votes. In short, we did not lose an election in 2010 due to our lack of appeal to middle class voters. We know this to be a fact because the numbers of middle class voters who voted for Labour during their 2005 victory was broadly the same as the numbers of middle class voters (AB) who voted for Labour in 2010. This analysis is now more commonplace than when I first argued it, having featured in Ed Miliband's leadership election campaign and in the analysis of Peter Kenyon/Jon Trickett. Thus, it is fair to say that there is something of a consensus among the Left that a lack of appeal to working class voters cost us the last election.

To some Labour strategists, Labour leaking working class voters need not be a problem. Those strategists point to the swelling ranks of the middle classes. They hark back to the Worcestershire Women, or the concept of Middle England. And – I'll be frank – I sympathise and understand their reasoning. But I think they are wrong and here is why. Generous NC-SEC classification that regards supervisors, technical operatives and sales reps as middling classes have the collective effect of swelling the ranks of those perceived to middle class. Taking workers alone, 15 million of 29 million workers are classified in the top categories (of 8). It was the categories of 5 and below that saw Labour lose the most votes and the number of workers in these categories have declined from about 10.5 million to 9.5 million over the course of the recession.

A lot of this misses the point. A taxi supervisor earns an extra 50p an hour to spy on his fellow drivers to ensure they are wearing ties. A chargehand in a cleaning team earns an extra 75 pence an hour to check her colleagues have mopped the floor correctly. A call centre worker might earn £6 an hour but they can be classified quite highly on an NC-SEC simply because they perform the highly technical task of making a phone call. A pizza takeaway supervisor gets to check the pizzas before they go in the scooter sack at midnight on Saturdays. I do not mean to demean their tasks; indeed, an early career spent washing wheelie bins by myself for 50p an hour taught me that the respect a job should command is in no way linked to salary. No, the point contained beneath these flippant examples is that we have indeed swelled the ranks of those workers who have increased status and power, but stagnating wages are evidence that with their new-found roles comes very little actual reward. Wages have only grown 300 pence per week this year but costs have grown by more than a £1,000 per year in just one year. I argue that this growing squeeze on living standards means that a lot of those categorized in NC-SEC 3 & 4 are significantly closer to the profile of a semi-routine worker than their job title or pay packet might suggest.

So, to those Labour strategists who perceive the growth in the numbers of middle class as evidence of an increasing need to appeal to Blairite centre-ground voters (aspirational/affluent class), I urge them to rethink this conclusion.

The other problem that Labour must now contend is a seat reduction to 600 MPs. This will hurt us to the tune of 13-4 seats against the Tories at the next election. If the election is to be a close one, that may well make the difference. All the evidence in the first 18 months of this administration is that the next election will indeed be closely fought, and so I caution you to prepare yourself for analysis in the second half of 2015 that show Labour may have won the election under the old 2010 boundaries. But the reduction to 600 MPs need not be a tragedy for Labour. The growing squeeze on living standards is in my view creating more *de facto* working class people every day.

There will also be new marginals as a result of the redrawing of boundaries. The merging of CLPs may well pool canvassing experience and mean that the Labour campaign is better organised. It is also the case that parties in power, whilst tending to stand a better chance of holding onto their seats, tend to do so with reduced majorities. It is also the case that the Tories did not win the last election, and if they are to win a majority this time out they'll need to win new seats. That is an especially hard task for an incumbent party to achieve, as a gradual drip effect of bad news government stories tends to leak voters, making it harder to gain seats. That said, do not view that analysis through the prism of current polling – it is not meant as such.

The reference to a leakage of voters is simply between the two reference points of GE 2010 and GE 2015. The fluctuation of polls can lead one in the false sense that voters are to-ing and fro-ing from party to party. Often it is the case that 'don't know(s)' or 'would not votes' suddenly become more exercised towards a firmer choice of party.

Of course, the key to any election victory from opposition is turnout. Evidence consistently shows that Tory voters are more likely to make it to the voting booths on Election Day. Labour voters are historically less likely to turn out. This is for lots of reasons, among which you can include:

- Poor voter registration due to Labour types being less likely to own homes, or live in long-term tenancies;
- Urban voters traditionally more likely to vote Labour are also much less likely to vote;
- Young voters who polling show lean more to Labour than Tory are less likely to vote, especially young women;
- Older, rural and wealthy voters, the type that tend to vote Tory, turn out in higher numbers.

Aside from this in-built historical disadvantage, hardened Labour types have, in recent years, stayed away from the polls. Whilst in some cases in must be accepted that this is because they live in safe seats, it is also the case that working class voters have switched off from civic participation in greater numbers than wealthier classes in recent years. This piece does not wish to tackle all of the reasons for that, but it is my contention that the closeness of the two political parties in the centre ground of UK politics as well as an increasing presidential style of government under Tony Blair impressed upon working class voters that they increasingly mattered less as a component of the political system. It is also the case that the de-industrialisation and growing indebtedness of working class regions have reinforced the belief among this class of voters that Parliament does not hold the key to their woes.

It cannot be the case that voters are too lazy to vote or that they are too stupid to make an informed choice, for that would ignore the historically high turnouts of working class voters before the neo-liberal consensus. No, I'm afraid to say that increasing numbers of Left-leaning working class people no longer feel that Labour has anything to offer them. On balance, it is hard to forcefully disagree with them since we know that these types of voters have saw increasing debt levels, rising obesity and mental health issues, as well as a growing living crisis as home ownership escaped them and they were left to rent squalid housing. I remain confident that an ambitious manifesto, geared to these people's needs, can inspire them to vote in greater numbers than ever before. A party from the Left that can inspire the working poor to vote in greater numbers could be the game changer at the next election. It is, in my view, the key to Labour's re-election.

My last point regarding the potential for Labour to win the 2015 General Election is this. If the key to winning is a) improving the turnout, and b) inspiring the working class voters to view politics as relevant and

Labour as their natural home, then we should have begun this task yesterday. We need to be imaginative and caring. We must be creative in thinking the unthinkable and caring in ensuring that our policies help real the concerns of real people.

This book I hope shows some understanding that people care about personal indebtedness, tax justice, affordable housing, value for money from their energy companies. I hope this book has added something to the debate about good capitalism. I wish that the book conveys a sense that a problem shared as a society, not as individuals, is a problem halved. Communitarianism and working together to create wealth in a sustainable way that rewards innovation with profit, but not in a way that the low paid cannot make ends meet. A living wage is crucial to show the working poor that Labour gets their plight. For after all, it was our abandonment of the working poor that thrust us from power. Ed Miliband has buried New Labour and that is to be welcomed. But if he is to win a General Election in 2015, he must repeat New Labour's greatest success – the 1997 manifesto.